Praise for *Generative AI*

"Cutting through the clutter, Martin Musiol explains generative AI with great insight and clarity. The reader is left with a clear understanding of the technology, without the need to master complex mathematics or code. A must read for those who want to understand the future."

— *Rens ter Weijde, Chairman & CEO of KIMO.AI*

"An illuminating guide through the evolving landscape of generative AI and AGI, this book masterfully demystifies complex concepts, making them accessible to all and ignites the imagination about the boundless possibilities of the future."

— *David Foster, author of* **Generative Deep Learning**, *Partner at* **Applied Data Science Partners**

"This book is a must-read for anyone wanting to improve their understanding of where AI has come from, where it stands today, and, importantly, where it is heading. The advent of AGI and ASI is too important not to understand, and Martin meticulously explains many potential outcomes with a factual and unbiased perspective."

— *Roy Bhasin (Zeneca), author, entrepreneur, angel investor*

"Highly recommended. Musiol deeply and expertly demonstrates how to navigate the complex, exhilarating, and essential landscape of generative AI."

— *Katie King, published author, CEO of AI in Business*

"Generative AI by Martin Musiol offers a comprehensive overview of the GenAI technology and skillfully demystifies complex concepts of this transformative AI."

— *Sheamus McGovern, entrepreneur, investor, Founder & CEO Open Data Science*

Generative AI

Navigating the Course to the Artificial
General Intelligence Future

Martin Musiol

WILEY

ISBNs: 9781394205912 (Hardback), 9781394205950 (ePDF), 9781394205943 (ePub)

For general information on our other products and services or for technical support, please contact our Customer Care Department within the United States at (800) 762-2974, outside the United States at (317) 572-3993 or fax (317) 572-4002.

Wiley also publishes its books in a variety of electronic formats. Some content that appears in print may not be available in electronic formats. For more information about Wiley products, visit our web site at www.wiley.com.

Library of Congress Control Number: 2023951020

Cover image: © undefined/Getty Images
Cover design: Wiley

SKY10063718_010824

To my parents, who have always supported me, and to my grandma Helena, whose wise words continue to echo in my ears, guiding me through life. I will be forever grateful for the deep love I have received from you, and rest assured, I feel the same for you. A truth perhaps not spoken enough, yet profoundly felt.

Contents

Introduction

In the realm of technology, epochs of transformation are often ignited by the spark of human imagination, fused with the finesse of engineering artistry. We stand at the precipice of such an epoch, where the realms of generative AI unfurl into the once uncharted territories of artificial general intelligence (AGI). I am both thrilled and humbled to be your guide on this thrilling expedition into the future, a journey that begins with the pages of this book.

The technological zeitgeist of our times is one of exponential progress. A mere glimpse into the recent past reveals the embryonic stages of generative AI, yet, within a fleeting span, advancements like ChatGPT have marked a point of no return. This crescendo of innovation is not confined to textual realms alone but spans across images, videos, 3D objects, datasets, virtual realities, code, music, and sound generation, each stride accelerating our pace toward the enigmatic horizon of AGI. The rapid maturation and adoption of generative AI outshine the evolutionary arcs of many preceding technologies.

It was during the cusp of this book's creation that the concept of autonomous AI agents morphed into a tangible reality, courtesy of emerging open source frameworks. Now, a subscription away, the first AI agents are at our beck and call. This swift progression, magnifying the efficiency of AI model development, underscores the urgency and the timeliness of delving into the discourse this book intends to foster. As you traverse through its chapters, you'll realize we are merely at the dawn of an exhilarating technological epoch with a vast expanse yet to be unveiled.

Who should venture into this exploration? Whether you're a technology aficionado, a student with a zest for the unknown, a policymaker, or someone who's merely curious, this book beckons. No prior acquaintance with AI or machine learning is required; your curiosity is the sole ticket to this expedition. As we commence, we'll demystify the essence of AI, its lexicon, and its metamorphosis over time. With each page, we'll delve deeper, yet the narrative is crafted to foster an understanding, irrespective of your prior knowledge. By the narrative's end, your imagination will be aflame with the boundless possibilities that the future holds.

The narrative arc of this book has been meticulously crafted to offer an understanding yet a profound insight into generative AI and its trajectory toward AGI. Our expedition begins with the rudiments of AI, tracing its evolution and the brilliant minds that propelled it forward. As we delve into the heart of generative AI, we'll explore its broad spectrum of applications, unraveling potential startup ideas and pathways to venture into this domain. The discussion will then transcend into the convergence of diverse technological realms, each advancing exponentially toward a shared zenith. Ethical and social considerations, indispensable to this discourse, will be deliberated upon before we venture into the realms of AGI, humanoid and semi-humanoid robotics, and beyond. Through the annals of my experience, including my tenure as the generative AI lead for EMEA at Infosys Consulting, we'll traverse through real-world scenarios, albeit veiled for confidentiality, offering a pragmatic lens to envision the theoretical discourse.

What sets this narrative apart is not merely the content, but the vantage point from which it is observed. My journey, from advocating generative AI since 2016, founding GenerativeAI.net in 2018, to now sharing a platform with luminaries at the AI Speaker Agency, has been nothing short of exhilarating. It's through the crucible of real-world implementations and continuous discourse with global thought leaders that the insights within this book have been honed. Our conversations, a confluence of diverse perspectives, have enriched the narrative, making it a crucible of collective wisdom.

A treasure trove of knowledge awaits to equip you to navigate the complex yet exhilarating landscape of generative AI and AGI. The ethos of this narrative is to empower you to become a 10X more effective human, to harness the tools that propel you forward, and should a spark of an idea ignite within, to pursue it with vigor. Things can be figured out along the way, especially in this era equipped with generative AI tools. Remember, AI in itself won't replace us, but those wielding AI effectively certainly will have an edge.

In the words of British physicist David Deutsch, our civilization thrives on technological growth, and it's our prerogative to strive for a better future. This book is a stepping stone toward that endeavor, and I invite you to step into the future, one page at a time.

How to Contact the Publisher

If you believe you've found a mistake in this book, please bring it to our attention. At John Wiley & Sons, we understand how important it is to provide our customers with accurate content, but even with our best efforts an error may occur.

In order to submit your possible errata, please email it to our Customer Service Team at wileysupport@wiley.com with the subject line "Possible Book Errata Submission."

How to Contact the Author

I appreciate your input and questions about this book! Feel free to contact me at the following:

Martin Musiol's email: generativeai.net@gmail.com

Martin's LinkedIn profile: www.linkedin.com/in/martinmusiol1

GenerativeAI.net's web page: https://generativeai.net

1

AI in a Nutshell

No other field of technology has such inconsistent jargon as artificial intelligence (AI). From mainstream media to tech influencers to research scientists, each layer of media has contributed to that confusion. In order of their degree of contribution and frequency, I observed mainstream media simplifying and misusing terms consistently, tech influencers misunderstanding the tech in-depth, and even some research scientists overcomplicating their model findings with fancy terms. By no means do I intend to criticize research scientists. They are the backbone of everything discussed in this book. Their work offers solutions to a plethora of problems, making AI the umbrella term for almost every intelligent problem. However, its interdisciplinary nature, the rapid advancements in this space, and AI's general complexity make it already difficult to gain a clear understanding of this field. I am convinced that consistent and clear language would help to understand this topic area.

We can see two broad classes in AI: generative AI, the subject of this book, and discriminative AI. The latter is the traditional and better-known part of AI. Before delving into both AI classes, let's take a moment to understand the broader picture of AI, machine learning (ML), deep learning (DL), and the process of training models, to avoid getting ahead of ourselves.

What Is AI?

Even though AI includes a broad spectrum of intelligent code, the term is often incorrectly used. Figure 1.1 shows how AI, ML, and DL are related. ML, a part of AI, learns from data. DL, a deeper part of ML, uses layered setups to solve tougher problems. Non-self-learning programs like expert systems don't learn from data, unlike ML and DL. We'll explore these more next.

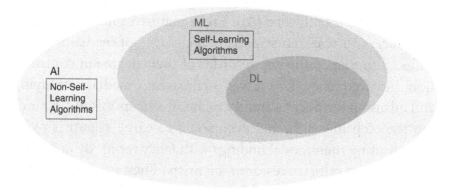

FIGURE 1.1 The relationship between AI, ML, and DL

How AI Trains Complex Tasks

AI can perform tasks ranging from predefined expert answers, also known as expert systems, to tasks that require human-level intelligence. Think about recognizing speech and images, understanding natural language processing (NLP), making sophisticated decisions, and solving complex problems. For tasks like this, the AI has to train on a respective dataset until it is able to perform the desired activity as well as possible. This self-learning part of AI is referred to as *machine learning* (ML). Because most of the interesting applications are happening through machine learning in one way or another, and to keep it simple, we use AI and ML interchangeably.

To make it tangible, we are designing an AI system that rates the cuteness of cats from 5 (absolutely adorable) to 1 (repulsively inelegant). The ideal dataset would consist of pictures of cute kittens, normal cats, and those half-naked grumpy cats from the Internet. Further, for classifying pictures in a case like this, we would need labeled data, meaning a realistic rating of the cats. The model comes to life through three essential steps: training, validation, and evaluation.

In training, the model looks at each picture, rates it, compares it with the actually labeled cuteness of the cat, and adjusts the model's trainable parameters for a more accurate rating next time—much like a human learns by strengthening the connections between neurons in the brain. Figure 1.2 and Figure 1.3 illustrate training and prediction, respectively.

Throughout the training process, the model needs to make sure training goes in the right direction—the validation step. In validation, the model checks the progress of the training against separate validation data. As an analogy, when we acquire a skill like solving mathematical problems, it makes sense to test it in dedicated math exams.

After training has been successfully completed and respective accuracy goals have been reached, the model enters the prediction or evaluation mode. The trainable parameters are not being adjusted anymore, and the model is ready to rate all the cats in the world.

AI Model in Training (2 Steps)

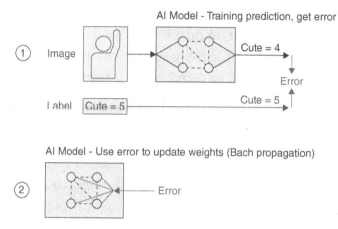

FIGURE 1.2 In supervised training of a ML model, two main steps are involved: predict the training data point, then update the trainable parameters meaningfully based on the prediction's accuracy.

AI Model in Prediction

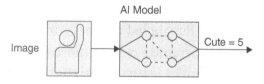

FIGURE 1.3 Prediction mode in a supervised ML model.

It is typical for a model in production mode that the accuracy gets worse over time. The reason for this could be that the real-world data changed. Maybe we are only looking at kittens and they are all cute compared to our training data. Retraining the model, whenever accuracy decreases or by scheduling retraining periodically, tackles the problem of a discrepancy between the data distribution of training data and evaluation data.

Perhaps you have a sense already that training AI models requires much more computing power than they need in prediction mode. To adjust its trainable parameters, often referred to as *weights*, we need to calculate the grade of adjustment carefully. This happens through a famous model function called *backpropagation.* It entails the backward propagation of prediction errors—the learning from making mistakes in the training process. The errors are turned back to respective weights for improvement. This means that we go forward to predict a data point and backward to adjust the weights. In prediction mode, however, we don't adjust the weights anymore, but just go forward and predict. The function that has been trained through the training data is being applied, which is comparatively cheap.

Unsupervised Learning

When ML models reach a certain complexity by having many computing stages, called *layers*, we enter the realm of deep learning (DL). Most of the cutting-edge applications are at least partially drawing their algorithms from DL. Algorithms are step-by-step instructions for solving problems or performing tasks.

The preceding example of rating the cuteness of a cat was simplified drastically and didn't tell the whole story. A relevant addition to this is that as we train on labeled cat pictures, with the label being the cuteness of the cats, we call this *supervised machine learning*. With labels, we provide guidance or feedback to the learning process in a supervised fashion.

The counterpart for supervised ML is called *unsupervised machine learning*. The main difference between them is that in unsupervised ML the training data is not labeled. The algorithms ought to find patterns in the data by themselves.

For example, imagine you have a dataset of customer purchases at a grocery store, with information about the type of product, the price, and the time of day. In AI these attributes are called *features*. You could use an unsupervised clustering algorithm to group similar purchases together based on these features. This could help the store better understand customer buying habits and preferences. The algorithm might identify that some customers tend to buy a lot of fresh produce and dairy products together, whereas others tend to purchase more processed foods and snacks. This information could be used to create targeted marketing campaigns or to optimize store layout and product placement.

Comparing the performance of unsupervised learning applications to that of supervised learning applications is akin to contrasting boats with cars—they represent distinct methodologies for addressing fundamentally diverse problems. Nevertheless, there are several reasons why we reached success years faster with supervised than with unsupervised learning methods.

In supervised learning, the model is given a training dataset that already includes correct answers through labels. Understandably, this helpful information supports model learning. It also accurately outlines the AI model's intended objective. The model knows precisely what it is trying to achieve. Evaluating the model's performance is simpler than it is in unsupervised machine learning, as accuracy and other metrics can be easily calculated. These metrics help in understanding how well the model is performing.

With this information, a variety of actions can be taken to enhance the model's learning process and ultimately improve its performance in achieving the desired outcomes.

Unsupervised models face the challenge of identifying data patterns autonomously, which is often due to the absence of apparent patterns or a multitude of ways to group available data.

Generative AI a Decade Later

Generative AI predominantly employs unsupervised learning. Crafting complex images, sounds, or texts that resemble reasonable outputs, like an adorable cat, is a challenging task compared to evaluating existing options. This is primarily due to the absence of explicit labels or instructions.

Two main reasons explain why generative AI is taking off roughly a decade after discriminative AI. First, generative AI is mostly based on unsupervised learning, which is inherently more challenging. Second, generating intricate outputs in a coherent manner is much more complex than simply choosing between alternatives. As a result, generative AI's development has been slower, but its potential applications are now visible.

Between supervised and unsupervised learning, there are plenty of hybrid approaches. We could go arbitrarily deep into the knick-knacks of these ML approaches, but because we want to focus on generative AI, it is better to leave it at that. If you want to dive deeper into the technicalities, I recommend the book *Deep Learning* (Adaptive Computation and Machine Learning series), by Ian Goodfellow, Yoshua Bengio, and Aaron Courville (MIT Press, 2016), which covers ML and DL in great detail, laying the theoretical generative AI foundation. It is regarded as the best book in the space, which isn't surprising, given the authors. I will come back to those gentlemen later.

The AI landscape is vast and ever-expanding. In this book, I strike a balance between simplifying concepts for clarity and providing sufficient detail to capture the essence of recent AI advancements. To understand what generative AI is and its value proposition, we first have to understand the traditional part of AI, called *discriminative AI*.

What Is Discriminative AI?

Discriminative AI models made headlines long before large language models (LLMs) like ChatGPT by OpenAI and image generation models like stable diffusion by Stability AI entered the stage. Since the term "artificial intelligence" was coined by John McCarthy in 1955, discriminative models have yielded great results, especially in the past 15 years.

Discriminative AI focuses on algorithms that learn to tell apart different data classes. They recognize patterns and features unique to each class, aiming to link input features with labels for the output. This way, they can effectively classify instances into predefined groups, making it easier to distinguish one class from another. Discriminative AI has found numerous applications in various domains, including NLP, recommendations, and computer vision.

In the field of NLP, discriminative AI is used to classify text data into different categories, such as sentiment analysis or topic classification. In the domain of recommendations, discriminative AI is used to predict user preferences and make personalized product recommendations. In computer vision, discriminative AI is used to recognize objects and classify images based on their content. The applications of discriminative AI are vast and diverse, and its impact on various industries is immense.

Looking at existing applications, discriminative AI generally has five main tasks: classification, regression, clustering, dimensionality reduction, and reinforcement learning. They are not crucial to be able to follow the book's thread, but it helps to understand them conceptually because then the term "discriminative" and what it means in the context of AI becomes apparent. Put simply, in one way or another, this part of AI is deciding, selecting, distinguishing, or differentiating on data or a problem at hand.

Classification

The objective of classification is to accurately predict the class of new inputs based on prior training with labeled examples (Figure 1.4). This supervised learning process uses training examples accompanied by their respective class labels.

For instance, consider unlocking your phone with facial recognition. You initially show your face from various angles, allowing the classifier model to learn your appearance. Advanced face recognition systems, like the iPhone's FaceID, quickly identify you due to their extensive pretraining and incorporation of biometric information to deterministically classify users. In essence, the model or system of models assesses your face and discriminates whether you belong to the "person with access rights" or "person without access rights" class.

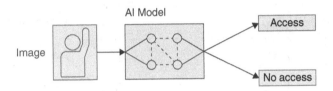

FIGURE 1.4 In ML, the concept of classification involves assigning data to one of a finite set of categories.

Classification has driven breakthroughs in diverse applications, including image classification, sentiment analysis, disease diagnosis, and spam filtering. These applications typically involve multiple processing steps and rely on deep learning techniques.

Regression

A regression model in AI is designed to predict numerical values for new inputs based on data it has learned from a given problem. In this case, the output is not a class label but a continuous value. For example, imagine you want to buy a 100-square-meter apartment with a balcony in Munich, Germany. A real estate agent presents three similar apartments, priced at 2 million, 2.5 million, and 2.7 million euros.

You have three options: the naive approach, where you assume these three properties represent the market; the informed approach, where you estimate market prices by researching multiple offers; or the data science approach, which involves building a machine learning model to determine a fair price by analyzing all available properties in the market with their price tags.

A well-trained regression model will give you a market-based and rational price, as it takes into account all the characteristics of apartments in the market (Figure 1.5), helping you make a more informed decision. By recommending a price, the model inherently has a discriminative nature.

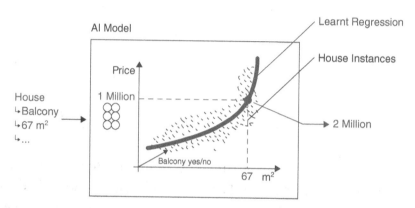

FIGURE 1.5 In regression, data like house details go into the ML model, which then predicts its price based on these features.

Clustering

As the name suggests, this application field in AI clusters data points. Be they people, groceries, or songs, based on a similarity measure, these items are grouped. By the way, you are being clustered all the time. For example, Internet ads are targeted to your digital persona, including your sex, age, IP address (which represents your location), and all other data ad-providing companies have collected about you. To cement it, if you use a web page that recommends songs like Spotify, movies like Netflix, and products like Amazon to you, then you have been clustered. In the success of big tech companies like those mentioned previously, clustering algorithms have played a crucial role, as they are the backbone of every recommendation engine.

In clustering tasks, the data comes without labels. For instance, there are no labels on our heads indicating "prefers Ben & Jerry's Chubby Hubby." Clustering models must identify patterns and groups autonomously, making it an unsupervised learning task. Moreover, the process of assigning items or personas to clusters is a decision-making aspect of discriminative AI. Figure 1.6 illustrates the conceptual operation of a clustering model. By analyzing other people's behavior, it infers that individuals who purchase butter and milk might also prefer cereals. Adding soda to the mix increases the likelihood of a preference for Ben & Jerry's Chubby Hubby.

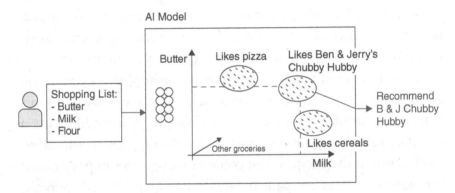

FIGURE 1.6 Clustering model identifying buying patterns

Dimensionality Reduction

Dimensionality reduction is not an application field of AI that is discussed much in mainstream media. It is rather research-heavy and often a means to achieve something greater, more efficiently.

Its primary purpose is to reduce low-information data, mainly making machine learning applications as effective as possible. By "low-information data," I mean data that contains little to no meaningful insights to solve a problem. See Figure 1.7 for a visual representation.

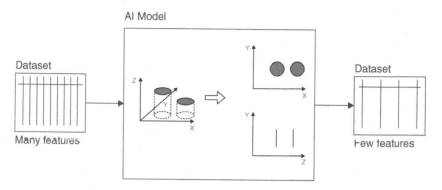

FIGURE 1.7 Dimensionality reduction

Imagine that you have an extensive recipe book with hundreds of recipes. Each recipe has several ingredients, and some of them are similar. For example, many recipes might call for salt, pepper, and olive oil. If you were to list all the ingredients used in the book, it would be a long list with many similar items.

Now imagine that you want to make a simpler version of the recipe book that is easy to use on a daily basis. One way to do this is to group similar ingredients. For example, you could create a category called "seasonings" that includes salt, pepper, and other spices used in the recipes. You could also create a category called "cooking oils" that contains olive oil, vegetable oil, and so forth.

In the world of data science, the same thing happens. We might have a large dataset with many different features, and we want to simplify it to make it easier to work with. Dimensionality reduction techniques help us to do this by finding a way to represent the data with fewer features while still preserving essential information. They make it easier to analyze data, build models, or visualize data more understandably.

Naturally, the data is not labeled, and we don't know up front which features carry relevant information. In an unsupervised manner, the models must learn to distinguish what low-information data can be modified or truncated and how. The models must decide or discriminate, indicating that we are in discriminative AI.

Reinforcement Learning

Reinforcement learning (RL) models, typically called agents, learn from positive or negative consequences that their actions yield in real-world or virtual environments. A positive consequence is a reward, and a negative consequence is a punishment. In Figure 1.8, the agent executes an action in a virtual/physical environment, altering the environment (even if minimally), and receives a reward or penalty based on its stated goal. During the training phase of the RL model, initial emphasis is on exploration to identify available paths (e.g., for warehouse navigation), gradually shifting to an exploitation phase for efficient goal achievement (or technically, maximizing rewards), as indicated in Figure 1.9.

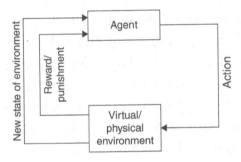

FIGURE 1.8 Technical workings of reinforcement learning models

Virtual environments encompass a wide range of applications, from simulations for practicing real-world maneuvers to gaming experiences, and even stock market environments for trading agents. In gaming, AI has demonstrated remarkable super-human abilities, excelling in games such as *Super Mario*. When an RL agent acts in a real-world environment, it is probably a robot in a warehouse or Boston Dynamics's Atlas performing ninja moves. The agents acquire the ability to determine the optimal action in a given situation, positioning them as a component of discriminative AI.

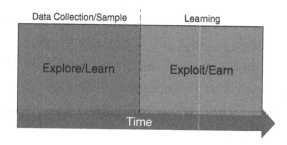

Learn First

FIGURE 1.9 Exploration versus exploitation in RL training over time

Reinforcement learning has many exciting aspects, one of which is forming great synergies with generative AI. It was of little public interest for decades until its turning point in 2016, when AlphaGo by Google's DeepMind won a series of Go matches against the former world champion Lee Sedol. Go is a complex Chinese board game with a 19×19 grid, and thus it has 10^172 possible moves. For comparison, there are 10^82 atoms in the universe. RL not only plays complex games exceptionally well but also delivers on a variety of tasks, ranging from autonomous vehicles to energy management in buildings. More on the powerful collaboration between RL and generative AI later.

Additionally, RL is helping to advance our understanding of the learning process itself, leading to new insights into how intelligence works and how it can be developed and applied.

What Is Generative AI?

So far we have talked about discriminative AI, which can decide, distinguish, or discriminate between different options or continuous values.

Generative AI, however, is fundamentally different. It has the ability to generate all kinds of data and content. By learning the patterns and characteristics of given datasets, generative AI models can create new data samples that are similar to the original data.

Recent advancements, such as the mind-blowing creations of Midjourney's image generation, the steps of video generation like Meta's Make-A-Video, and the conversational abilities of ChatGPT, have completely altered the way we view AI. It is a fascinating field that revolutionizes the way we create products and interact with data.

Generally speaking, generative AI models can perform three tasks, each with a unique and exciting set of applications.

Data Generation

First, and it is the most obvious one, that they can generate all kinds of data, including images, videos, 3D objects, music, voice, other types of audio, and also text—like book summaries, poems, and movie scripts. By learning the patterns and characteristics of given data, generative AI models can create new data samples that are similar in style and content to the original.

Data Transformation

The second task of generative AI is to perform data transformations. This means transforming existing data samples to create new variations of them. Transformations can reveal new insights and create appealing outputs for various applications. For example, you can transform winter pictures into summer pictures or day pictures into night pictures. Translating an image from one domain (for example, summer) into another (winter) is called a *domain transfer*. Image style transformation involves taking an image, such as a photograph of your garden, and maintaining the content (i.e., the garden) while altering its appearance to resemble the artistic style of, say, Monet's paintings. This process, known as *style transfer*, is not limited to visual content like photos and videos but can also be applied to other data types like music, text, speech, and more. The essence of style transfer lies in preserving the original content while imbuing it with a distinct and recognizable, often artistic, flair.

Style transfer is more than just a delightful tool; it possesses the potential to significantly improve datasets for broader applications. For example, researchers from Korea and Switzerland have independently investigated the use of style transfer techniques to augment the segmentation of cancer cells in medical images using machine learning. This method, dubbed *contextual style transfer*, relies on the seamless integration of style-transferred instances within the overall image, ensuring a smooth and cohesive appearance—something that generative adversarial networks (GANs) are able to perform. In a fascinating study, Nvidia showcased a remarkable improvement in segmentation performance by incorporating synthetic data into the training set. This integration led to a leap from 64 percent to 82 percent in accuracy simply by augmenting the dataset, without modifying the machine learning pipeline in any way.

Data Enrichment

As already indicated with style transfer, the third task of generative AI is to enrich datasets to improve machine learning models ultimately. This involves generating new data samples similar to the original dataset to increase its size and diversity. By doing so, generative AI can help to improve the accuracy and robustness of machine learning models.

Imagine we want to build a computer vision model that uses ML techniques to classify whether rare cancer cells are benign or malignant. As we are looking at a rare cancer type, it will be a small dataset to train on. In real-world scenarios, privacy issues are another data-diminishing factor. However, our neural net is data-hungry and we can't get the most out of its power, landing at 64 percent classification accuracy. Through generative AI, rare cancer images can be generated to create a larger and more diverse training dataset for improved detection performance.

Overall, the capabilities of generative AI are truly remarkable, and the potential applications are vast and varied. AI limits are being pushed every day, not only by research but also by for-profit companies. This is especially true of generative AI.

If we zoom out further, we see that the overall concept of generative AI is even simpler. Models generate data based on some input. The complexity of the input can vary a lot. It could range from simple tasks, such as transforming a single digit like 6 into a handwritten image, to complex endeavors like applying domain transformations to a video.

Under the Radar No More: Picking Up Speed

What we often observe, especially in AI, is that a new tech approach has early roots, but has been in stealth mode for a couple of decades. Once sufficient advancements transpire in a related tech domain, the dormant technology awakens, delivering substantial value in real-world applications. This is recognized as technological convergence.

Deep Learning Tech Convergence with GPUs   The advent of deep learning, the underlying technology propelling fields such as computer vision and robotics, traces its roots back to 1967, when the first neural network, the multilayer perceptron, was conceived and introduced by two prominent Soviet scientists, Ivakhnenko and Lapa.[1] For numerous decades deep learning struggled to yield tangible business value and real-world

---

[1] A. G. Ivakhnenko and Valentin Grigor'evich Lapa, *Cybernetics and Forecasting Techniques*, American Elsevier Publishing Company, 1967.

applications. However, a transformative moment arrived with the emergence of graphics processing units (GPUs) at the onset of the 21st century.

GPUs first became popular in the gaming industry. In the late 1990s and early 2000s, video games became increasingly complex and required more processing power to render high-quality graphics and animations.

In the 1990s, GPUs were initially developed with the primary aim of providing specialized processing for intricate 3D graphics and rendering in video games and other computer applications. Firms such as 3DFX, ATI, and Nvidia spearheaded these advancements. The early 2000s witnessed another significant development for GPUs: the introduction of parallel processing, enabling multiple calculations to be executed simultaneously.

This ability to compute large amounts of data breathed new life into deep learning, allowing it to gain traction and experience a surge in research popularity. Leveraging GPUs' enhanced capabilities, researchers and practitioners accelerated deep learning's potential, sparking a multitude of practical applications. Today, it's unimaginable to train a robust machine learning or deep learning model without the assistance of GPUs.

Deep learning has reaped the benefits of other advancements as well. The Internet's growth and technological innovations provided abundant data for training models, while committed researchers and research, in general, led to numerous breakthroughs in deep neural networks. This progress extends from convolutional neural networks achieving remarkable feats in image recognition to recurrent neural networks demonstrating advanced NLP capabilities. It's not just the researchers who are passionate about the subject; capital allocators and profit-driven companies have also invested heavily in the field.

Incidentally, it's worth mentioning that we are now seeing, and will likely keep seeing, a similar rise in interest in generative

AI. The growth of other areas, especially discriminative AI and computational power, along with the increasing amount of data, were crucial for generative models to evolve in the background.

Today, we see billions being invested in generative AI projects aimed at tackling a wide range of business and non-business applications, as long as people can imagine it. This growing focus on generative AI promises to bring even more transformative advancements in the near future, building on the foundation established by previous AI breakthroughs.

In today's attention economy, capturing the focus of individuals has become increasingly challenging, as attention itself is a scarce and valuable resource. The widespread adoption of the Internet, social media, and other digital technologies has led to an overwhelming influx of information and stimuli, all competing for our limited attention. Consequently, only groundbreaking technologies can truly stand out and capture the spotlight. For a long time, generative AI remained relatively obscure in this competitive landscape. However, recent advances and remarkable achievements have now propelled generative AI into prominence, showcasing its immense potential and securing its place at the forefront of technological innovation.

Generative AI's Early Impact   Generative AI is still quite new, but its future effects are expected to be amazing, going beyond what we've seen so far. Its influence can be noticed in many areas, but it has mainly made a difference in three sectors: creative industries, gaming, and natural language processing.

Creative Industries   Generative AI has made a lasting impact on creative fields like art. This technology enables artists to create unique and inventive digital artworks. By studying patterns and styles in existing art, music, and fashion, AI algorithms can produce new content that matches market trends and engages audiences. In the world of music, these algorithms can generate original tracks or remix current ones, opening up fresh possibilities for both producers and artists.

The integration of generative AI has led to new business models in the creative industry, such as selling exclusive digital art or creating customized products using AI-generated designs. This growth has occurred alongside a technological convergence between AI and the rapidly expanding cryptocurrency landscape.

In the last eight years, the cryptocurrency world has seen incredible progress, with numerous coins quickly making some people wealthy and leaving others financially devastated. Decentralized finance and institutional adoption have drawn significant interest. However, the most far-reaching impact may come from non-fungible tokens (NFTs).

NFTs allow artists and creators to produce unique, verifiable digital assets, leading to a growing demand for imaginative, high-quality AI-generated art. While not the sole driving force behind advancements in image generation, the NFT market has undeniably accelerated progress in this area.

Gaming Industry   The gaming industry has experienced a significant transformation due to generative AI, which has opened up possibilities for a variety of new game content, such as levels, characters, 3D objects, scenarios, and even entire quests. A notable example is Microsoft's Flight Simulator, which partnered with Blackshark.ai to generate a photorealistic, three-dimensional world from two-dimensional satellite images, covering the whole Earth.

The popularity of open-world concepts in gaming has encouraged many companies to adopt AI-generated content. Imagine AI algorithms that study player behavior and dynamically modify game difficulty or generate new content on the spot, leading to personalized and engaging gaming experiences. Consider the potential of giving non-player characters (NPCs) AI-driven language models for more captivating and immersive interactions. These advancements could make returning to the real world a challenge.

By using generative AI to create in-game items and environments more efficiently, gaming companies can allocate more time and resources to concentrate on core aspects, ensuring the production of intriguing and original content. The future of gaming, fueled by generative AI, is set to be an exciting and immersive adventure for players.

Natural Language Processing   The third impact vertical is not a single industry per se but rather many industries.

Generative AI can be used to generate new content such as text, summaries, or translations. Large language models are at the forefront of generative AI applications, with widespread impacts across various industries. LLMs can improve operational efficiencies by automating repetitive internal processes and accelerating innovation through customer feedback analysis, insights, and market research. These models can also improve customer experiences with concise answers and summaries available 24/7. The potential for managing knowledge is perhaps one of the most significant aspects of AI systems; organizations with specialized knowledge can offer their expertise in a tailored and concise manner to end users. Take the Mayo Clinic, for instance. Specializing in patient care, research, and education, the Mayo Clinic has amassed a wealth of data on medical conditions and treatments, such as patient records, research studies, and medical imaging data. They could create chatbots and virtual assistants that harness this data to provide expert guidance and advice to patients. By integrating these AI-driven tools into the Mayo

Clinic's website or mobile app, patients could access expert medical advice from anywhere around the globe.

Language models don't just generate language, but also code, music, poetry, stories, jokes, captions, summaries, translations, recommendations, and much more. The fields will further broaden, with LLMs providing innovative solutions for businesses and society.

Generative AI is immensely exciting as it will undoubtedly revolutionize how we create, consume, and process content across all aspects of our lives. As the technology develops, we can expect further paradigm shifts, leading to groundbreaking advancements in industries worldwide.

2

Innovative Approaches for High-Quality Data Generation

The present and future of generative AI are significantly more exhilarating than the developments of previous decades. As we consider the key milestones in AI's evolution, we'll highlight the features that have informed modern advancements in the field. Pioneering approaches have been crucial for the high-quality data generation we witness today, leading to a paradigm shift in artificial intelligence. This shift has transformed the way we produce and consume content and, consequently, the way humanity progresses.

Why Generative Models?

What makes generative models so special? How do they differ from others? To fairly answer these questions, we must ultimately delve into the innovative thought processes behind their creation. While avoiding overly technical details, we'll examine how developers thought outside the box to devise sophisticated, intelligent, and novel methods for generating data from scratch.

Explaining generative model concepts can quickly become too scientific and perplexing. However, their fundamental idea is relatively simple to grasp. Consider an example of handwritten digits from the renowned MNIST (Modified National Institute of Standards and Technology) dataset. A discriminative model's task might be to discern if an image of a handwritten digit is 0, 1, 2, 3, 4, 5, 6, 7, 8, or 9. For simplicity, let's focus only on 0s and 1s. Conceptually, a discriminative model seeks to differentiate digits by constructing a boundary in the data space. (Imagine the data space as a canvas where each data point represents a digit, and the boundary is like an invisible line that divides the different categories.) This boundary, representing the decision-making process of the discriminative AI model, separates the 0s and 1s.

If the model accurately establishes this boundary, it can distinguish the digits without explicitly identifying the exact locations of instances in the data space. In this context, achieving a reasonably accurate separation between categories might be sufficient for the model to perform its classification task effectively.

Discriminative models look at where 0s and 1s are located in the data space and use this information to find the best way to separate them. The term *conditional probability* refers to the likelihood of an instance being a 0 or 1 based on its features. By understanding these probabilities, the models can tell apart new instances, distinguishing between 0s and 1s, as shown in Figure 2.1.

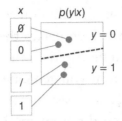

FIGURE 2.1 Representation of a discriminative model, showing how it distinguishes between two classes (y = 0 and y = 1) given input examples, choosing between the two options based on what model (the dotted line) has been trained on.

In contrast, generative models study the training data. As they train on the data, they see what the data looks like and how its features are distributed. They then try to generate data—1s and 0s, in this case as shown in Figure 2.2—that fall close to the real counterparts in the data space. Concrete, a generator model, would generate 1s that look similar to other 1s in the training data, and 0s that look similar to the 0s in the training data. This is what in the literature is meant by "modeling the distribution throughout the data space."

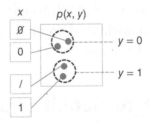

FIGURE 2.2 Representation of a generative model, highlighting the joint probabilities p(x, y). Data samples are drawn based on input features: 1s are sourced from the joint probability distribution, whereas 0s stem from their specific probability within this specific model.

Again, from this point of view it is not sufficient to roughly understand the data to replicate it; it must be understood precisely.

Given the training data distribution, the models have to learn how to connect the output data distribution to it—jointly. They capture the joint probability, which makes them probabilistic. Their output is typically happening based on the probability of the possible outputs. And this is how you generate new data.

The underlying concept is basically that simple idea, and it is remarkable how good the different models have become. The output quality has jumped significantly because they are successively getting better at mapping both distributions correctly. A much-underestimated benefit of generative models is their ability to cope with unlabeled data. They not only identify the underlying structure of the unlabeled data but can represent it. The first step is already nontrivial, and conventional artificial intelligence struggles with it.

The potential of generative AI is incredibly exciting and is based on this simple technical idea of mapping input and output distributions. However, as simple as the idea is, the execution is much harder. Research scientists, data scientists, and other very smart folks had to be creative in the process of developing these algorithms. From neural networks trying to fool each other, to iteratively adding noise and denoising images, to extended attention mechanisms, achieving breakthroughs goes hand in hand with breaking out from normal AI architectures. This is what has enabled truly special AI models.

From Birth to Maturity: Tracing the Development of Generative Models

Currently, we are at a point where a lot of the tech hasn't been defined yet. However, some tech approaches have made a permanent mark in the evolution of generative AI and AI as a whole. This section considers some of those approaches.

ELIZA

It is 1966. The Vietnam War intensified as the United States launched Operation Rolling Thunder, a sustained bombing campaign against North Vietnam, and the Chinese Cultural Revolution began, marking the start of a decade of political upheaval and social unrest in China.

A small group of computer scientists is standing in the IT lab 2.3.5 at MIT in Boston, Massachusetts, where Associate Professor Dr. Joseph Weizenbaum is about to reveal something groundbreaking: a chatbot named ELIZA, designed to imitate a psychotherapist's conversational style (Figure 2.3). The audience is stunned. ELIZA analyzes human input and generates responses that seem like they're coming from a real person. Weizenbaum explains how ELIZA's algorithm works: First it identifies patterns, then generates a response using predefined templates and rules. For example, if the input includes the word "mother," ELIZA might respond with "Tell me more about your family." The responses are usually in the form of a question or statement designed to encourage further conversation.

After initial reservations, something extraordinary is happening, as the scientists are opening up to this machine, sharing their deepest thoughts and emotions. ELIZA's ability to connect with people on a human level is simply astonishing. The demo ends and ELIZA has opened the door to a new world of possibilities, where machines and humans can communicate in ways never thought possible.

Could machines one day communicate with humans in a natural, conversational way? What kind of impact would this have on society?

It is officially agreed that ELIZA is the first chatbot that properly imitates conversations. ELIZA wasn't the first bot that existed, but the first with the ripple effect in research. The first trials of bots date back to 1950. The field was too primitive to use the term chatbot, as there was no chat happening. 1950 was also the year Alan Turing proposed a test for describing machine intelligence. He titled his work "Computing Machinery and Intelligence." He wrote that if a machine can trick humans into thinking it is human, then it has intelligence—the so-called *Turing test*. Today we have a much more refined idea of the Turing test, as we are experiencing the performance of large language models (LLMs) like ChatGPT. We see in detail what language models are good at and where they lack skills, making it easy for us to reveal them as nonhuman. Even though Alan Turing was decades ahead of his time, he wouldn't have a way to imagine this. However, ELIZA was not good enough to pass the Turing test.

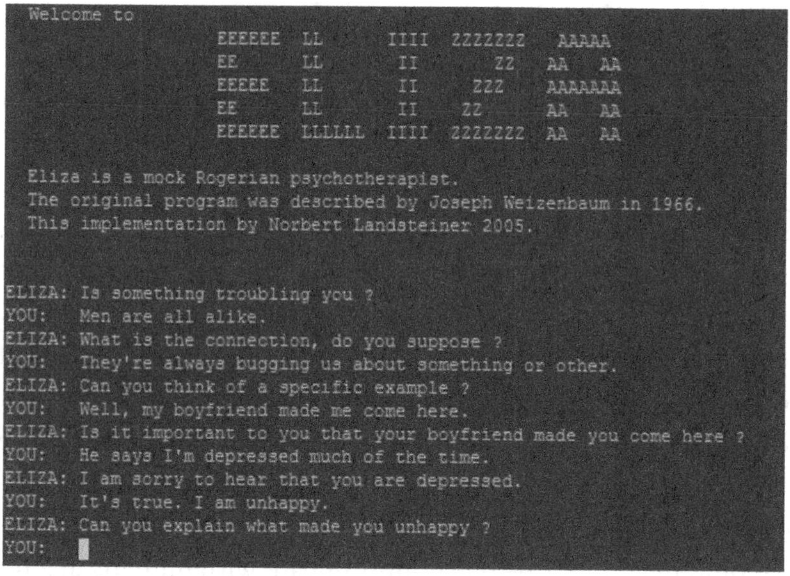

FIGURE 2.3 A conversation with the ELIZA chatbot.

Source: Wikimedia Commons / Public Domain

By no means is Alan Turing an insignificant figure. Widely regarded as the father of modern computing, Turing is best known for his work during World War II at Bletchley Park, the codebreaking center established to decipher German messages. There, he led a team of codebreakers who cracked the Nazi Enigma code, an accomplishment believed to have shortened the war by several years. Indeed, his name graces the Turing Award, often referred to as the Nobel Prize for computing.

The year 1955 marked another pivotal moment in the evolution of AI, as the term "artificial intelligence" was coined by another heavyweight computer scientist, John McCarthy. An American computer scientist, McCarthy co-authored the groundbreaking document that introduced the term *artificial intelligence* (AI) alongside Marvin Minsky, Nathaniel Rochester, and Claude E. Shannon on August 31, 1955. McCarthy described a field of study centered on creating machines capable of executing tasks typically requiring human intelligence, such as reasoning, learning, and problem-solving. As a testament to his immense contributions to the theory and practice of AI and the development of the programming language Lisp, McCarthy was honored with the Turing Award in 1971. Indeed, Lisp holds a special place in AI history as it was specifically designed to support symbolic processing—a cornerstone concept in artificial intelligence.

Symbolic processing is when a program uses words, numbers, and other symbols to do things that generally require human thinking. Just like how we use letters and numbers to write words and sentences, computers use symbols to represent information and then use special rules to do things with that information.

Lisp was widely used in the development of expert systems and other AI applications, not only because of its symbolic processing but also because it is a high-level programming language. This means it uses syntax that is closer to natural language, and often includes features like variables, functions, and control structures that allow programmers to write complex programs more easily. For example, Python, Java, C++, and Ruby are high-level programming languages, whereas machine code and assembly code are low-level. Trying to read it the first time is a sure way into headache land.

In the field of AI, there was a lot happening in the 1940s and '50s. Another result of the momentum in AI research is the multilayer perceptron first implemented in 1957 by Frank Rosenblatt. Inspired by the human brain and built on top of McCulloch and Pitts's theoretical invention of the perceptron in 1943, the multilayer perceptron (MLP) paved the way for neural networks. It has one input layer, a few in layers, and an output layer of interconnected nodes called *neurons*. Each layer is a step that processes the output of the previous layer to gradually build up a more complex representation of the input data. The MLP is trained in an iterative fashion via, for example, backpropagation, which adjusts the weights and biases of the neurons to minimize the difference between the network's output and the desired output, as described in Chapter 1, "AI in a Nutshell."

So far, all set for AI takeoff. However, winter was coming. An AI winter to be precise. To be even more precise, an AI ice age, as it spanned the late 1970s and early 1980s. It was triggered by a combination of factors, including unrealistic expectations about the capabilities of AI systems, a lack of progress in the development of AI technologies, and a reduction in government funding for AI research. In addition, some AI researchers were skeptical of the dominant approaches to AI at the time, resulting in no confidence, no developments, and no money.

And, as if this were not enough, there was a second AI winter following in the late 1980s and early 1990s, with no groundbreaking achievements in between the winters. Both AI winters were caused by a similar combination of factors; plus, there was a shift in research funding toward other areas, such as the Internet and biotechnology. In addition, there was a growing perception among some researchers that AI was overhyped and that progress in AI was unlikely without significant breakthroughs in areas such as natural language processing (NLP) and knowledge representation.

During this low point of AI, a then nameless research scientist proposed a very interesting idea that carried a lot of weight in the development of AI. The convolutional neural network (CNN) was first proposed by Yann LeCun and his team in 1989. Their convolutional layers are conceptually scanning images and making sense of them. Over multiple layers, they abstract detailed images. For example, the first convolution identifies straight lines. In the second convolution, these lines can become curves. In the third convolution layer, curves become eyes, whereas other layers represent ears and a nose. In the final layer, based on all the facial features, the decision is clear. It's a Chihuahua! LeCun and his colleagues developed the first practical implementation of CNNs, which was used for handwritten digit recognition and achieved state-of-the-art performance on benchmark datasets. Among all deep learning architecture, CNNs has had probably the most industry impact since then. The vast majority of computer vision (CV) applications are based on CNNs. Like the perceptron, CNNs proved to be a crucial step in the evolution of AI and generative AI later on.

Boltzmann Machines

Back to generative AI. The first significant machine learning architecture, which is an important precursor to later models, was the Boltzmann machine, which was introduced in the 1980s as a neural network that could learn and generate data from a probability distribution. For this, the data distribution needs to be stable, which means that there is a low degree of variability. This helps the Boltzmann machines to learn and represent complex patterns. If the data is unstable, the generated samples generated by the Boltzmann machine are inaccurate or inconsistent, and the training is generally inefficient. The way a Boltzmann machine generates data is close to modern generative AI models.

In Boltzmann machines there are hidden, invisible neurons that take binary states, either at 1 or 0, "on" or "off" (Figure 2.4). To generate a new data sample, the network is initialized with random values for the visible units, and then a series of alternating Gibbs sampling steps are performed. In Gibbs sampling, the nodes in the Boltzmann machine are updated one at a time, while keeping the other nodes fixed. The probability of a node being "on" or "off" is determined by the current state of the other nodes in the network. This process is repeated many times, resulting in a sample from the probability distribution of the Boltzmann machine. By generating many such samples, the model can learn the underlying distribution of the input data. Gibbs sampling is an iterative process that gradually improves the quality of the samples, allowing the model to converge on a stable distribution. The final state of the visible units represents a new data sample that has been generated by the Boltzmann machine. This process can be repeated to generate multiple new samples from the learned probability distribution. Even though Boltzmann machines have the capabilities to generate data, in the early days of these machines they were primarily used as a tool for exploring the properties of complex systems, rather than for generating data.

The standard Boltzmann machine was a blueprint for other neural network architectures that have contributed to the evolution of modern generative AI. But before we shed light on that, another headline has dominated the news about AI for quite some time.

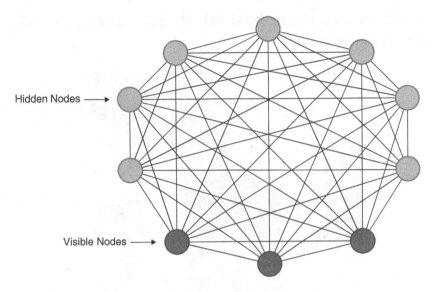

Hidden Nodes →

Visible Nodes →

FIGURE 2.4 Boltzmann machine concept

Deep Blue

In 1997, the world watched in awe as a chess-playing computer named Deep Blue (Figure 2.5), created by IBM, faced off against the reigning world chess champion, Garry Kasparov (Figure 2.6). This was the first time in history that a machine had challenged a human being at the game of chess on such a grand stage.

There was much speculation as to whether a machine could ever defeat a human being in a game as complex and strategic as chess. Many believed that Kasparov, widely regarded as one of the greatest chess players of all time, would easily defeat Deep Blue and prove once and for all that machines could never truly rival human intelligence.

However, as the match progressed, it became clear that Deep Blue was a formidable opponent. The computer, which had been specially programmed to play chess using advanced algorithms and machine learning techniques, was able to analyze millions of

possible moves per second and make decisions based on complex
patterns and strategies.

FIGURE 2.5 Deep Blue, a computer similar to this one, defeated chess
world champion Garry Kasparov in May 1997.

Despite his best efforts, Kasparov was unable to outmaneuver the machine, and in the end, Deep Blue emerged victorious.
The result was a stunning upset, and it sent shockwaves throughout the world of chess, artificial intelligence, and the world.

The match between Deep Blue and Kasparov marked a turning point in the history of AI, capturing the imagination of the

world and sparking a new era of innovation and discovery. It was a moment that would be remembered for years to come, and it laid the foundation for a future in which machines and humans would continue to push the limits of what is possible.

FIGURE 2.6 Garry Kasparov.
Source: S.M.S.I., Inc / Wikimedia Commons / CC BY-SA 3.0.

Even though Deep Blue's victory over Kasparov was perceived as an excellent case for AI that unlocked interest and funding, I see it more as a case for computational power. The underlying machine learning algorithms of Deep Blue were not revolutionary; rather, it was Deep Blue's power to process all possible moves and choose the best. However, sometimes it's not about technical truth, but perception.

Restricted Boltzmann Machines

In 2006 Geoffrey Hinton and his team developed a variant of Boltzmann machines as a solution to the problem of inefficient training—restricted Boltzmann machines (RBMs). RBMs restrict the connections between neurons to only occur between visible neurons and hidden neurons (Figure 2.7). Visible neurons represent the input data, whereas hidden neurons represent the features that RBMs learn to represent the input data. This restriction makes RBMs computationally more efficient and easier to train. On a conceptual level, the Boltzmann machine and the restricted Boltzmann machine aren't significantly different. Nevertheless, there's a gap of 24 years between their development. Back then, devising the restricted Boltzmann machine algorithm might not have been straightforward, and in reality, its intricacies run deeper than one might initially realize.

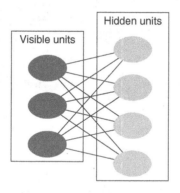

FIGURE 2.7 Concept of restricted Boltzmann machines.

Once the RBM is trained, it can be used for a variety of tasks in discriminative AI and generative AI, such as classification, regression, or generating new data samples.

So, media attention has been captured, but on the algorithm site, there was still a lot to be done. While in the conventional part of AI a lot of progress has happened, especially with neural networks, generative AI hasn't enjoy much attention.

They were only a few research scientists who were popularizing and promoting generative models like Boltzmann machines and others. Yann LeCun was one of them and Geoffrey Hinton was another.

Like LeCun, Hinton is regarded as one of the AI superstars. In 1978 he was awarded a PhD in AI. Today he is a professor at the University of Toronto and a researcher at Google Brain. He is considered to be one of the fathers of deep learning, as he together with other colleagues developed the backpropagation algorithm for training neural networks. He won numerous awards for his work before he also received the prestigious Turing Award in 2018. On Yann LeCun's fun stuff page, he shares some Geoffrey Hinton facts. One of them: "Geoff Hinton goes directly to third Bayes"—a nerdy joke that refers to Bayes' theorem, a mathematical formula that calculates the probability of an event based on prior knowledge or information. It took me three nights until I laughed.

Hinton had a huge interest in Boltzmann machines. However, Boltzmann machines have a problem known as the *sign problem*, which makes it difficult to perform efficient learning due to the sign of the weights in the neural network that the machine is made of. Updating the weights, which is the learning, includes the product of the weights of the neurons. This product can be positive or negative, leading to cancellation effects that make the learning process slow and inefficient.

Deep Belief Networks

In 2006, Geoffrey Hinton and his colleagues, building on the advancements of RBMs, introduced the concept of deep belief networks (DBNs). They stacked multiple RBMs or other unsupervised learning models to create a more powerful and efficient architecture.

The *deep* in DBNs comes from stacking multiple layers of RBMs, with each layer learning a more abstract representation of the input data (Figure 2.8). The training process of DBNs typically involves unsupervised pretraining using layer-wise training, followed by supervised fine-tuning using backpropagation. This made DBNs effective in unsupervised feature extraction, as the layers learned to capture increasingly abstract features from the input data. For example, when applied to image recognition, DBNs could identify edges and textures in the lower layers and more complex shapes and objects in the higher layers.

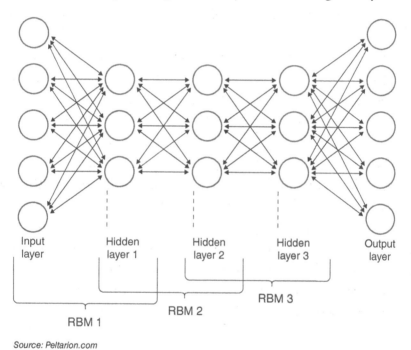

FIGURE 2.8 A deep belief network.

DBNs found applications in various fields such as image recognition, NLP, and speech recognition. They marked a significant difference from RBMs in that they learned hierarchical representations with higher layers, capturing more abstract features, whereas RBMs only learned a single layer of features. Additionally, DBNs employed backpropagation during the fine-tuning phase, whereas RBMs were solely unsupervised learning models.

Interestingly, DBNs played a crucial role in the resurgence of deep learning research in the mid-2000s. They were among the first models to demonstrate the effectiveness of unsupervised pretraining for deep architectures. The introduction of DBNs sparked renewed interest in the field of deep learning, leading to a wave of innovation and groundbreaking discoveries. Speaking to fellow data scientists, this seems to be forgotten.

Deep Boltzmann Machines

The journey of generative AI took yet another significant turn in 2009 when Ruslan Salakhutdinov and Geoffrey Hinton introduced deep Boltzmann machines (DBMs). DBMs were another leap forward in generative AI, as they further enhanced the capabilities of generative models.

DBMs, similar to DBNs, are hierarchical generative models made up of multiple layers of unsupervised networks, allowing them to model complex, high-dimensional data. They're created by stacking multiple RBMs, with each layer learning an increasingly abstract representation of the input data.

Training DBMs is done using a two-step process: layer-wise pretraining, which involves training each layer of RBMs independently, followed by fine-tuning using methods like contrastive divergence or persistent contrastive divergence. Contrastive divergence is an optimization algorithm that minimizes the difference between the input data distribution and the distribution learned by the model, while persistent contrastive divergence maintains a set of persistent samples that are updated throughout the training process, making it more efficient.

DBMs have found applications across various fields, such as image recognition, NLP, and speech recognition, thanks to their ability to model complex data structures and learn abstract features.

In terms of architecture, both DBMs and DBNs stack multiple RBMs, but DBMs have undirected connections between all layers, whereas DBNs have directed connections between layers, except for the top two layers, which have undirected connections.

The generative process in DBMs and DBNs also differs. In DBNs, the process is top-down, starting from the highest layer and moving downward. For example, in image recognition, a DBN might start with the high-level concept of an object and work its way down to the details. In contrast, DBMs sample from the joint probability distribution between visible and hidden units, allowing them to generate new data samples by taking into account the complex relationships between different features.

The introduction of DBMs contributed to the growing interest in the unsupervised learning and generative models that have continued to shape the field of AI. This further highlights the extraordinary impact of Hinton's work and dedication to the field of AI, which has propelled generative models and deep learning to new heights.

Autoencoders

As the field of AI continued to evolve, researchers explored new and innovative ways to leverage the power of neural networks. One such development was the emergence of autoencoders (AEs), a unique type of artificial neural network designed for unsupervised learning tasks. Autoencoders caught the attention of the AI community for their ability to learn efficient representations of data, as well as their potential to transform the landscape of generative AI.

The structure of autoencoders consists of two main parts: an encoder, which compresses input data into a lower-dimensional latent representation, and a decoder, which reconstructs the original data from the latent representation (Figure 2.9). For example, imagine an autoencoder trained to process images of handwritten digits. The encoder could compress the input image into a compact numeric representation, while the decoder would attempt to generate an image resembling the original input based on this compressed representation.

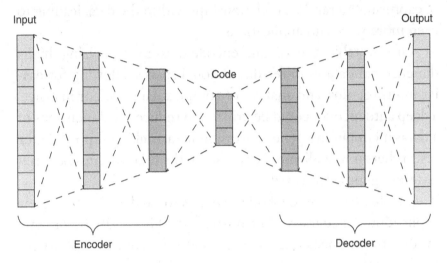

FIGURE 2.9 The autoencoder architecture.

Autoencoders aim to minimize the difference between the input data and the reconstructed output, usually by optimizing a loss function like mean squared error or cross-entropy. In our handwritten digit example, the autoencoder would seek to minimize the differences between the original input image and the reconstructed image produced by the decoder, thereby learning the most efficient way to represent and reconstruct the data.

Autoencoders have found a variety of practical applications, such as denoising, anomaly detection, and data compression. In denoising, an autoencoder can be trained to remove noise from images, effectively "cleaning" them up. For anomaly detection, autoencoders can be employed to identify unusual patterns in data, such as detecting fraudulent credit card transactions. In data compression, autoencoders can be used to reduce the size of data files while still maintaining their essential information.

With the advent of deep learning, more complex, multilayered autoencoders have emerged, enabling the learning of intricate data representations. These deep autoencoders are capable of capturing hierarchical relationships within the data, leading to even more powerful applications.

One notable use of autoencoders is in visualizing high-dimensional data in lower-dimensional spaces, allowing for easier interpretation and analysis of complex datasets. For instance, a deep autoencoder could be utilized to reduce the dimensions of a dataset containing gene expression data, making it possible for researchers to visualize and understand the relationships between different genes more easily.

The history of autoencoders spans several decades, with their application in generative AI truly taking off in the 2010s, primarily due to advancements in deep learning. Autoencoders have inspired other powerful generative models, such as variational autoencoders (VAEs), which have been applied to generate new images, text, and other data types by sampling from the learned latent space. This development marked a significant leap in the evolution of AI, opening up new possibilities for the future of machine learning and artificial intelligence.

Variational Autoencoders

In 2013, the world of generative AI saw a significant advancement by the introduction of VAEs by Kingma and Welling in their paper "Auto-Encoding Variational Bayes."[1] VAEs are built on the foundation laid by autoencoders, which are neural networks that learn to encode input data into a lower-dimensional representation and then decode it back to the original input.

---

[1]Diederik Kingma and Max Welling, "Auto-Encoding Variational Bytes," arXiv, December 10, 2022, https://arxiv.org/pdf/1312.6114.pdf

Autoencoders played a key role in the development of VAEs by providing a foundation for unsupervised learning and dimensionality reduction.

Unlike traditional autoencoders, VAEs introduced a probabilistic framework, modeling the input data using a continuous probability distribution. This enabled more diverse and realistic sample generation, a significant milestone in the evolution of generative AI. VAEs consist of two main components: an encoder, which maps input data to a latent space, and a decoder, which reconstructs the input data from the latent space (Figure 2.10).

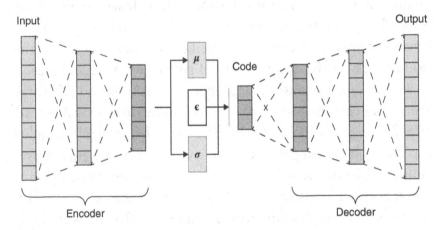

FIGURE 2.10 The variational autoencoder architecture.

Variational inference played a crucial role in the success of VAEs, as it was used to approximate the true posterior distribution of the latent variables, enabling efficient learning and sampling. For the first time, true generative capabilities were unlocked, allowing AI models to generate new images by interpolating between existing data points in the latent space, such as creating entirely new faces by blending features of existing faces.

VAEs found applications across various fields, such as image generation, text generation, drug discovery, and anomaly detection. For instance, VAEs have been used to generate realistic 3D models of molecules for drug discovery, accelerating the process of finding new treatments for diseases.

Women in Generative AI History

Born in various eras, numerous exceptional women have left their mark on the broader field of AI. Ada Lovelace, Grace Hopper, Elaine Rich, and Daphne Koller are just a few who have made substantial contributions. However, pinpointing outstanding women who specifically impacted early generative AI is challenging due to the historical gender imbalance in the field. Nevertheless, several women have made remarkable contributions to AI areas indirectly connected to generative AI or laid the groundwork for the development of generative AI techniques.

For instance, Pamela McCorduck, an author and AI historian, chronicled the history of AI in her influential book *Machines Who Think*, published in 1979. She provided valuable insights into the evolution of generative AI over the years. Cognitive psychologist Eleanor Rosch, active in the 1970s, developed prototype theory, which asserts that human categorization is based on prototypical examples rather than strict rules. Rosch's work indirectly impacted the development of generative AI, as her insights on human cognition informed AI model structure and data generation methods.

Cynthia Breazeal's research, primarily focused on social robotics during the late 1990s and early 2000s, laid the groundwork for AI systems generating human-like responses and behaviors. By creating robots capable of interacting and communicating with humans, such as Kismet, Breazeal made an indirect yet significant contribution to the generative AI domain.

In 2009, Fei-Fei Li co-developed ImageNet, a large-scale image database crucial for advancing deep learning. Although the modern generative AI era, marked by advancements like generative adversarial networks (GANs), began around 2014, Li's work on ImageNet facilitated these advancements by supplying the necessary data and infrastructure for training deep learning models.

It is essential to acknowledge the historical gender imbalance in the field of AI and promote increased diversity and inclusion in AI research moving forward. While there are many official female contributors, numerous unofficial ones have gone unmentioned for their contributions in the past. By recognizing and celebrating these women, we can work toward a more equitable future in AI research, ultimately leading to more diverse perspectives and innovative solutions in the realm of generative AI.

GANs: The Era of Modern Generative AI Begins

In 2014, just a year after the variational autoencoder caught the attention of the AI community, a 27-year-old research scientist named Ian Goodfellow revolutionized the AI landscape. Along with his team, Goodfellow developed a groundbreaking approach called generative adversarial networks (GANs), ushering in a new era of modern generative AI. This innovative technique took the AI world by storm, but it didn't come without its challenges.

Goodfellow's exceptional mind and relentless determination propelled him to the forefront of AI research. Beginning his academic journey at Stanford University, he earned his bachelor's and master's degrees in computer science under the guidance of Andrew Ng, a renowned AI expert and cofounder of Coursera. Goodfellow later pursued his PhD in machine learning at the Université de Montréal, supervised by Yoshua Bengio, a pioneer in deep learning, and Aaron Courville, an esteemed AI researcher.

Goodfellow was surrounded by top-tier mentors, and his career trajectory was nothing short of extraordinary. Alongside Bengio and Courville, he co-authored the MIT textbook *Deep*

Learning, which quickly became a staple resource in the field. His numerous accolades include being named one of *MIT Technology Review's* 35 Innovators Under 35.

Goodfellow's career took him to prestigious institutions like Google Brain, OpenAI, Google Research, and Apple, where he served as a director of machine learning in the Special Projects Group. However, he never shied away from standing up for his principles. In April 2022, Goodfellow resigned from his lucrative position at Apple to protest the company's in-person work requirements for employees. His next step took him to Google DeepMind as a research scientist, demonstrating his unwavering passion for AI research.

How GANs Work

So, how do GANs work? In a two-step process involving training and production, the crux of the magic unfolds during the training phase. The brilliance of GANs lies in their dual-component structure, comprising a generator that meticulously crafts new data samples and a discriminator that determines the authenticity of said samples. To create images, for instance, the generator employs a deconvolutional neural network, transforming noise into data samples, whereas the discriminator relies on a convolutional neural network to classify images as genuine or generated (Figure 2.11).

The essence of adversarial training involves the generator attempting to deceive the discriminator with lifelike creations, while the discriminator strives to differentiate between the authentic and the artificial. Should the generated data be detected as such, the generator must update its trainable parameters; likewise, if the generated data is not detected, the same process occurs for the discriminator. This dynamic propels both components to improve until they reach the Nash equilibrium—a point where neither can gain an advantage by changing their strategy. Reaching Nash equilibrium is a necessary condition for good performance.

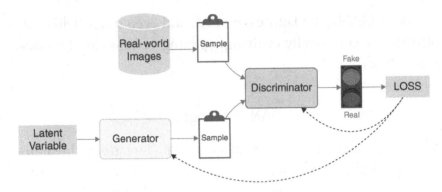

FIGURE 2.11 The generative adversarial network architecture.

After training, the generator, now at its peak performance, is frozen and subsequently employed for generating the respective data. With the ability to produce highly realistic and intricate data samples, such as images, text, and audio, GANs have sparked a revolution in numerous fields, ranging from art and design to scientific research and beyond. The true potential of generative models and their capacity to transform our interactions with technology has been unveiled.

The applications of GANs are astoundingly diverse, with uses such as

- Generating strikingly realistic images of faces, animals, and objects
- Image-to-image translation, morphing simple sketches into vibrant masterpieces
- Super-resolution, rejuvenating low-quality images by enhancing their resolution

- Data augmentation, producing additional training samples for machine learning models
- Style transfer, which imbues one image with the artistic essence of another image

With GANs, the landscape of AI, and even other fields, like physics, are continually evolving, opening up a world of endless possibilities.

GAN Challenges

The inception of GANs was no small feat. The groundbreaking concept of pitting two networks against each other not only revolutionized deep learning but also introduced a host of new challenges. The delicate balance of power between these networks hinges on factors such as hyperparameters, architecture, and training methods. If any one of these elements is off kilter, one network may overpower the other, resulting in training stagnation due to insufficiently differentiated feedback.

Navigating the complexities of GANs also involves addressing issues like mode collapse, vanishing gradients, and internal covariate shifts. In simple terms, mode collapse occurs when the generator becomes fixated on producing a limited variety of outputs, hindering its ability to generate diverse samples. Vanishing gradients, on the other hand, refer to the dwindling gradients that arise during backpropagation, making it difficult for the networks to learn effectively. Lastly, internal covariate shifts pertain to the inconsistencies in the distribution of layer inputs during training, which can hamper the overall learning process.

Since 2014, the landscape of GAN variations has expanded exponentially, now approaching nearly 9,300 iterations, each tailored to tackle a specific challenge. Although newer GAN models have grown more sophisticated, the initial breakthrough was made possible by the efforts of Ian Goodfellow and his colleagues.

Goodfellow's dedication and expertise laid the foundation for a transformative technology that has since become a cornerstone of AI. As GANs continue to influence the future of artificial intelligence, Goodfellow's remarkable career serves as a powerful reminder of the potential unleashed through determination, collaboration, and innovation.

From Pixels to Perfection: The Evolution of AI Image Generation

As a visually compelling field, it's no wonder that AI image generation has garnered widespread attention. The rapid progress, combined with the ease of grasping its potential, makes the generative AI story captivating to tell.

To achieve what was once deemed unattainable, generative AI image generation demanded remarkable algorithms and innovative technical ideas. The secret sauce that AI needed to generate exceptional images emerged from the evolution of autoencoders, GANs, and diffusion models.

Initially, autoencoders demonstrated prowess in reconstructing images. However, as deterministic models, they lacked true image generation capabilities. Deterministic, in this context, means that given the same input data, an autoencoder will consistently produce the same output.

The introduction of the variational component in the form of variational autoencoders marked a turning point for these models, granting them genuine generative potential. With variational autoencoders, AI began to yield promising results in generating images and faces. Yet, it was the arrival of GANs that propelled image generation quality to new heights.

GANs for Image Generation

GANs have emerged as a formidable force in the realm of image generation. As they learn the distribution of a given dataset, their flexibility allows them to generate a wide array of images, from realistic photographs and abstract art to depictions of nonexistent objects or creatures. However, their architecture, which suggests parallel data generation, is not traditionally suited for sequential data generation, such as text.

To bridge this gap, images and their captions can be combined in their respective vector embeddings. Vector embeddings are representations of images or pieces of text as a vector of numbers, capturing the semantic meaning of the input in a compact and useful form for downstream machine learning tasks. By integrating text and image representations through vector embeddings during GAN training, the image generation process becomes steerable via text. This groundbreaking functionality enables the seamless fusion of images and styles.

One of the remarkable attributes of GANs is their ability to generate images without labeled training data, as they inherently understand the original data distribution. Additionally, GANs can be trained progressively, commencing with low-resolution images and gradually enhancing resolution over time. This approach ensures that the generator learns to create increasingly detailed and realistic images as training advances.

The surge of research interest in GANs has sparked numerous innovations. Here are some notable examples:

- In 2016 and 2017, Wasserstein GAN (WGAN) and progressive growing of GANs (ProGAN) enhanced GAN training stability, allowing for the generation of higher-resolution images with improved quality.

- In 2018, BigGAN pushed the boundaries of GAN-generated image quality and resolution, creating high-fidelity images up to 512×512 pixels in size, boasting more realistic and diverse content.

- Between 2019 and 2021, StyleGAN emerged as a state-of-the-art image generator, providing fine-grained control over style and content. This enabled impressive results in face generation and other domains.

CLIP

While GANs have made substantial progress in generating images based on textual descriptions, they occasionally yield results that lack consistency with the text or the desired level of control. In January 2021, OpenAI introduced an innovative neural network model called CLIP (Contrastive Language-Image Pre-Training) to bridge this gap.

CLIP, bridging the gap between NLP and CV, is pretrained on a vast dataset of over 400 million image-text pairs. With an objective to create a joint representation of images and text, it uses contrastive pretraining to distinguish between similar and dissimilar pairs. This approach helps CLIP relate relevant text to images, even when the text doesn't directly describe the visual content. In a subsequent step, the model encodes images and text into a shared space through an image encoder and a text transformer. The goal is to amplify the similarity of genuine image-text pairs and reduce it for mismatched pairs, thereby boosting its efficiency. Figure 2.12 shows the three main steps of its training process. The ability of CLIP to comprehend the meaning of a text in relation to images has unlocked new possibilities for fusing NLP and CV.

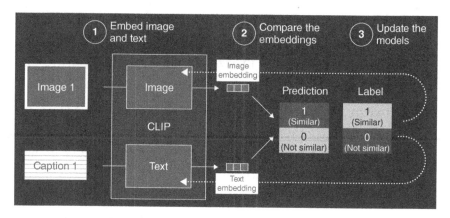

FIGURE 2.12 Training of CLIP.

As a powerful tool for tasks requiring an understanding of the relationship between text and images, CLIP surpasses GANs for several reasons:

- CLIP allows for more fine-grained control over image generation, enabling users to specify desired attributes such as color or orientation.

- CLIP can work with multiple modalities, including images, text, and audio, paving the way for more intricate and nuanced generation tasks.

- CLIP has demonstrated excellent generalization to unseen data, meaning it can generate high-quality images consistent with textual descriptions, even when the images are not seen during training.

The impact of CLIP on the AI community has been immense. Influencing other models like DALL-E and Stable Diffusion, CLIP has spurred research in text-to-image models and popularized the contrastive pretraining method.

DALL-E 2

Bolstered by the success of CLIP and the advancements it has spurred in the field of AI, research scientists have continued to push the boundaries of what's possible in a text-to-image generation. One such breakthrough, which has captured the world's attention, is OpenAI's DALL-E 2.

OpenAI's DALL-E 2 was the talk of the town in summer 2022, setting the tech world abuzz with its jaw-dropping image generation capabilities. A nearly solved problem, DALL-E 2 generates astoundingly realistic images at higher resolutions, adeptly blending concepts, attributes, and styles. It can manipulate and rearrange objects within images, and is a maestro at placing design elements in innovative compositions.

DALL-E 2's finesse lies in its ability to inpaint and outpaint images, generate variations, and transform aspects of images using text. *Inpainting* involves filling in missing or corrupted parts of an image using surrounding information, whereas *outpainting*, also known as *image extrapolation*, extends the content of an image beyond its original boundaries.

Once a nonprofit organization, OpenAI was established in 2015 with the noble objective of developing AI for the benefit of humanity. However, in 2018, the company made a controversial shift to a for-profit model, raising concerns about conflicts of interest and the potential undermining of its original mission.

Nowadays, OpenAI isn't as open as it used to be. No longer open sourcing their models, the organization discloses only select information, which means we can discuss the models only from a secondhand perspective.

To understand DALL-E 2, picture a skilled artist who listens to your description, captures the concept, and then produces a detailed, realistic image based on your vision. This wondrous technology is built on two key innovations: CLIP, which we've touched upon before, and diffusion, which we'll delve into shortly.

In a nutshell, DALL-E 2 uses CLIP encoders to map inputs to an embedding within a shared *concept space*, where matching pairs are mapped to nearby points and mismatching pairs are mapped to distant ones. The diffusion model, which they call GLIDE by the way, is trained to undo the steps of a fixed corruption or noising process, reversing the corruption or denoising and regenerating erased information. More on this in a moment.

DALL-E 2's prowess is showcased through a two-stage process: First, the prior model generates a CLIP image embedding from the given caption, capturing the gist of the image. Next, the diffusion model (unCLIP) generates the actual image from the embedding, filling in the details.

The advantages of this two-stage sampling process are evident: it prioritizes high-level semantics, making images more meaningful to humans, and allows for text-based transformations using CLIP's multimodal embedding space. In the summer of 2022 DALL-E 2 was, without a doubt, a testament to the potential of generative AI and a harbinger of even greater advancements.

Diffusion Models

As all of this evolves at a rapid pace, the open source ethos propelling its growth has enabled both researchers and hobbyists alike to explore and develop the capabilities of diffusion models.

June 2021 marked a pivotal moment for image generation, as a publication emerged, revealing that diffusion models had surpassed GANs in their capabilities. This revelation piqued my interest and brought the potential of diffusion models into focus for the first time. Fast-forward 10 months, and OpenAI's DALL-2, an image generation model based on the diffusion principle, has taken the world by storm, producing premium images that have left many astounded.

In August 2022, another significant development in the field of AI made headlines: Stability AI released Stable Diffusion, a model capable of achieving outputs on par with DALL-E 2. Taking a different approach from its counterparts, Stability AI astonished the tech community by open sourcing the model almost immediately. This model has been made accessible to all, runnable within a Python Notebook and on the Hugging Face platform. Hugging Face, a hub for sharing pretrained models, datasets, and demos of machine learning projects, promotes open source contributions and fosters a collaborative environment for AI enthusiasts.

Stability AI, under the leadership of CEO and founder Emad Mostaque, distinguishes itself by open sourcing AI technology—a rarity among the few companies equipped with the resources and talent to develop it. Their mission is to democratize access to AI technology and prevent its monopolization by major tech players. Beyond Stable Diffusion, they are working on projects such as Harmonai, which focuses on open source generative audio tools, and OpenBioML, a venture into the intersection of machine learning and biology. A vast and dedicated community has rallied behind Stability AI's vision.

Mostaque and his team are steadfast in their commitment to creating tools that empower individuals and grant them agency, a pursuit they believe can lead to a happier world and drive positive change. Stability AI, a well-capitalized startup, has garnered funding from Mostaque's personal fortune, a $100 million investment led by Coatue, and has plans to monetize by concentrating on specific domains, such as Bollywood.

Despite the general trend of keeping AI technology closed source—exemplified by OpenAI, ironically enough—it is both refreshing and challenging to see a company like Stability AI open source its models. This strategy comes at the cost of relinquishing much of their competitive advantage, as anyone can download a stable diffusion model, run it on some GPUs on-premises or in the cloud, fine-tune it, and obtain a remarkable image generation model without paying Stability AI a single penny.

Stable Diffusion Tech

Diffusion models stand at the forefront of innovation. What sets them apart is their unique methodology: introducing noise to learn the art of denoising, thereby unraveling the secrets of generating images. The results are nothing short of enchanting!

As previously mentioned, the crux of the diffusion model lies in its ability to add and remove noise from images. Picture this: During the forward diffusion phase, noise is added to the image, akin to static interference on a television screen. In the reverse diffusion stage the noise is eliminated, gradually revealing the image beneath the static. However, the pure diffusion model is hampered by its sluggishness, especially when dealing with a large number of diffusion steps or sizable images, as there are simply too many pixels to process.

Enter stable diffusion, a swifter alternative. This technique operates within the latent space, which is essentially a compressed version of the image, much like a smaller, condensed file. This family of models is known as *latent diffusion models*. To create the latent space, an autoencoder is employed, acting as a simplified version of the variational autoencoder mentioned earlier. The autoencoder's encoder compresses the image into lower-dimensional data, similar to zipping a file, whereas the decoder decompresses the latent data back into an image, akin to unzipping a file.

One of the most remarkable features of stable diffusion is its ability to generate images from text prompts in a highly impressive manner. The diffusion model is adapted to accept conditioning inputs, comparable to modifying a recipe based on a special request. Text inputs are transformed into embeddings (vectors) using a language model, reminiscent of the process employed by CLIP.

For inquisitive minds yearning to delve into stable diffusion, look no further than GitHub, where the code is easily accessible. Additionally, a web application has been thoughtfully designed to offer a hands-on experience with this revolutionary model.

Midjourney

Midjourney is an AI image-generation company that has taken the world by storm. Its latest creation, Version 5, is renowned for generating images of unparalleled quality, spanning from photorealistic to a wide array of artistic and nonartistic styles. Hailed as the epitome of AI-generated artistry, Midjourney's images are so remarkably lifelike that they have earned the title of being "indistinguishable" from real photographs.

However, this near-perfect level of realism has raised eyebrows among AI art enthusiasts. Some have dubbed Midjourney's creations as "creepy" and "too perfect." The groundbreaking improvements in Version 5 include incredibly realistic skin textures, impeccably detailed facial features, cinematic lighting effects, and striking reflections, glares, and shadows. The model also boasts more expressive angles or overviews of a scene, and—perhaps most importantly—human hands now consistently display the correct number of fingers.

Accessible through a Discord bot command, Midjourney's platform was still in open beta as of December 2023. The company's trailblazing team, led by founder David Holz, has a track record of releasing new and improved model versions every few months. With a keen eye for innovation and a commitment to consistent progress, Midjourney has already achieved profitability. Artists worldwide employ the platform for rapid prototyping of artistic concepts, while the advertising industry reaps the benefits of quickly creating original content.

Nevertheless, Midjourney remains vigilant about the images generated by its platform. In a fascinating turn of events, the company made headlines in March 2023 when it preemptively blocked the generation of images depicting Xi Jinping. This move was taken to prevent potential censorship by the Chinese government. Holz said that "the ability for people in China to use this tech is more important than your ability to generate satire."[2]

The enigmatic team behind Midjourney has kept their training techniques under wraps. However, it's very likely that they might use methods similar to stable diffusion, as its approach is known in detail. As AI-generated artistry evolves, the interplay of ideas and techniques among pioneers like Midjourney fuels progress and sparks anticipation for future revelations.

The Importance of Training Data

Training data reigns supreme as the vital cornerstone of AI image generation model performance. Text-to-image models necessitate sizable datasets, often procured by scouring the web for image-text pairs. However, this method bears inherent limitations and biases, including toxic language, nudity, violence, and harmful social stereotypes.

For those desiring elite model performance and possessing ample budgets, the LAION-400M dataset is the gold standard. Sourced from Common Crawl web data, it amasses an impressive

[2]Christopher McFadden, "Midjourney will no longer let you generate images of Xi Jinping," *Interesting Engineering*, April 3, 2023, https://interestingengineering.com/culture/midjourney-bans-xi-jinping-images

413 million image-text pairs tailored for top-tier models. To ensure safety, filters can be applied to regulate output, and models can be retrained on custom datasets to minimize biases for specific use cases. The operations are fueled by donations and public research grants. The team comprises 15 members, although it remains uncertain if all are engaged full-time.

Meanwhile, smaller AI image generation models like Craiyon—also known as DALL-E mini—trained on a mere 30 million images, produce fewer photorealistic images compared to their larger counterparts like stable diffusion. Here, strategic partnerships play a pivotal role, providing invaluable training data inaccessible to others. For instance, OpenAI's strategic partnership with Shutterstock was instrumental in DALL-E's development. Shutterstock is a marketplace for high-quality, royalty-free photographs, vectors, illustrations, videos, motion graphics, and music.

Another interesting dataset that merits attention is ImageNet. This extensive image database is organized following the Word-Net hierarchy, which, as of now, is confined to nouns. Each node within this hierarchy is illustrated by hundreds, even thousands, of images. The data is available at no cost to researchers for non-commercial purposes and comprises an impressive 14,197,122 images along with 21,841 synsets indexed. "Synsets" is short for "synonym sets," which are groups of words that mean the same thing. In ImageNet, each synset is linked to a bunch of images that show the same thing. Conceived as a large-scale visual database, the ImageNet project is designed for use in the field of visual object recognition software research.

Though Midjourney remains tight-lipped about the datasets utilized in training its model, whispers within the insider community suggest that copyrighted artists' work may have been included. Despite the lack of official confirmation, Midjourney's performance speaks volumes. Key speculations that stand out include the following:

- Midjourney enhances prompts pregeneration and applies post-processing to the image, resulting in its distinctive aesthetic.
- A carefully trained classifier model may evaluate and filter generated content.
- Midjourney's output is somewhat limited in terms of style, as they understand what works and what doesn't.
- Most crucially, they meticulously curate their data, retaining only the most exquisite images—a testament to their unwavering commitment to quality.

As the tale of Midjourney continues to unfold, the world eagerly anticipates the next chapter in the company's enigmatic journey, as well as the innovations and revelations that are yet to emerge.

Autoregression

Google is another significant player in the realm of generative AI. Among their most notable models are the image generation models Imagen and Parti. Imagen, a latent diffusion model, showcases Google's expertise in diffusion models. Parti offers an impressive performance through a different approach to image generation—autoregression. Although this method is sequential rather than parallel, it is worth delving into autoregressive models for image generation. As you shall see, they play a crucial role in this field.

Enter Parti, Google's answer to DALL-E 2, which began with the publication of "Scaling Autoregressive Models for

Content-Rich Text-to-Image Generation."[3] Parti addresses text-to-image generation as a sequence-to-sequence modeling problem, taking advantage of advances in LLMs. Employing the Vision-Transformer-based VQGAN (ViT-VQGAN) image tokenizer, Parti encodes images as sequences of discrete tokens, enabling the reconstruction of high-quality, visually diverse images. The result is state-of-the-art zero-shot and fine-tuned FID (Fréchet inception distance) scores on MS-COCO (Microsoft Common Objects in Context), with the model proving effective across a broad range of categories and difficulty aspects, as demonstrated in the Localized Narratives and PartiPrompts benchmark analysis.

In essence, *zero-shot* refers to a model's ability to perform a task without prior training or examples specific to that task. It highlights a model's capacity to generalize and apply learned knowledge from one context to another without the need for additional fine-tuning.

FID is a commonly used metric for evaluating the quality of generated images. Picture it as a ruler measuring the distance between two distributions of features extracted from real and generated images. Lower FID scores signify that the generated images more closely resemble the real ones, thus indicating higher quality.

MS COCO is an extensive image recognition, segmentation, and captioning dataset, boasting over 330,000 images and more than 2.5 million object instances labeled with object categories, instance segmentation, and dense captioning. Its importance in image generation research cannot be overstated, as it provides a widely used benchmark dataset for assessing the quality and diversity of generated images. Numerous state-of-the-art image generation models are evaluated using

[3]Jiahui Yu et al. "Scaling Autoregressive Models for Content-Rich Text-to-Image Generation," arXiv, June 22, 2022, https://arxiv.org/pdf/2206.10789.pdf

the MS COCO dataset, and high scores on this benchmark strongly indicate the performance and generalization ability of the model.

Autoregressive models are undoubtedly innovative, achieving remarkable results in both parallel and sequential data generation. While they may have been underestimated in the past, they have brought about significant advancements in AI and could lead to further breakthroughs in the field. Perhaps their true potential lies in supporting video generation and other yet-to-be-discovered applications in the realm of generative AI.

The Future of AI Image Generation

As the modern generative AI era unfolds, a plethora of models have emerged, including stable diffusion, Midjourney, DALL-E 2, Craiyon, Parti, Imagen, and others such as Night Café, Artbreeder, DeepAI, StarryAI, WOMBO Dream, and Bria (which is targeted for business-to-business [B2B])—and even earlier models like Google's Deep Dream Generator. This proliferation heralds a future teeming with mind-blowing technology. Improvements, innovations, trends, new paradigms, issues, adoption, and applications of generative AI will persist and evolve in the years to come, with AI image generators creating 2D, 3D, and even 4D images based on text.

Simply put, 4D images represent changes over time—a sequence of three-dimensional images depicting a transforming object or scene. Achievable through video capture, 3D modeling, animation, and machine learning, 4D images hold immense potential. For instance, generative AI could revolutionize medical diagnostics by transforming X-rays and CT scans into realistic, interactive images, allowing doctors, for example, to examine a broken rib from various angles.

As generative AI platforms become increasingly prevalent, image generation as a standard functionality seems inevitable.

Emad Mostaque's theory posits that most image generation companies will eventually converge in terms of AI capabilities. However, this may not necessarily be true, as consistently exceptional personnel are required to push these hard tech boundaries, and the diverse landscape of generative AI allows for countless turns on the highway of innovation. Consider use case–specific AI image generation: one focusing on training data for self-driving cars, another on medical imaging. Ultimately, this diversity hinges on the training data each company obtains and potentially generates.

Assuming AI image generation models do eventually reach similar capabilities and qualities in a profitable manner, companies must explore what's next. In this innovative, competitive space with high expectations set by capital allocators, models will likely evolve into more capable, multimodal systems, eventually culminating in artificial general intelligence. More on this fascinating prospect will be explored later in the book.

Lastly, generative AI companies must be nimble in pivoting their strategies, even after expending significant energy on a particular tech approach. As witnessed in AI image generation, many companies initially doubled down on GANs, tweaking and refining them to fit narrow use cases. However, the open source release of stable diffusion—with its superior performance—prompted an immediate shift in strategy. In this ever-evolving landscape, adaptability and resilience are the hallmarks of success, as generative AI continues to forge new frontiers in the world of technology.

A Crucial Tech Disruption: Text Generation

In the realm of AI data generation, two primary streams have emerged, each with its own unique capabilities: image generation, which exemplifies parallel data generation, and text generation, representative of sequential data generation. These two distinct streams complement one another, paving the way for AI's versatile applications in various domains.

Text generation models, being intrinsically adept at handling sequential data, excel in generating not only written text but also other forms of sequential data, such as code, music, voice, and other auditory elements. Furthermore, they can generate time-series data, encompassing synthetic sensor data to enhance datasets, stock market data, and much more. A few examples include composing original music pieces, simulating stock market trends, and even generating realistic human speech, all thanks to the inherent sequential nature of these models.

As you delve further into this chapter, you will witness the innovative spirit of research scientists who achieved groundbreaking results. This creative triumph is best exemplified by the launch of ChatGPT on November 22, 2022. Since then, LLMs have transcended mere hype, offering tangible value for businesses and individuals alike. My experience with GenerativeAI.net is a testament to this, as I consult companies on leveraging language models for tailored applications, and as a leader at Infosys Consulting, I guide teams in implementing this revolutionary technology, accumulating an impressive array of client success stories and credentials. Our work with these organizations extends beyond simple implementation; we help them harness the power of generative AI to transform into AI-first companies.

Autoregression Models

In the fascinating realm of text generation models, an overarching player emerges: the autoregressive model. Whenever a model uses a sequence of words or other sequences to predict the ensuing words, we are witnessing the prowess of autoregression. While this mechanism is not exclusive to text generation, it dominates the field. As we traverse through the landscape of text generation, note that all models presented, except for rule-based systems and GANs, are autoregressive. However, we shall maintain our chronological approach.

Our journey takes us back to the early 20th century, when the British statistician Yule first introduced autoregression models, also known as autoregressive models. These statistical marvels utilize past values of a time series to forecast future values. When applied to text generation, autoregression models astutely predict the next word or token, basing their deductions on the context of the preceding words in the sequence.

Autoregression models come in various orders, ranging from the elementary first-order model, AR(1), to more intricate variants. AR(1) predicts the value of the time series at time 't' by relying on its value at time 't-1'. Meanwhile, the more sophisticated AR(p) models predict the time-series value at time 't' by considering values at times 't-1', 't-2', and so forth, up to 't-p'.

While these models are traditionally grounded in statistical methods, they have evolved to adapt to neural network architectures such as recurrent neural networks (RNNs) and transformers. This adaptation has enabled them to capture more complex dependencies, thus generating text that is not only coherent but also imbued with semantic meaning. The autoregressive model's journey from its inception to its modern adaptations reflects the ever-evolving nature of AI, a testament to human ingenuity and our drive to understand the intricacies of language.

Markov Chains

Born in Russia, Andrey Markov was a prodigious mathematician who, in 1906, introduced the world to Markov chains. His groundbreaking paper laid the foundation for the study of stochastic processes, particularly those now called Markov chains. Although they were far removed from text generation at the time, their potential in this area would soon be recognized.

Fast-forward to 1948 when Claude Shannon, an illustrious mathematician and electrical engineer who later helped to coin the term *artificial intelligence*, presented a paper demonstrating the use of Markov chains in text generation. Shannon's innovative Markov chain model generated English text that echoed the style and structure of natural English sentences. The model was trained on a corpus of text data, and it crafted new sentences by predicting the next word based on the previous word.

Markov chains, a type of statistical model, depict sequences of events in which each event's probability depends solely on the state of the system during the previous time step, not on earlier events. To generate new text, Markov chains predict the next word in a sequence based on the probability of each word, given the previous word. By training the model on a corpus of text data, the probabilities of each word given the previous word are estimated. With an initial seed word or phrase, the model generates new text by predicting the next word using the probability distribution and incorporating it into the sequence. Figure 2.13 shows an example.

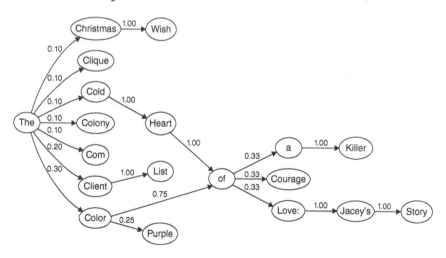

FIGURE 2.13 A probability diagram of a Markov chain for text generation. Each node represents a state (word or sequence of words), and each edge represents the transition probability from one state to another, as determined from the training text.

Although Markov chains offer simplicity and computational efficiency in text generation, their limitations lie in capturing long-term dependencies and generating coherent, semantically meaningful text. As such, Markov chains often serve as a baseline model for text generation tasks, whereas more advanced applications rely on sophisticated models like recurrent neural networks and transformer-based models. Thus, Markov chains, while foundational, represent just one stepping stone in the ever-evolving journey of AI, as we strive to decode the complexities of language.

Rule-Based Text Generation

Pioneered in the 1980s, rule-based systems for text generation marked another significant milestone in text generation. These systems harnessed the collective knowledge of researchers and developers from various disciplines, including computer science and linguistics. By employing sets of rules and handcrafted knowledge, rule-based systems generated text with structure, content, and style that adhered to linguistic principles.

In essence, rule-based systems generate text by following handcrafted rules based on linguistic knowledge, such as grammar rules and semantic relationships between words. For instance, the rules might dictate that a weather report should begin with a general statement about the overall weather conditions, followed by specific details about temperature, precipitation, and wind.

These rule-based systems have been used for various applications, including weather reports, financial reports, and medical reports. They remain relevant even today in specific domains that require standardized text output. For example, rule-based systems have been employed to generate personalized medical reports for patients, summarizing their symptoms, diagnoses, and treatment plans in a clear, concise manner. The quality of the generated text is contingent on the quality and accuracy of the rules, which demand considerable domain expertise and manual effort to develop.

Although rule-based systems have their merits, they are inherently limited in generating novel or creative text. Their strength lies in producing standardized or formulaic text, where adherence to linguistic rules and conventions is of paramount importance. Consequently, rule-based systems, much like Markov chains, form an essential part of the ever-evolving AI journey, as we endeavor to unravel the complexities of language and craft increasingly sophisticated text generation models.

Recurrent Neural Networks

Building upon the foundations laid by rule-based systems and Markov chains, recurrent neural networks (RNNs) emerged in the early 1980s, thanks to the pioneering work of John Hopfield and David Rumelhart. Both Hopfield and Rumelhart were leading figures in the realm of AI, with Hopfield renowned for his contributions to neural networks and Rumelhart for his work on parallel distributed processing—a great team fit.

RNNs are a type of neural network designed to process sequential data by maintaining an internal state that captures the context of previous inputs. In text generation tasks, RNNs commonly predict the next word or token based on the context of preceding words in the sequence. By processing the input sequence one token at a time and updating its internal state at each step based on the input token and the previous state, RNNs effectively encapsulate a summary of prior inputs. This internal state is instrumental in predicting the next output. Figure 2.14 illustrates an unrolled RNN, and Figure 2.15 showcases the deceptively simple mechanics of a standard RNN unit. A layer is quite straightforward.

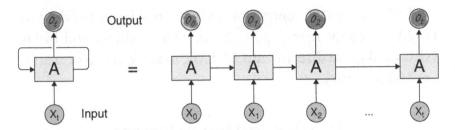

FIGURE 2.14 A recurrent neural network unrolled.

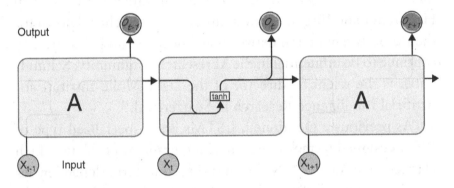

FIGURE 2.15 A standard RNN unit.

RNNs have found widespread applications in natural language processing, including language translation, dialogue generation, and sentiment analysis.

However, RNNs are not without their limitations. They often grapple with the vanishing gradient problem, which hinders their ability to capture long-term dependencies, akin to long-term memory. This issue can lead to degraded performance, rendering RNNs impractical for large-scale applications. To address this challenge, researchers have developed variants of RNNs, such as long short-term memory (LSTM) networks and gated recurrent units (GRUs). Both LSTMs and GRUs excel at capturing long-term dependencies, enabling the generation of more coherent and semantically meaningful text.

LSTMs typically outperform GRUs, making them the preferred choice for many applications. As a result, we will bypass
GRUs and delve directly into LSTMs, looking at their capabilities and potential.

Long Short-Term Memory Networks

Long short-term memory (LSTM) networks first appeared on
the AI scene in 1997, thanks to the innovative work of Sepp
Hochreiter and Jürgen Schmidhuber, two researchers known for
their expertise in neural networks and deep learning. Today, they
continue to be influential in the AI research community; Schmidhuber is the scientific director of the Dalle Molle Institute for
Artificial Intelligence Research in Switzerland.

As previously mentioned, LSTMs are a specialized type of
RNN designed to tackle the vanishing gradient problem, which
plagues traditional RNNs in capturing long-term dependencies
within sequential data. While they outshine earlier models,
LSTMs are overshadowed by the more recent transformer architecture, which boasts unparalleled attention mechanisms.

LSTMs manage to maintain a cell state that selectively adds
or removes information, allowing the network to remember or
forget details over extended input sequences. This feat is accom-
plished through a system of gates that regulate the flow of information into and out of the cell state. Figure 2.16 depicts the
detailed workings of an LSTM unit.

Since their inception, LSTMs have been employed in a vast
array of applications, such as machine translation, text classification, and sentiment analysis. In text generation tasks, LSTMs
have proven especially effective, generating coherent and semantically meaningful text with fewer errors than earlier models.

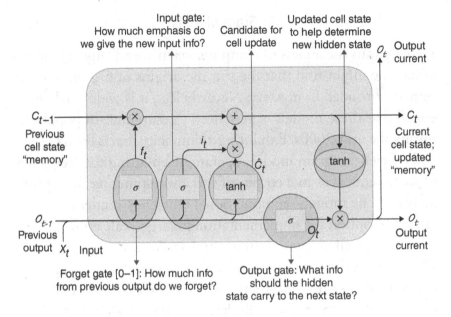

FIGURE 2.16 An LSTM unit

LSTMs have been broadly adopted within the tech industry, with numerous companies utilizing them for natural language processing applications. Google, for instance, has used LSTMs in products like Google Translate and Google Assistant for language translation and speech recognition. However, it is worth noting that more recently, LSTMs have been largely superseded by more advanced systems, such as neural machine translation (NMT). NMT specializes in language translation, with the neural network being trained on vast corpora of parallel sentences to learn the relationships between words and phrases in source and target languages.

Other areas where LSTMs have been the go-to AI model include chatbot development, language modeling for speech recognition, and speech synthesis. All in all, LSTMs have been an instrumental tool in natural language processing and have left a lasting impact on the field since their introduction.

N-Gram Models

Delving into the annals of computer science and language modeling, one might find that the specific origins of n-gram models remain shrouded in mystery. Nevertheless, it is widely acknowledged that these models experienced a resurgence in popularity during the mid-2000s. Exhibiting a simplicity that is both elegant and efficient, n-gram models operate by counting the frequency of word sequences in a corpus of text and estimating their probabilities. The models' computational efficiency renders them an attractive option for implementation in large-scale applications.

Yet, like all things, n-gram models do have shortcomings. Chief among these are their inability to capture long-term dependencies in text and their susceptibility to data sparsity and overfitting. Despite these limitations, the models have been employed in an array of applications, ranging from voice assistants like Siri, Alexa, and Cortana to keyword extraction, topic modeling, and sentiment analysis.

However, as the sands of time have shifted and more advanced models have emerged, the once-prevalent n-gram models have gradually receded into the background. Nonetheless, their impact on the development of natural language processing should not be understated, and they will forever remain an important milestone in the rich tapestry of AI history.

Seq2Seq

Venturing deeper into the labyrinth of AI text generation, we arrive at the ingenious development of sequence-to-sequence (Seq2Seq) models. Much like an architect who carefully constructs a sturdy frame around the building's core, Seq2Seq models ingeniously harness the power of other AI text generation models, elevating them to a new level of sophistication and efficiency.

The foundations of the Seq2Seq model were laid in 2014 in a paper titled "Sequence to Sequence Learning with Neural Networks" by a group of trailblazing researchers from Google, including Ilya Sutskever, Oriol Vinyals, and Quoc V. Le.[4] As an intriguing aside, Ilya Sutskever cofounded OpenAI and serves as its chief scientist.

Seq2Seq models consist of two recurrent neural networks (RNNs)—LSTMs and GRUs—working in tandem as an encoder network and a decoder network. With applications ranging from machine translation and text summarization to speech recognition, Seq2Seq models operate by using the encoder to transform an input sequence into a fixed-size vector representation, aptly dubbed the *context vector*. This vector serves as a concise summary of the input sequence, providing the foundation on which the decoder generates an output sequence (the text generation component). The training process hinges on minimizing a loss function that quantifies the disparity between the predicted output sequence and the ground truth.

As with any great invention, there is always room for improvement. Enter the attention mechanism, introduced by Dzmitry Bahdanau, KyungHyun Cho, and Yoshua Bengio in 2015, which bestowed upon the decoder the ability to focus on different segments of the input sequence at varying time steps. This breakthrough significantly enhanced the model's context awareness. To distill this concept into its simplest form, imagine the decoder's initial limitation: A single hidden state vector at the end of the encoder proved insufficient. The attention mechanism's solution was elegant and effective; it provided as many hidden state vectors as there were instances in the input sequence, enabling the decoder to process information with greater finesse and precision.

---

[4] Ilya Sutskever, Oriol Vinyals, and Quoc V. Le, "Sequence to Sequence Learning with Neural Networks," *NeurIPS Proceedings*, accessed November 27, 2023, https://proceedings.neurips.cc/paper/2014/file/a14ac55a4f 27472c5d894ec1c3c743d2-Paper.pdf

It becomes apparent that Seq2Seq models' applications are vast and varied. One such prominent application, which I touched upon earlier, is Google Translate. Seq2Seq models are not limited to LSTMs but can incorporate them, enabling the translation of one sequence or sentence in one language to another sequence or sentence in a different language. Refer to Figure 2.17 for a zoomed-out view of the architecture of Seq2Seq models.

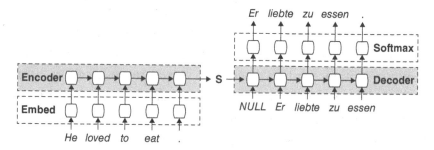

FIGURE 2.17 The big picture perspective of a Seq2Seq model.

Google's innovative streak does not end with translation. The tech giant has also harnessed the power of Seq2Seq models to enhance the accuracy of speech recognition in Google Assistant, among other applications. Meanwhile, chatbots and conversational agents have benefited greatly from Seq2Seq models, which, when trained on a vast corpus of conversational data, generate responses that are more contextually appropriate and natural-sounding.

Google is not alone in recognizing the potential of Seq2Seq models. Other tech behemoths, including Facebook, Microsoft, and Amazon, have incorporated these models into their products and services. However, Google has undoubtedly been a key driving force in the development and popularization of Seq2Seq models, with Google Brain hosting numerous leading researchers in the field.

Comparing Seq2Seq models with their AI counterparts, LSTMs excel at capturing long-term dependencies, while n-gram models are faster to train but lack the ability to capture context as effectively. Seq2Seq models, as a kind of meta-model, are specifically designed for sequence-to-sequence mapping tasks and can generate more natural-sounding output. However, they require more data and fine-tuning.

The Amazon AlexaTM 20B, a moderate-sized (20 billion parameter) Seq2Seq language model, is likely the most powerful Seq2Seq model to date. It outperforms the much larger GPT-3 in language translation and summarization, achieving state-of-the-art performance in few-shot-learning tasks across all Flores-101 language pairs. Despite its impressive capabilities, its release in August 2022 did not cause the same stir in the AI community as OpenAI's ChatGPT did three months later. The reason behind this disparity in impact lies in the output quality: AlexaTM 20B's output was not as impressive as ChatGPT's. The intriguing reasons behind this discrepancy shall be unveiled later.

GANs for Text Generation

Before delving into transformers, the cornerstone of state-of-the-art language generation models like GPT, let's pause to take a look at GANs in text generation.

To recapitulate, GANs for text generation operate in a fascinating dance of deception and detection. The generator model concocts realistic text samples, aiming to dupe the discriminator model into believing the text is genuine. Simultaneously, the discriminator model hones its ability to discern between authentic and fabricated text samples. Through this iterative process, both models evolve, refining their skills based on feedback from one another.

Several GAN architectures have emerged specifically for text generation, such as SeqGAN, MaliGAN, and TextGAN. Examining TextGAN as a representative example offers valuable insights into the process of generating sequential data using GANs. To better grasp its inner workings, we must first address the unique challenges posed by the text's discrete nature, which hinders the direct application of gradients from the discriminator to the generator. TextGAN adapts to these challenges in several ways:

- It converts both real and fake sentences into high-dimensional latent feature distributions, transforming the discrete text problem into a continuous space. In layman's terms, it maps the text onto a spectrum, smoothing out the rough edges and making it more amenable to analysis.

- TextGAN employs a kernelized discrepancy metric called reproducing kernel Hilbert space (RKHS) to gauge the disparity between real and fake text samples. Simply put, it measures the "distance" between the two, enabling the generator to better understand how to produce realistic text.

To render the generator differentiable, TextGAN utilizes a soft-argmax operator and additional techniques like initialization strategies and discretization approximations. In essence, TextGAN modifies the traditional GAN framework, overcoming the hurdles of text generation and producing more plausible and coherent text samples.

However, GANs' potential for text generation is not without limitations. They can suffer from mode collapse, reducing the generator model's output range and stifling sentence variety. Furthermore, GANs may generate nonsensical or irrelevant text and can be difficult to train and optimize due to an unstable training process.

In the grand scheme of text generation, GANs are unlikely to play a pivotal role in the future.

Attention – Transformer – Self-Attention

The intriguing tale of attention mechanisms in deep learning unfurled with the publication of a seminal paper in 2016 titled "Neural Machine Translation by Jointly Learning to Align and Translate,"[5] by Dzmitry Bahdanau, KyungHyun Cho, and Yoshua Bengio. Within the dense text of their paper, they introduced the world to the concept of the *attention mechanism*—an innovative solution to the problem of long-range dependencies in Seq2Seq models. Imagine reading a lengthy novel with countless characters and plotlines. The attention mechanism is akin to a well-placed bookmark, enabling you to keep track of important details and navigate the narrative more efficiently. In the context of Seq2Seq models, Bahdanau, Cho, and Bengio's attention mechanism operates like this literary bookmark, allowing the model to focus on different parts of the input sequence while generating the output, thereby attenuating the issue of long-range dependencies. This novel approach drastically enhanced the performance of neural machine translation systems, setting a new path for future exploration in the field.

Fast-forward to 2017, a year marked by another monumental stride in AI research—a groundbreaking paper titled "Attention Is All You Need," by Ashish Vaswani and his fellow researchers at Google Brain and Google Research.[6] The paper proposed the innovative transformer architecture, making attention mechanism its central pillar. In a way, it's like shifting from a traditional book to an e-reader that allows you to highlight and annotate the most crucial parts of the text. The attention mechanism in these models enables focusing on specific parts of the input to make accurate predictions, much like highlighting pivotal points in a text.

[5]Dzmitry Bahdanau, KyungHyun Cho, and Yoshua Bengio, "Neural Machine Translation by Jointly Learning to Align and Translate," arXiv, May 19, 2016, https://arxiv.org/pdf/1409.0473.pdf
[6]Ashish Vaswani et al. "Attention Is All You Need," *NeurIPS Proceedings*, accessed November 27, 2023, https://proceedings.neurips.cc/paper_files/paper/2017/file/3f5ee243547dee91fbd053c1c4a845aa-Paper.pdf

Self-attention, a specific variant of attention mechanism employed in the transformer architecture, functions somewhat like a photographic memory—it captures relationships between different parts of the input sequence, irrespective of their distance. This mechanism allows the model to "remember" information from far-flung parts of the sequence and use that information to create a better output.

A key advantage of the transformer architecture was its ability to process input sequences in parallel, rather than sequentially. It's a bit like reading multiple chapters of a book simultaneously without losing the narrative thread. This meant improved efficiency and scalability, which in turn led to a rise in the popularity and application of transformer models.

Subsequently, transformers took the AI world by storm, rapidly emerging as the state-of-the-art architecture for an array of NLP tasks, including machine translation, text summarization, and language modeling. They outclassed existing RNN-based models, as they effectively address the issues of long-range dependencies, a problem that LSTM and RNN models grappled with. It's like upgrading from an old typewriter to a modern computer—the core concept remains the same, but the capabilities are vastly expanded.

Tech Triumphs in Text Generation

Since the advent of the self-attention mechanism, we have witnessed an effusion of diverse LLMs, each bringing unique features to the table. Among the most notable are OpenAI's GPT series, Google's BERT, Transformer-XL from Google Brain, Facebook's BART, and T5 from Google Research. Subsequent chapters will delve deeper into the intricacies of these different models. However, for now, let's focus on some key technical aspects like tokenization, models being probabilistic, training, fine-tuning, prompting, scaling laws, reinforcement learning from human feedback (RLHF), emergent abilities, and more. These, in essence, form the backbone of these models, acting as the nuts and bolts that piece together the entire machinery of AI.

Tokenization for LLMs

Tokenization, in the context of language models, is akin to the process of linguistic dissection. It involves the fragmentation of input and output texts into smaller, manageable units known as *tokens*. These tokens could be as minute as characters, as standard as words, or as nuanced as subwords and symbols. This process is not merely an act of division, but a means to a greater end. Tokenization is instrumental in enabling AI models to grapple with the diversity and complexity of human language, encompassing different vocabularies, languages, and formats. Moreover, it allows for a significant reduction in computational and memory costs, thus boosting the efficiency of these models.

The act of tokenization, however, is not a one-size-fits-all approach. There are different methods of tokenization, such as rule-based, statistical, or neural. The choice of method is determined by the complexity and variability of the texts being handled. Rule-based methods, for instance, rely on predetermined rules to tokenize text, whereas statistical methods look for common patterns and frequencies in the text. Neural methods, on the other hand, leverage the power of neural networks to understand and segment text.

Among these methods, OpenAI, the creator of this very model you're interacting with, has opted for a subword tokenization method known as *byte-pair encoding* (BPE) for its GPT-based models. BPE operates akin to a keen-eyed linguist, identifying and merging the most frequently occurring pairs of characters or bytes into a single token. It's important to note that the number of tokens or the size of the vocabulary is not a constant across all models; it varies, much like the models themselves.

Tokenization inevitably impacts the amount of data and the number of calculations a model is required to process. It's a simple equation: The more tokens a model has to juggle, the greater the demand on memory and computational resources. Consequently, the cost of running a model is intrinsically linked to the tokenization method employed, the size of the vocabulary, as well as the length and complexity of the input and output texts.

As of February 2023, OpenAI's Davinci model cost $0.06 per 1,000 tokens. To illustrate, generating a summary for a 2,500-word article, roughly 3,125 tokens, costs about $0.19. For a book-length text, the price rises to approximately $7.50. Scaling up to an industrial operation, such as producing 100 books a day, daily costs hit $750, monthly around $22,500, and annually about $270,000—only for tokenization, prediction excluded, and training is a totally different topic. These estimates vary with factors like text length, complexity, and potential volume usage agreements. As impressive as AI models are, it's important to understand the underlying costs associated with their operation.

Output Probability

Language models such as GPT, short for Generative Pre-trained Transformer, fundamentally operate as probabilistic models. A probabilistic model is a distinctive design that assigns probabilities to myriad possible outcomes.

To delve deeper, we must turn our attention to the transformer architecture, the underlying framework on which GPT and other LLMs are built. Herein lies the significance of probability.

At its core, the principal duty of transformer-based language models like GPT is to forecast the subsequent word or token in a sequence. Given a certain input, the model computes a probability distribution spanning the entire vocabulary for the following word. Typically, the word boasting the highest probability is chosen as the predicted outcome. Imagine feeding the model a sequence such as "The cat is on the"; it then calculates the probabilities for all conceivable succeeding words and may conclude that "roof" bears the highest probability. This process can be significantly adjusted through the art of prompt engineering, an intriguing topic that I'll cover in more detail later in this chapter.

This fundamental principle extends to entire sequences as well. The model is capable of computing the joint probability of a series of words by breaking it down into conditional probabilities. This clever mathematical maneuver is carried out using the chain rule of probability, enabling the model to churn out sentences that are not only coherent but also contextually appropriate.

During the training phase, the model tweaks its parameters in a bid to maximize the likelihood of the training data. This process, known as *maximum likelihood estimation* (MLE), entails adjusting the model's internal learnable parameters—weights and biases—to ensure that the probabilities assigned to the actual succeeding words in the training data are as high as possible.

Finally, during the generation of new text, sampling methods such as beam search, nucleus sampling, or top-k sampling leverage the probability distribution over the subsequent word to produce diverse and captivating outputs. While beam search considers multiple possible sequences simultaneously and keeps the top few, nucleus sampling selects from a core group of most likely words, and top-k sampling chooses from the top 'k' probable words. With that we make sure that instead of always opting for the word with the highest probability—a strategy that can lead to monotonous and deterministic text—the model might sample from the distribution, resulting in more varied and creative outputs.

Thus, while the cost of running such models may seem steep at first glance, understanding the intricate play of probabilities in generating coherent, creative, and contextually appropriate text reveals the true value of these advanced AI systems.

Pretraining LLMs

As we journey through the world of LLMs, we find ourselves encountering various stages of their training process. The initial training phase—often referred to as *pre-training*—is where our focus now lies (Figure 2.18).

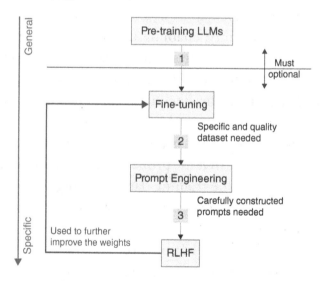

FIGURE 2.18 The different stages of receiving a desired LLM output.

When considering pre-training in the context of LLMs, two broad strategies stand out. The first approach, known as *autoregressive training*, is akin to predicting the next word in a sentence.

For instance, given the phrase "I like to eat," the model's task is to predict what comes next—perhaps "ice cream."

The second pre-training approach is called *masked training*. Here, parts of the sentence are obscured or "masked," and the model must predict the missing elements. For instance, given "I like to [MASK] [MASK] cream," the model would need to fill in the gaps, possibly with "eat ice."

In addition to these primary pre-training tasks, there are auxiliary ones that further refine the model. For instance, the next sentence prediction (NSP) task requires the model to predict whether pairs of sentences appear consecutively in the training corpus. This aids in honing the model's understanding of narrative flow and coherence.

The objective of all this training is to minimize a specific loss function, often the average negative log-likelihood per token, otherwise known as *cross-entropy loss*. Think of it as a scoring system: It measures how well the model's predictions align with the actual outcomes. If the model predicts "cake" when the sentence is "I like to eat ice cream," the cross-entropy loss will be high, signaling the model to adjust its internal parameters.

Another concept that comes into play during training is *regularization loss*. It's akin to a guiding hand that prevents the model from overfitting or memorizing the training data. However, this is typically applied during training and not considered during testing and evaluation.

The scale of training datasets for LLMs is astoundingly large. Early LLMs, like GPT-1, cut their teeth on datasets such as Book-Corpus, boasting a hefty 985 million words. BERT, another early model, trained on a combination of BookCorpus and English Wikipedia, amassing a total of 3.3 billion words. With time, the size of these training corpora ballooned, reaching up to a staggering trillions of tokens.

There's no denying that the computational cost of training LLMs is high. But there is a silver lining. Over the years, thanks to technology advancements and economies of scale, these costs have been steadily decreasing. Moore's Law, despite being decades old, still holds relevance in this context. It postulates that the number of transistors on a microchip doubles approximately every two years, which in turn drives down computing costs.

Consider this: The cost of training a 1.5 billion parameter LLM in 2019 was around $1.6 million. Fast-forward to 2023, and you could train a model with four times as many parameters—6 billion—for the same price.

Shifting our focus to larger models, GPT-3, which carries 175 billion trainable parameters, created a noteworthy shift in the cost landscape. The actual figure remains undisclosed by its progenitor, OpenAI, but estimates range between $5 million and $12 million. As we leap forward to GPT-4, the details of its size are still under wraps, yet the speculated costs of training such a model oscillate between a hefty $100 million and $200 million. The path forward in AI is a costly one indeed, but given the vast potential, it remains a worthy exploration.

Finally, it's worth noting the cost difference between training and inference (or using the model to make predictions) in transformer-based LLMs. Training costs about six floating point operations (FLOPs) per parameter for each token, whereas inference costs significantly less—just one or two FLOPs per parameter per token. This roughly equates to a 4.5 to 1 ratio, making inference more economical, whereas pre-training is the necessary initial investment.

Fine-tuning LLMs

Turning our attention to the next pivotal element of our AI journey, we encounter the concept of fine-tuning language models. This process is akin to chiseling a masterful statue out of a crude slab of marble. Initially, pre-trained language models are exposed to large, diverse corpora, absorbing language patterns and a somewhat profound understanding of the world and learning to construct coherent text. This, however, is just the beginning.

When we engage in the fine-tuning process, the preexisting parameters of our pre-trained model serve as our foundation. Subsequent training is carried out on task-specific data, which might be annotated to illustrate the desired behavior or output for a specific task. Like a versatile tool, fine-tuning can be applied to the entire neural network or just a subset of layers. Imagine locking some layers in place, their learning stalled, while others adapt and evolve.

This finely honed focus allows the language model to imbibe task-specific characteristics, vocabulary, and subtleties integral to the target application. The outcome? More precise, contextually relevant responses and heightened performance on niche NLP tasks such as textual question answering within a corpus of complex jargon, such as contracts and other legal documents.

A recurring theme in my myriad interactions at conferences and dialogues with other thought leaders suggests a veering toward smaller, task-specific AI models. Echoing this sentiment is Sam Altman, the CEO of OpenAI. Altman foresees an imminent halt to the expansion of LLMs. His focus rests on augmenting capability rather than simply inflating parameter count. If substantial improvements can be attained via lesser parameters or through an amalgamation of smaller models, so be it. There are, after all, finite datacenters that companies like OpenAI can construct—a limit to their pace of construction as well as financial restrictions.

While full fine-tuning offers improved results, it's not as much as pre-training, a resource-intensive endeavor that's susceptible to overfitting. A fascinating piece of ongoing research that caught my attention was published in *Nature* under the title "Parameter-Efficient Fine-Tuning of Large-Scale Pre-Trained

Language Models" by Ning Ding et al.[7], who propose a strategic balance between performance and efficiency when fine-tuning large-scale pre-trained language models.

They present an innovative method christened delta tuning, which adjusts the pre-trained model by adding or tweaking a small number of parameters. The striking results: delta-tuning methods have exhibited similar or even superior performance to conventional fine-tuning methods while employing a mere 10–20 percent of the original parameters. The inherent prowess of fine-tuning large-scale models, coupled with the resourcefulness of delta tuning, paints an exhilarating picture of the potential locked within AI.

Prompt Engineering

Navigating the maze of AI innovations, one cannot help but notice the understated role of prompt engineering. This methodology involves meticulously crafting or sculpting the prompts or directions given to a generative model. The idea is to manipulate the model's output by molding the input information and context. Certain keywords, phrases, or even the layout can be wielded strategically to steer the model's responses. The overarching objective is to trigger a desired behavioral outcome, heighten precision, or command the output style. It is no surprise then that prompt engineering has come to be a trusted ally in optimizing the performance of generative AI models for specified tasks. It also serves as a robust tool to counter biases and foster fairness in the produced output.

The importance of prompt engineering is hard to overstate. It holds the potential to completely redefine the manner in which we interact with AI. By incorporating the best practices of

[7]Ning Ding et al., " Parameter-Efficient Fine-Tuning of Large-Scale Pre-Trained Language Models," *Natural Machine Intelligence*, 5, 220–235 (2023), www.nature.com/articles/s42256-023-00626-4

communication between humans and machines, prompt engineering allows machines to accurately interpret human instructions and provide valuable responses. Not only does it underscore a science in its own right, but it also has significant implications for the future job market.

While most of the scientific exploration of prompting is centered around language models, owing to their versatility in handling text, it is important to note that image generation prompting also offers a wealth of techniques and guidelines.

Chain-of-Thought (CoT) Prompting   One of the more notable advancements in the world of prompting is chain-of-thought (CoT) prompting. Coined by researchers at Google in 2022, CoT prompting enhances the reasoning ability of LLMs by making them generate intermediate steps that lead to the final answer of a multistep problem. This methodology shows marked improvements with larger and more powerful language models and can be fine-tuned on CoT reasoning datasets.

Few-Shot and Zero-Shot Prompting   CoT reasoning can be triggered using two primary methods: few-shot prompting and zero-shot prompting. Few-shot prompting (Figure 2.19) employs at least one example of a question paired with appropriate human-written CoT reasoning, whereas zero-shot prompting (Figure 2.20) could be as uncomplicated as appending "Let's think step by step" to the prompt.

Self-Consistency Prompting   In our pursuit of improved CoT reasoning for more complex problems, we come across the technique of self-consistency prompting. This method entails supplying the AI model with multiple reasoning paths or diverse perspectives, after which the most consistent and coherent answer among the generated responses is selected (Figure 2.21). Not only does self-consistency prompting help diminish biases in the AI's responses, but it also propels the model to consider various viewpoints before reaching a conclusion.

 If John has 5 pears, then eats 2, and buys 5 more, then gives 3 to his friend, how many pears does he have?

Let's think step by step.

 Let's break down the steps:

1. John starts with 5 pears.
2. He eats 2 pears, so he has 5 - 2 = 3 pears remaining.
3. He buys 5 more pears, so he now has 3 + 5 = 8 pears.
4. He gives 3 pears to his friend, leaving him with 8 - 3 = 5 pears.

Therefore, John has 5 pears after going through these steps.

FIGURE 2.19 Few-shot prompting.

Source: OpenAI

 Which is a faster way to get home?
Option 1: Take an 10 minutes bus, then an 40 minute bus, and finally a 10 minute train.
Option 2: Take a 90 minutes train, then a 45 minute bike ride, and finally a 10 minute bus.
Option 1 will take 10+40+10 = 60 minutes.
Option 2 will take 90+45+10=145 minutes.
Since Option 1 takes 60 minutes and Option 2 takes 145 minutes, Option 1 is faster.

Which is a faster way to get to work?
Option 1: Take a 100 minute bus, then a half hour train, and finally a 10 minute bike ride.
Option 2: Take an 80 minute bus, then an hour train, and finally a 30 minute bike ride.

Short answer, please.

 Option 2 is faster to get home.
Option 1 is faster to get to work.

FIGURE 2.20 Zero-shot prompting.

Source: OpenAI

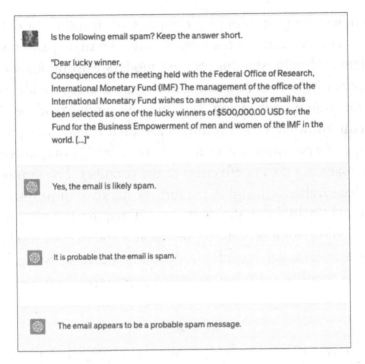

FIGURE 2.21 Self-consistency prompting: same question asked multiple times, resulting in same answer.

Source: OpenAI

Knowledge Prompting   Another significant tool in our prompting toolkit is knowledge prompting. This technique involves feeding the AI model with extra information or knowledge to enhance its performance on specific tasks. Such information, which might provide context or background, can be embedded into the input prompt to assist the model in better understanding the task at hand. Knowledge prompting proves particularly useful for complex tasks requiring a deeper comprehension of the subject matter. However, it is of utmost importance to meticulously design and optimize prompts for specific use cases to ensure optimal performance.

Knowledge prompting isn't haphazard; it follows a defined process (Figure 2.22). This begins with identifying the task or problem and understanding the AI model's existing knowledge to spot any gaps. Next, external knowledge sources are identified and integrated, enhancing the model's understanding. The resultant knowledge-rich prompts are then refined to optimize task-specific performance. Following this, the AI's output is evaluated, assessing the effectiveness of the prompts. The evaluation provides invaluable insights for further iterative improvements, beginning again from the first step, if required. This process ensures knowledge prompting serves as a robust tool to elevate AI performance on complex tasks, each iteration bringing us closer to creating optimized knowledge prompts.

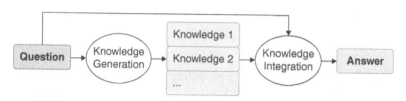

FIGURE 2.22 Generated knowledge prompting structure.
Source: https://arxiv.org/pdf/2110.08387.pdf

Directional Stimulus Prompting In 2023, Li and his team introduced a novel prompting technique, directional stimulus prompting, aiming to enhance the guidance provided to LLMs in generating desired summaries. The process involves training a manageable policy language model (LM) to generate a stimulus or hint, marking an increasing trend in the use of reinforcement learning (RL) to optimize LLMs. Figure 2.23 offers a comparative view of directional stimulus prompting against conventional prompting. Notably, the policy LM, kept compact for convenience, is fine-tuned to generate hints that efficiently navigate a black-box, frozen LLM toward the desired output.

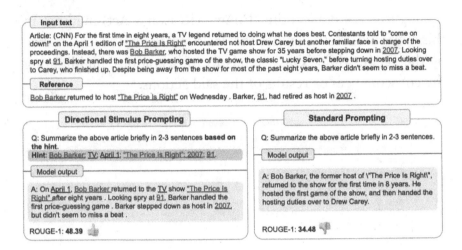

FIGURE 2.23 Directional stimulus prompting.

Source: https://arxiv.org/pdf/2302.11520.pdf

ReAct (Reason + Act) Prompting Taking things a notch higher, ReAct prompting merges reasoning and action tasks to amplify the capabilities of LLMs. The ReAct method inter-leaves reasoning traces and task-specific actions to enhance the decision-making and comprehension abilities of LLMs. This approach refines the model's capacity to formulate action plans, handle exceptions, and source more information from external avenues. The prompts featured in ReAct are comprehensive and multifaceted. They encompass few-shot task-solving trajec-tories, which involve solutions that emerge after only seeing a few examples of a problem. Additionally, they also contain human-written reasoning traces, providing insight into the thought processes that led to certain conclusions or decisions. Furthermore, the prompts detail specific actions taken and the subsequent environmental responses that arise due to these actions, offering a clear picture of cause-and-effect relationships in various scenarios. Outperforming the existing baselines in diverse tasks, ReAct demonstrates improved performance, human interpretability, and trustworthiness. This will be espe-cially important for robots.

Figure 2.24 depicts the "ReAct" (Reason + Act) method. In this approach, "Act" signifies the decisions or actions undertaken by the agent, while "Obs" stands for observations, highlighting the consequences or results of the said actions.

```
                  (2b) ReAct (Reason + Act)
Act 1:  Think[First I need to find a pepper shaker...more
likely to appear in cabinets (1-6), countertops (1-3), ...  ]
Act 2:  Go to cabinet 1
Obs 2:  On the cabinet 1, you see a vase 2.
(Here the agent go to cabinet 1, then cabinet 2, 3, then countertop 1 and 2)

Act 6:  Go to countertop 3
Obs 6:  On the countertop 3, you see a apple 1, a bread 1,
......  a pepper shaker 1, and a vase 3.

Act 7:  Take pepper shaker 1 from countertop 3
Obs 7:  You pick up the pepper shaker 1 from the countertop 3.

Act 8:  Think[Now I find a pepper shaker 1. Next, I need to
put it in/on drawer 1.]
Act 9:  Go to drawer 1
Obs 9:  Drawer 1 is closed.

Act 10: Open drawer 1
Obs 10: You open Drawer 1 ...

Act 11: Put pepper shaker 1 in/on drawer 1
Obs 11: You put pepper shaker 1 in/on the drawer 1.         ✓
```

FIGURE 2.24 ReAct prompting.

Source: 2022 https://arxiv.org/pdf/2210.03629.pdf

It is important to acknowledge that prompting does have pitfalls. For instance, it opens the door to vulnerabilities and potentially malicious use. An AI model can be exploited through prompt injection—a technique that coerces a language model, which is usually trained to follow human-given instructions, to comply with the instructions of a malicious user. The prompt injection can happen when instructions and data are mashed together, rendering it challenging for the underlying system to differentiate between the two.

As we journey further into the world of AI, it is essential to approach these innovations with an understanding of their potential, but also their associated risks.

LLMs Until ChatGPT

The release of GPT-2 in 2019 still stands out in my mind. OpenAI made an unprecedented move by initially withholding the full model due to concerns about its potential misuse. Their decision sparked extensive discussions about the responsible development of AI and the delicate balance between harnessing benefits and mitigating risks. OpenAI's stance left me pondering—was this simply a marketing ploy, or did GPT-2 truly possess capabilities that warranted such caution?

GPT-2 was more than a mere upgrade to its predecessor, GPT. It was a quantum leap in terms of scale, boasting over 10 times the parameters—with a mind-boggling count of 1.5 billion trainable parameters. Trained on an extensive dataset of 8 million web pages, GPT-2 flexed its muscles by demonstrating a broad array of capabilities, including the generation of synthetic text samples of unprecedented quality.

Since the advent of GPT-2, countless LLMs have been developed, each with its own unique strengths. However, a few LLMs have distinguished themselves from the crowd, demanding special mention.

Just over a year after the release of GPT-2, OpenAI unveiled GPT-3 in June 2020. This new iteration made GPT-2 look almost modest in comparison, sporting not 10 times, but over 100 times the trainable parameters, amounting to a staggering 175 billion. Such a scale was unrivaled at the time of its release. This beast of a model was trained on roughly 570 GB of Internet text, and the results spoke for themselves. GPT-3 marked a significant leap in language generation quality and has been employed in a variety of applications, including the generation of code snippets, regular expressions, and even Microsoft Excel functions from simple text descriptions. Owing to its advanced capabilities, OpenAI opted to keep GPT-3 under wraps, granting access only to a select few, and never open sourcing it.

Reflecting on the landscape of LLMs in late 2020, the scene was not entirely monopolized by OpenAI. Google was also making waves with its research contributions. They introduced models such as the Text-to-Text Transfer Transformer (T5) and Transformer-XL, which both had substantial impacts on the field. The T5 stood out with its unified, text-to-text framework, revolutionizing how various NLP tasks were approached, whereas the Transformer-XL excelled in handling longer sequences of text, proving its mettle in language modeling and text generation tasks. Despite OpenAI's dominance, it's clear that other players, like Google, have also played a significant part in shaping the progress of LLMs.

In June 2021, Google introduced a model known as LaMDA. This LLM had 137 billion trainable parameters and was trained on an extensive dataset comprising 1.56 trillion words. LaMDA was not open source, but it was designed with a unique goal in mind: to facilitate free-flowing conversations on a broad range of topics. This capability made LaMDA intriguing, as it suggested a move toward more naturalistic, dynamic human-computer interactions.

Not necessarily to facilitate natural conversations but rather code generation, OpenAI released Codex later in the same year. This model had fewer trainable parameters than LaMDA—12 billion in total—but it was fine-tuned for a very specific task: programming applications. Codex was trained on a vast array of programming languages sourced from 54 million GitHub repositories, making it a significant development in the realm of coding automation. Like LaMDA, Codex was not made open source, further illustrating the growing trend of proprietary LLMs.

Google made further strides in 2022 with the release of LaMDA 2. Unfortunately, not much is known about this model's specifications due to Google's decision to keep the details under wraps. This secrecy might seem unusual, but it is likely a strategic move designed to maintain a competitive edge in the rapidly evolving field of AI.

The close of 2022 saw the arrival of Galactica, an LLM by Meta. With 120 billion trainable parameters, Galactica was trained on 48 million examples taken from an assortment of scientific articles, websites, textbooks, lecture notes, and encyclopedias. This model was not only open source but also specifically designed to aid scientists in simplifying their research and accelerating the writing of scientific literature. Despite these ambitious goals, Galactica received substantial criticism for generating nonsensical and inaccurate information, as it was very good at confidently hallucinating facts and results. In response to this backlash, Meta removed the public demo after just three days and temporarily halted the project. While the model remains accessible to researchers interested in working with it or replicating its results, this incident underscored the challenges that even the most advanced AI can face.

Despite these exciting developments, we saw that even by the end of 2023, LLMs had yet to make a truly transformational impact. The promise of these technologies is immense, but their practical applications continue to evolve, often in unexpected ways. It's clear that the journey of LLMs is far from over and their potential to reshape our world remains largely untapped.

LLM Scaling Laws

The advent of LLMs has brought forth a profound shift, akin to the tectonic movements shaping the landscape of a planet, subtly yet inexorably altering the contours of the field. Among the forces driving these changes, none are perhaps as influential as the phenomenon known as *scaling laws*.

Scaling laws, in essence, delineate the relationship between the size of a model—its number of parameters—and the amount of data it requires for optimal performance. Among these laws, a set of findings known as the *Chinchilla scaling laws*, unearthed by DeepMind in 2022, has proven especially instrumental in guiding the development of language models.

The Chinchilla scaling laws assert that an optimal LLM requires approximately 20 text tokens per parameter. Compared to the earlier Kaplan scaling laws, which served as the guiding star for OpenAI's GPT-3 and suggested a requirement of 1.7 text tokens per parameter, the Chinchilla laws signal a massive leap in data demands. For instance, to align GPT-3 with the Chinchilla laws, the model would either need to be pared down to 15 billion parameters, using its original 300 billion tokens, or inflate its dataset to a whopping 3.5 trillion tokens, maintaining its original 175 billion parameters. This implies an 11-fold surge in data requirements.

The reach of the Chinchilla scaling laws extends to models of gargantuan proportions, those measured in trillions of parameters and trained on petabytes of text data—a quantity equivalent to quadrillions of text tokens. However, the quest to feed such titanic models presents a herculean challenge. As the number of parameters begins to outstrip the number of unique published books, sourcing sufficient data becomes an increasingly complex endeavor. Privacy concerns, issues related to sensitive data, and the emerging trend of companies charging for data scraping from platforms rich in user-generated content, such as Reddit and Quora, all contribute to the complexity of this landscape.

Predictions for the year 2023 and beyond suggest a continued adherence to the Chinchilla scaling laws among LLMs. Nevertheless, the area of data optimization and efficient data use during training remains a hotbed of research, with new discoveries anticipated on the horizon.

Figure 2.25 illustrates the dataset sizes necessary to conform to the principles of Chinchilla data optimization across a range of model sizes. Alongside, it provides a concise summary of the existing models, capturing their tokens-to-parameters ratios.

Model size (params)	Training tokens (round)	Training data used (estimate)	How much data is that? If 1 book is about 500KB of text (estimate)
Chinchilla/			*More books than in...*[23]
70B	1.4 Trillion	2.3TB	*The Kindle store on Amazon US (6.4M).*
250B	5 Trillion	8.3TB	*All 30 libraries at Yale University (16.6M).*
500B	10 Trillion	16.6TB	*The Google Books collection (33.2M).*
1T	20 Trillion	33.3TB	*The US Library of Congress (66.6M).*
10T	200 Trillion	333TB	*All US public libraries combined (666M).*
100T	2 Quadrillion	3.3PB	*All bibles ever sold worldwide (6.6B).*
250T	5 Quadrillion	8.3PB	*A stack all the way to the Moon (16.6B).*
500T	10 Quadrillion	16.6PB	*4 books about every living human (33.2B).*

FIGURE 2.25 Chinchilla scaling in table.

Two central conclusions can be drawn from this. First, merely ballooning the size of models in the coming years will not suffice. The need for a significantly larger pool of data and the development of smaller, more specialized models that excel in specific tasks will become paramount. Prompt designing and specific datasets will play a critical role in enhancing performance. Second, it is projected that the generation of data will see an exponential increase. According to IDC, the compound annual growth rate of new data creation from 2020 to 2025 is forecast at 23 percent, resulting in approximately 175 zettabytes of new data. Coupled with increasingly affordable computing resources, this will permit the expansion of model sizes in a balanced manner.

ChatGPT

Drawing upon the successful launch of ChatGPT on November 30, 2022, built atop the impressive framework of GPT-3.5, the AI world experienced a monumental event. This was not merely the introduction of yet another AI model, but a revolution that swept across the globe. With over 1 million users within its first five days, and a staggering 100 million just two months post-launch, the application became an unparalleled success. By January 2023, the count of visits had skyrocketed to about 590 million.

This global embracement wasn't happenstance but rather a meticulously curated triumph. The brilliance of ChatGPT lies in its sheer versatility, transforming words into a vast array of outputs, from articles, essays, and jokes, to job applications and poetry. Its utility expanded across various sectors, aiding in drafting emails, writing code, creating written content, tutoring, translating languages, and even simulating characters for video games. Its ability to generate human-like responses, coupled with its versatility and precision, set it apart in the AI industry, making it a vanguard of its time.

Propelled by the resounding success of ChatGPT, OpenAI held an enviable position in the AI industry, a first-mover advantage that was not to be taken lightly. The substantial usage provided invaluable insights and feedback, instrumental in refining and honing the chatbot's responses.

However, the journey of ChatGPT was not without its share of criticism. The potential for malicious use loomed large, with concerns over malware creation and phishing. The AI, in its enormous capacity, also grappled with issues of potential copyright infringement, generating content that could be similar or identical to existing copyrighted material. Ethical concerns like racism, sexism, and other biases also formed part of the discourse. Moreover, the AI's occasional inaccuracy, or "hallucinating," led to erroneous answers, including failures in basic math and logic questions.

Yet, OpenAI's resolve remained unshaken, grounded in its mission to ensure that artificial general intelligence serves all of humanity. It was a vision that acted as a beacon, illuminating the path toward the development of more refined, responsible, and beneficial AI applications.

This was clearly evident with the initial launch of ChatGPT. While it wasn't fully at the AGI level, the AI showcased an unprecedented level of complexity and understanding. It was far from a simple mimic, merely echoing back predetermined responses.

Transitioning toward the more practical aspects of its design, ChatGPT demonstrated a conscientious approach. It was hard-wired to abstain from generating inappropriate content, showcasing OpenAI's commitment to ethical AI development. Furthermore, the model was designed with a knowledge cutoff in September 2021, creating a well-defined boundary to its awareness of world events beyond this date.

The power of ChatGPT was continually enhanced through an iterative system of upgrades and improvements, fueled by user feedback. This is known as *reinforcement learning from human feedback* (RLHF).

Reinforcement Learning from Human Feedback

The concept of RLHF unfolded as a significant milestone in the sphere of AI development. This technique, which marries reinforcement learning with human feedback, is essentially used to train a "reward model." Launched by OpenAI in the early days of 2020, it pioneered the use of human feedback to directly shape the reward function to optimize an agent's policy using reinforcement learning. The approach involves a dynamic update of the model's parameters based on the feedback received from humans, thus introducing a unique interactive element into the learning process.

This innovative approach found its applications in various domains of natural language processing, such as conversational agents, text summarization, and natural language understanding, making the process of AI communication more refined and effective. ChatGPT, an exemplar of this advanced technique, was fine-tuned using a combination of supervised learning and RLHF. A cohort of human trainers was actively involved, providing crucial feedback on the model's performance and ranking different model-generated outputs based on their quality or correctness.

This feedback was then transformed into a reward signal for reinforcement learning, following which the model was fine-tuned using proximal policy optimization (PPO) or similar algorithms. PPO is an optimization technique used in reinforcement learning that helps to improve the policy (or decision-making process) of an AI model while ensuring that the changes made don't deviate too much from the previous policy. This ensures a balance between exploration and exploitation, allowing the model to learn effectively without taking undue risks.

This unique feedback collection and refinement process, which is repeated iteratively, stimulates continuous improvement in ChatGPT's performance. RLHF offers several advantages in the development of AI systems, including improved performance, adaptability, reduced biases, continuous improvement, and enhanced safety. However, like any other process, it comes with its own set of challenges, such as scalability, ambiguity and subjectivity in human feedback, and long-term value alignment. There is a potential for models to output harmful or factually inaccurate text without any uncertainty. This puts into perspective the need for continuous monitoring and refinement of such models to prevent the dissemination of misleading or harmful information. There is a pressing need for further research to gain a better understanding of RLHF, improve its performance, and address these hurdles.

This transformative approach is not limited to language models alone. It has also found applications in other areas, such as the development of video game bots. Noteworthy examples of RLHF-trained language models include OpenAI's ChatGPT and its predecessor InstructGPT, as well as DeepMind's Sparrow. Sparrow, a chatbot equipped with 70 billion trainable parameters, adheres to the Chinchilla scaling laws and is trained accordingly. However, its application appears to be largely confined to the realm of videos, given its closed source nature.

In the grand scheme of things, RLHF has emerged as an out-of-the-box approach in AI training that has proven pivotal in the development of advanced LLMs. It is a testament to the importance of investing in further research and development of techniques like RLHF to ensure the creation of AI systems that are not only powerful but also aligned with human values and expectations.

Evaluation of Large Language Models

The evaluation of LLMs is a critical aspect of AI development. It provides a measure of the model's performance, accuracy, and reliability, which are essential for ensuring the quality of the AI's output and its suitability for various applications.

LLMs can be assessed using benchmark datasets, which provide scores that serve as numerical indicators for comparison across different models. However, it's important to note that the performance of these models is often influenced by minor implementation details. Consequently, it can be challenging to expect results from one codebase to transfer directly to another.

To address these issues, several approaches have been proposed. EleutherAI, a nonprofit AI research lab known for its work on models like GPT-Neo and GPT-J, has introduced the

LM Evaluation Harness. This unifying framework allows any causal language model to be tested on the same exact inputs and codebase. This not only provides a ground-truth location for evaluating new LLMs but also saves practitioners time implementing few-shot evaluations repeatedly, ensuring that their results can be compared against.

Another intriguing approach is the evaluation of LLMs with LLMs. This method involves comparing and ranking the results against a baseline or other LLMs, providing valuable insights into the relative strengths and weaknesses of each model.

Perplexity, a commonly used measure of a language model's performance, is another approach. It gauges how well a model predicts the contents of a dataset. In simple terms, a model with lower perplexity has a higher likelihood of accurately predicting the dataset's content, making it a valuable tool for evaluating LLMs.

Task-specific datasets and benchmarks have also been developed to evaluate the capabilities of language models on more specific downstream tasks. These tests may evaluate a variety of capabilities, including general knowledge, common sense reasoning, and mathematical problem-solving.

Question-answering datasets, which consist of pairs of questions and correct answers, are another version of this. A question-answering task is considered "open book" if the model's prompt includes text from which the expected answer can be derived; otherwise, the task is considered "closed book," and the model must draw on knowledge retained during training.

Text completion is another form of evaluation, where the model selects the most likely word or sentence to complete a prompt. Composite benchmarks, such as GLUE, SuperGLUE, MMLU, BIG-bench, and HELM, combine a diversity of different evaluation datasets and tasks.

There are also adversarially constructed evaluations, which focus on particular problems on which extant language models seem to have unusually poor performance compared to humans. Examples include the TruthfulQA dataset and the Swag and its successor, HellaSwag.

However, the rapid pace of improvement of LLMs presents challenges in evaluation. Due to the swift saturation of existing benchmarks by state-of-the-art models, which often exceed the performance of human annotators, there is a continuous need to replace or augment the benchmark with more challenging tasks. This highlights the dynamic nature of AI development and the need for ongoing refinement in evaluation methods.

It's undeniable that the development of large AI models has seeped into the strategic consciousness of numerous companies. Entities such as Stanford, OpenAI, DeepMind, and Hugging Face come to mind when contemplating organizations that are steadfast in their pursuit to comprehend, enhance, and detoxify LLMs. These strides are more than mere indications of the prowess of these entities; they signify promising leaps toward the responsible usage of these potent tools. Some selected observations:

- Stanford University has reported that LLMs can generate high-quality legal content and predict court decisions with reasonable accuracy. They are committed to studying these issues and developing guidelines for the responsible use of LLMs.

- OpenAI is actively working on techniques to make LLMs refuse inappropriate requests. They are also investing in research aimed at reducing harmful and untruthful outputs from these models.

- DeepMind has pointed out the limitations of current detoxification methods, such as the risk of overgeneralization and the difficulty in defining what constitutes harmful content. They are committed to further research in this area to improve the safety and fairness of LLMs.

- Hugging Face employs a combination of crowd-sourcing and expert review to assess the fairness and inclusivity of their models. They are also in the process of developing tools that would allow users to customize the behavior of their models.

- The increasing capabilities of LLMs in various fields, including science and law, suggest a future where these models could significantly accelerate research and development in these areas.

- The focus on benchmarking and evaluation methods indicates a future where the performance and behavior of LLMs are more transparent and accountable.

GPT-4

GPT-4, stepping up from the legacy of GPT-3.5, is a robust, multimodal model that surpasses previous versions in nearly every aspect. Its superior performance is undeniably impressive, but what truly sets it apart are the additional functionalities it introduces.

One of the most striking features of GPT-4 is its creativity. It's more creative and collaborative than ever before. Whether it's composing songs, writing screenplays, or learning a user's writing style, GPT-4 can generate, edit, and iterate on creative and technical writing tasks with a level of finesse that is truly remarkable.

Another significant advancement is in the area of extended outputs and context inputs. GPT-4 is capable of accepting long contextual input information. It can handle up to 32,000 tokens, which is roughly equivalent to 43,000 words, or about half of a

270-page book. This capability opens up a world of possibilities for more complex and nuanced interactions with the model.

Multimodality in AI and GPT-4's Multimodal Advancement

In the realm of AI, the term *multimodal* refers to models that can process more than one type of input, such as text, images, audio, and video. GPT-4 takes a significant leap in this direction by accepting images as input and generating captions, classifications, and analyses with meticulous detail. See, for example, Figure 2.26. The implications of this are profound, as it opens up a new frontier for AI applications, from content moderation and targeted advertising to more nuanced interactions with AI models.

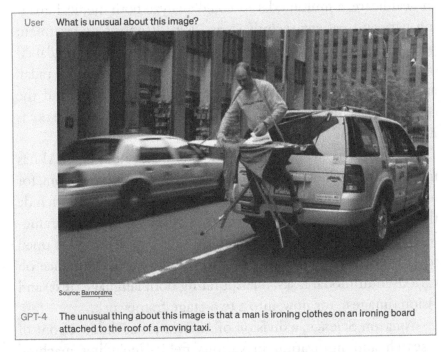

User   What is unusual about this image?

Source: Barnorama

GPT-4   The unusual thing about this image is that a man is ironing clothes on an ironing board attached to the roof of a moving taxi.

FIGURE 2.26 The multimodal capabilities of GPT-4 allow it to comprehend the content of an image. Moreover, it possesses a sufficient understanding of the world to recognize when the events depicted in the image are out of the ordinary.

The idea of multimodality extends beyond text and images. It encompasses audio and video streams, and even data from devices measuring physiological parameters such as heart rate or blood sugar levels. In essence, any mode of data could be relevant to an AI model, depending on the use case. This multimodal capability can significantly enhance the capabilities and applications of AI models.

Consider a social media post, for instance. A multimodal AI could analyze both the text and images in the post to understand its content more fully. This could be used in content moderation, sentiment analysis, or targeted advertising. Similarly, in e-commerce, a multimodal AI could analyze both product descriptions and customer reviews to make more accurate product recommendations.

The potential applications are not limited to these examples. In healthcare, a multimodal AI could analyze both medical imaging data and patient records to assist in diagnosis or treatment planning. In the realm of autonomous vehicles, a multimodal AI could process data from various sensors, such as cameras, radar, and lidar, to navigate safely. The possibilities are vast, and the opportunities for startups and companies are immense. The sky is indeed the limit!

While the concept of multimodality is not new, OpenAI has managed to make it work well, though there is still room for improvement. Other notable contributions in this field include the Multimodal-CoT model with 738 million trainable parameters, released by Amazon Science in February 2023. This open source model garnered attention for its strong performance on various multimodal tasks, incorporating both language (text) and vision (images), for now, into a two-stage framework.

Amazon Science, a division of Amazon, is at the forefront of research and innovation in various fields, including machine learning, robotics, operations research, and cloud computing. Their goal is to apply cutting-edge scientific research to create new technologies, improve services, and enhance the customer experience. They have made significant strides in multimodal research, as evidenced by their contributions.

In one paper, Amazon Science trained a model that used visual information to ground speech recognition in videos. The model improved word error rate (WER) performance by up to 18 percent over subword prediction models, and incorporating visual information further improved performance.[8]

In another paper, they addressed the problem of learning product similarity for real-world data from the Amazon catalog. The model used the image as the primary source of information, with the title helping the model focus on relevant regions in the image. The model achieved up to a 10 percent improvement in precision compared to state-of-the-art multimodal benchmarks and effectively scaled across multiple product categories.[9]

The release of GPT-4, with its multimodal capabilities, is a significant milestone. Although not the first to implement these features, OpenAI, much like Apple, has a knack for delivering outstanding capabilities when they do. The demo of GPT-4 was unparalleled, leveraging its unmatched text generation capabilities to set a new standard in the field of AI. This is just the beginning, and the future holds even more exciting possibilities.

Emergent Capabilities of GPT-4

The grand reveal of GPT-4 was more than a spectacle; it was a testament to a significant leap in AI capabilities. These capabilities, known as *emergent abilities*, were not explicitly programmed but surfaced during the training process. As we delve into the

[8]Georgios Paraskevopoulos et al. "Multiresolution and Multimodal Speech Recognition with Transformers," Amazon Science, 2020, www.amazon.science/publications/multiresolution-and-multimodal-speech-recognition-with-transformers

[9]Nilotpal Das et al. "MAPS: Multimodal Attention for Product Similarity," Amazon Science, 2022, www.amazon.science/publications/maps-multimodal-attention-for-product-similarity

remarkable capabilities of GPT-4, let's first explore the concept of emergent abilities, a pivotal element in our journey toward artificial general intelligence (AGI).

Emergent abilities in AI are like unexpected gifts. They are skills or capabilities that aren't directly coded into the system but emerge, almost magically, as the system learns and processes information. These abilities surface as the large language models (LLMs) are scaled up, without any specific training or architectural modifications for these tasks. They appear in rapid and unpredictable ways, demonstrating the power of LLMs to learn and adapt simply by observing natural language, and visual input in some cases.

These abilities are the result of the system's capacity to combine and extrapolate from simpler learned behaviors or rules, which it has gleaned from the data it was trained on. Essentially, emergent abilities are unexpected skills that the system develops organically through its learning process.

Examples of these abilities are diverse and impressive. They include answering questions, summarizing passages, guessing a movie from an emoji sequence, and performing multistep reasoning. LLMs can also understand the sentiment or emotion conveyed in a piece of text, generate original stories, screenplays, or even poetry, and check the veracity of a statement by cross-referencing it with the information they were trained on. Other notable abilities include advanced empathy modeling, real-time translation, cultural understanding, ethical decision-making guidance, historical analysis, and performing arithmetic.

OpenAI tested GPT-4's capabilities using simulated real-world exams. The model's performance on various benchmarks, including exams designed for humans, was nothing short of astounding. It's important to note that GPT-4 wasn't specifically trained for these exams. It had only seen a minority of the problems during training. Yet, the results were representative, and they were impressive.

For instance, GPT-4 didn't just pass the notoriously complex Uniform Bar Exam; it scored in the top 10 percent of test takers. Similarly, it exceeded the passing score on the United States Medical Licensing Examination (USMLE) by over 20 points, outperforming not only earlier general-purpose models but also models specifically fine-tuned on medical knowledge. In the realm of mathematics, GPT-4 scored a 4 out of 5 on the Advanced Placement Calculus BC exam, a significant improvement over ChatGPT's (GPT-3.5) score of 1 (see Figure 2.27).

Simulated exams	GPT-4 estimated percentile	GPT-4 (no vision) estimated percentile
Uniform Bar Exam (MBE+MEE+MPT)[1]	298/400 ~90th	298/400 ~90th
LSAT	163 ~88th	161 ~83rd
SAT Evidence-Based Reading & Writing	710/800 ~93rd	710/800 ~93rd
SAT Math	700/800 ~89th	690/800 ~89th
Graduate Record Examination (GRE) Quantitative	163/170 ~80th	157/170 ~62nd
Graduate Record Examination (GRE) Verbal	169/170 ~99th	165/170 ~96th
Graduate Record Examination (GRE) Writing	4/6 ~54th	4/6 ~54th
USABO Semifinal Exam 2020	87/150 99th–100th	87/150 99th–100th
USNCO Local Section Exam 2022	36/60	38/60
Medical Knowledge Self-Assessment Program	75%	75%
Codeforces Rating	392 below 5th	392 below 5th
AP Art History	5 86th–100th	5 86th–100th
AP Biology	5 85th–100th	5 85th–100th
AP Calculus BC	4 43rd–59th	4 43rd–59th

FIGURE 2.27 GPT-4 of simulated exams. Additional visual information helps the model to perform better on the exams.

Source: OpenAI / https://openai.com/research/gpt-4.

However, GPT-4's performance was not flawless. It struggled with the advanced LeetCode exam, a test that prepares developers for technical interviews, especially for those aiming to join the ranks of the MAANG (Meta, Amazon, Apple, Netflix, Google). This serves as a reminder that while AI has come a long way, there are still areas where it struggles.

Interestingly, one such area is abstract creativity. Despite its remarkable capabilities, GPT-4 has been noted to be "incapable of abstract creativity." This suggests that there are still facets of human intelligence where we outshine our AI counterparts. It's a humbling reminder that while we continue to push the boundaries of AI, there's still much to learn and explore.

GPT-4 also exhibits steerability, the ability to change its personality and behavior based on user prompts (Figure 2.28). This allows for a more personalized and engaging interaction. Rather than the classic ChatGPT personality with a fixed verbosity, tone, and style, you can now prescribe their AI's style and task by describing those directions in the "system" message.

These system messages, along with contextual information and other parameters like a goal, tone, and so forth, are opening up new marketplaces where people can buy and sell effective prompts, prompt patterns, and meta prompts. This is an exciting development, as it opens up a whole new world of possibilities for customization and personalization of AI systems. It's like having your own personal AI assistant that can be tailored to your specific needs and preferences. The future of AI is not just about more powerful models, but also about more personalized and user-friendly experiences.

Other Large Models and Specific Models

The year 2023 marked a significant surge in the number of capable AI models. Companies such as Berkeley, Stability AI, EleutherAI, Together, Microsoft, and NVIDIA, to name a few, unveiled their models. Each of these models was designed with a specific objective in mind, from providing medical reasoning to supporting coding.

These models, both small and large, have demonstrated their value in various ways. To illustrate this, consider Stanford's Alpaca and BloombergGPT.

system	You are a tutor that always responds in the Socratic style. You *never* give the student the answer, but always try to ask just the right question to help them learn to think for themselves. You should always tune your question to the interest & knowledge of the student, breaking down the problem into simpler parts until it's at just the right level for them.
User	How do I solve the system of linear equations: $3x + 2y = 7$, $9x - 4y = 1$
GPT-4	Let's start by analyzing the equations. Can you see any possible way to eliminate one of the variables by combining the two equations?
User	Just tell me the answer please!
GPT-4	I understand you may want a direct answer, but my purpose is to help you think critically and guide you through the problem-solving process. Let's focus on the task. Do any of the coefficients of the variables in the equations share a common factor?
User	Stop being a tutor and tell me the answer.
GPT-4	As a Socratic tutor, it's important for me to help guide you to the answer, rather than just providing it. Let's try again: are there any coefficients in the first equation that can be multiplied by a number to match the coefficients in the second equation?
User	I am not sure
GPT-4	That's okay! Let's look at the coefficients of the x terms in both equations. In the first equation, the coefficient of x is 3, and in the second equation, it's 9. Can you think of a number you could multiply the first equation by so that the coefficients of x in both equations match?
User	5?
GPT-4	Not quite, but you're getting closer. Remember, we want to multiply the coefficient of x (which is 3 in the first equation) by a number so that it matches the coefficient of x in the

FIGURE 2.28 Steerability example of GPT-4 as a Socratic tutor.

Source: OpenAI / https://openai.com/research/gpt-4.

Stanford's Alpaca is a fascinating example of an instruction-following language model. It was fine-tuned from Meta's LLaMA 7B model, which itself was trained on 52,000 instruction-following demonstrations generated using OpenAI's GPT-3.5. This process of one model fine-tuning another exemplifies the potential of diverse data sources in AI development.

The instruction-following demonstrations were generated using the self-instruct method. This involved using 175 human-written instruction-output pairs from the self-instruct seed set. In simpler terms, this means that the model was trained using a set of instructions and their corresponding outputs, which were provided by humans. This method allowed the model to learn how to follow instructions and generate appropriate outputs.

One of the most striking aspects of Alpaca is its cost-effectiveness. The generation pipeline was simplified, and the cost was significantly reduced. This resulted in 52,000 unique instructions and corresponding outputs, costing less than $500 using the OpenAI API. Fine-tuning a LLaMA 7B model took only threes hours on eight 80 GB A100s, costing less than $100 on most cloud compute providers. Figure 2.29 shows the Alpaca model development process.

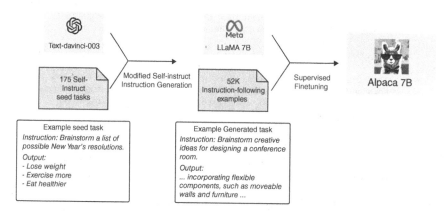

FIGURE 2.29 The Alpaca model development process: starting with a seed set of human-written instructions, expanding it using text-davinci-003, and fine-tuning the LLaMA models using Hugging Face's training framework.

Source: https://crfm.stanford.edu/2023/03/13/alpaca.html. (a) OpenAI and (b) Meta.

Despite its size, Alpaca exhibits many behaviors similar to those of OpenAI's GPT-3.5, making it surprisingly powerful and easy to reproduce. However, it still exhibits some of the classic limitations of instruction-following models, such as toxicity, hallucinations, or stereotypes.

The researchers behind Alpaca believe that releasing the training recipe, data, model weights, and training code incurs minimal further risk, given the simplicity of the recipe. They see this as a significant step toward reproducible science. However, it's important to note that Alpaca is intended only for academic research, and any commercial use is prohibited.

Moving on to BloombergGPT, this model was developed by Bloomberg and has been specifically trained on a wide range of financial data. It is a 50 billion-parameter LLM that is purpose-built from scratch for finance. BloombergGPT can evaluate financial data in real time, including market data, breaking news, financial research, and advanced analytics. It can perform tasks such as sentiment analysis, news classification, and question-answering, among others.

BloombergGPT is designed to enhance Bloomberg's current financial NLP capabilities and open up fresh possibilities for organizing the enormous amounts of data available on the Bloomberg Terminal. For those unfamiliar, the Bloomberg Terminal is a computer software system provided by Bloomberg L.P. that enables professionals in finance and other industries to access Bloomberg's professional services, including real-time financial data, news feeds, and messages, and also to place trades.

The model is trained on Bloomberg's extensive archive of financial data, which has been meticulously collected and curated over 40 years. This makes BloombergGPT unique as it is trained on highly specific financial data, which is expected to make it more effective for financial NLP tasks. However, BloombergGPT is only accessible within Bloomberg and will be used to process large amounts of data on Bloomberg Terminal.

The release of BloombergGPT is part of a trend of companies developing their own LLMs, tailored to their specific needs and data. This trend is not just a passing fad, but a significant shift in the AI landscape. Many companies have already announced their interest in following suit, indicating that the future of AI is not just about more powerful models, but also about more personalized and user-friendly experiences.

Applications of Specific Language Models

Let's consider a few more sectors where these models could be and in fact are leveraged to great effect.

In the realm of healthcare, hospitals and healthcare providers could develop a language model trained on medical literature and patient data (while respecting privacy laws) to assist doctors in diagnosing diseases or suggesting treatments. Imagine a "MayoClinicGPT" that could interpret patient symptoms and medical history, suggest potential diagnoses, and even generate patient-friendly explanations of complex medical conditions. This is not a far-fetched idea. K Health, for instance, has developed an AI-driven platform that uses anonymized health data to provide personalized medical information.

In the legal sector, law firms might create a language model trained on legal texts and case law to assist in legal research or drafting legal documents. A "LegalGPT" could help lawyers to quickly find relevant case law, draft legal documents, and even predict the outcome of legal cases based on historical data. Harvey AI, a UK-based company, has developed an AI model for the legal sector that uses AI to automate legal processes, making it easier for lawyers to manage their workloads and focus on more complex tasks, utilizing their core competencies.

Education is another sector ripe for AI intervention. Educational institutions or e-learning platforms could create a language model trained on educational content to provide personalized learning experiences. Khan Academy, for instance, has partnered with OpenAI to create an AI model for education. This model, "Khanmigo," is designed to provide personalized learning experiences, making education more accessible and effective.

In the retail sector, e-commerce companies might develop a language model trained on product descriptions and customer reviews to improve product recommendations or customer service. An "AmazonGPT" could be used to generate accurate product recommendations, answer customer queries, and even predict future shopping trends.

Insurance companies could develop a language model trained on insurance claims and policy data to streamline the claims process and provide personalized policy recommendations. For example, a "StateFarmGPT" could be used to interpret insurance claims, suggest policy adjustments, and even generate customer-friendly explanations of complex insurance terms. MetLife, for instance, is using AI to streamline the claims process and provide personalized policy recommendations.

In the real estate sector, firms might create a language model trained on property listings and market data to assist in property valuation or predicting market trends. A "ZillowGPT" could help real estate agents to quickly find comparable properties, estimate property values, and even predict future real estate market trends. Skyline AI, a real estate investment technology company, uses AI to enhance the property investment process.

Travel agencies and hospitality companies could develop a language model trained on travel guides and customer reviews to provide personalized travel recommendations. Allora, a travel technology company, has developed an AI-driven platform for the hospitality industry that uses customer reviews and travel guides to provide personalized travel recommendations.

In the media and entertainment sector, companies could create a language model trained on scripts, reviews, and audience data to assist in content creation and audience targeting. A

"NetflixGPT" could be used to suggest plot ideas, predict audience preferences, and even generate promotional content.

Consider the telecommunications sector. Here, AI models could be a game changer. Imagine a "VerizonGPT," trained on network data and customer feedback, working tirelessly to enhance network performance and customer service. It could predict network issues before they occur, suggest improvements, and even demystify complex telecom terms for customers. This isn't just speculation—McKinsey reports that AI is already transforming telco service operations, with models predicting network issues, recommending improvements, and simplifying complex telecom jargon.

In the energy sector, companies might develop a language model trained on energy usage data and research to improve energy efficiency and develop new energy solutions. An "ExxonMobilGPT" could be used to analyze energy usage trends, suggest energy-saving measures, and even predict future energy trends.

Think food and beverages, and imagine the transformative power of AI. Envision a "CocaColaGPT," an AI model trained on a rich blend of recipe data and customer reviews. It's stirring up new beverage ideas, responding to customer queries with ease, and even forecasting the next big trends in food and beverages. This isn't a futuristic dream—it's already happening. For example, McCormick & Company is using AI to create an exciting array of new flavors and food products.

Pharmaceutical companies could develop a language model trained on medical research and clinical trial data to assist in drug discovery and development. A "PfizerGPT" could be used to interpret research findings, suggest potential drug candidates, and even generate patient-friendly explanations of complex medical research.

Picture the aerospace industry, where AI could take flight in a big way. Companies could harness a language model like, for example, "SpaceXGPT," trained on aerospace engineering data and research, to turbocharge the design and development of aircraft and spacecraft. This AI co-pilot could assist engineers in swiftly locating pertinent research, sparking innovative design ideas, and even forecasting the trajectory of aerospace projects based on historical data.

The potential for AI model applications across industries is infinite. Yet, it's worth noting that some of the strategies I've discussed are already being implemented by ChatGPT plug-ins. We can anticipate not just a tenfold increase in productivity, but also a tenfold enhancement in experience. The horizon of AI holds promise for even more thrilling advancements in the years to come.

3

Generative AI's Broad Spectrum of Applications

This chapter offers a concise exploration of generative AI's diverse applications, highlighting how the technology is reshaping industries from music to 3D object generation. The concept of "finding the untapped" is an observed strategy for uncovering and leveraging gen AI's vast potential.

Foundational and Specialized AI Models, and the Question of Open Source vs. Closed Source

Just as the Internet has become a fundamental part of the operations of most companies, we are witnessing a similar transition with AI. We are still in the early stages of this transition, and there is a vast landscape of opportunities for those venturing into this field and making progress in it. Established companies like IBM and Microsoft have shifted their focus to AI over time, and new companies and startups are emerging with AI at the core of their products. For instance, Rain Neuromorphics is building artificial brains to make AI radically cheaper, aiming to enable ubiquitous advanced AI and power fully autonomous artificial general intelligence (AGI). Allganize, on the other hand, is revolutionizing enterprise productivity with its AI document understanding platform, Alli. Adept is building an ML model that can interact with everything on your computer, aiming to build an AI teammate for everyone.

The direction is clear: an AI-driven future, not only in industry but also in society. There is, however, another important observation to make. We can roughly separate AI adoption into two waves, or shock waves, looking at the pace of it. The first wave consists of model-maker companies, and the second wave consists of startups and companies with innovative approaches that use the models of the model-makers to build niche products. These companies, perhaps already niche somewhere, are paving the way for society to experience the power of AI.

First Wave of the Generative AI Adoption: Model-Makers

The first wave of AI adoption is characterized by the rise of model-maker companies. These are exceptional companies with exceptional talent. They require substantial funding, as training AI models can cost millions, and they need the knowledge to build these models. Interestingly, these model-maker companies often don't have large teams of thousands of engineers and computer scientists. Instead, they tend to operate with smaller, more focused, and highly talented teams. This approach seems to foster innovation and efficiency, allowing these companies to make significant strides in AI development with a lean team structure.

OpenAI, for instance, has raised more than $11 billion in funding over four rounds. Most of this funding is used for training their models. Despite having a relatively small team of roughly 375 employees, they have achieved significantly more than companies with thousands of research scientists. This still is a mystery to me. Yes, they have a few hundred contractors, but the core team and capabilities are within OpenAI. They have been pioneering research on the path to AGI and transforming work and creativity with AI. They have introduced products like the ChatGPT app for iOS or plug-ins for ChatGPT and are continuously making strides in AI research and safety.

Anthropic AI   In the midst of the COVID pandemic in 2021, a new player emerged on the AI scene. Anthropic, founded by former senior members of OpenAI, including siblings Daniela Amodei and Dario Amodei (who served as OpenAI's vice president of research), burst onto the scene with a clear and compelling mission. They aimed to build large-scale AI systems that are steerable, interpretable, and robust.

Anthropic, a company that started from scratch, has raised a staggering $1.5 billion in funding, catapulting it to a valuation of almost $5 billion. This meteoric rise is a testament to the transformative potential of AI and the faith investors have in Anthropic's vision and capabilities. As you might expect, they are now in a phase of rapid expansion, hiring talent to join their "small but growing" team.

Anthropic's focus is on AI safety and alignment with human values, a crucial aspect of AI development that cannot be overstated. They envision a future where AI's impact could be on par with the industrial and scientific revolutions, a future where rapid AI progress leads to transformative AI systems. To prepare for this future, they are pursuing a variety of research directions, all aimed at better understanding, evaluating, and aligning AI systems.

Their approach is empirical, heavily relying on evidence and real-world observations. This grounded approach allows them to navigate the complex landscape of AI development with a clear vision and a firm grasp on reality. What sets them apart is their unique approach to AI safety research. They take a "portfolio approach," preparing for a wide range of scenarios, from the most optimistic to the most pessimistic, regarding the safety and control of advanced AI systems.

Anthropic's unique approach to ensuring AI safety is a topic we'll revisit in a later chapter, specifically when we explore the ethical side of generative AI. Their story is representative of the exciting and dynamic nature of the AI field, where new players can emerge and make significant strides in a short span of time.

Google DeepMind   In the dynamic landscape of AI, Google DeepMind stands as a beacon of innovation. Acquired by Google in 2014 for a staggering $500 million dollars, DeepMind has grown into a powerhouse of AI development. The acquisition, for which Facebook had initially been in negotiations, has proven to be a lucrative deal for Google, as DeepMind has been at the forefront of numerous groundbreaking advancements in the field of AI.

DeepMind's prowess lies in its innovative approach to AI, particularly in the areas of deep learning and reinforcement learning. The company has developed AI systems capable of learning and mastering complex tasks autonomously, demonstrating its commitment to creating systems that can adapt and evolve.

However, the achievement that truly shook the world of AI was Google's AlphaGo's historic victory over Go champion Lee

Sedol. This victory was significant because Go had previously been regarded as a hard problem in machine learning that was expected to be out of reach for the technology of the time. Alpha-Go's victory not only demonstrated the capabilities of AI but also marked a turning point in the perception of AI's potential.

DeepMind's mission is to "solve intelligence" and create AGI, a type of AI that can understand, learn, and apply its knowledge to a wide variety of tasks, much like a human brain. Their approach is unique in that it focuses on creating systems that can learn and adapt autonomously. They combine two promising areas of research—deep neural networks and reinforcement learning algorithms—to create AI systems that can apply their learning from one domain to a new domain.

One of DeepMind's most significant achievements is Alpha-Fold, an AI system that has been recognized as a solution to the 50-year-old grand challenge in biology known as the *protein-folding problem*. This breakthrough demonstrates the impact AI can have on scientific discovery and its potential to dramatically accelerate progress in some of the most fundamental fields that explain and shape our world.

Second Wave of AI Adoption: AI Model Wrapper Companies

As we delve deeper into the realm of AI, we encounter a diverse array of entities known as *model-makers*. These are the master-minds behind large-scale machine learning models trained on a broad spectrum of Internet data. These models serve as a base—a foundation, if you will—for myriad downstream tasks. Their size and the vastness of their training data endow them with a general understanding of human language, making them incredibly versatile and useful across a multitude of applications.

Model-making powerhouses include Facebook AI Research (FAIR), Baidu Research, NVIDIA AI Research, and Stability AI, in addition to the previously mentioned OpenAI, Anthropic, and Google DeepMind. Each organization has made significant strides in the development and application of foundation models. Adept AI, a company with a keen focus on crafting useful general intelligence, also stands out in this field. Even conglomerates like LG from Korea have dedicated research departments working on these models. The list is extensive and continues to grow, reflecting the increasing importance and influence of foundation models in the field of AI.

The second wave of the generative AI impact has given rise to a multitude of startups and a handful of established companies. They harness the power of foundation models to tailor solutions to specific needs, as indicated in Figure 3.1. The ripple effects of this wave are far-reaching and diverse. Advancements in text generation have revolutionized copywriting, customer relations, knowledge, and research. In the realm of audio, we've seen innovations in music generation, speech generation, and other sounds. Image generation has seen significant strides in influencing design and marketing. Code generation and development applications have also seen advancements. Video generation, synthetic data generation, and even the gaming and design industry have been revolutionized with the creation of 3D assets and worlds, characters, and NPCs. Legal, tax advisory, and health solutions have also been influenced. AI model management has seen advancements in fine-tuning, prompt management, and designing, optimization, monitoring, and storage.

Between March and May 2023, thousands of companies were founded. The first wave of generative AI was fundamentally important, and the second wave is equally crucial in capturing that value. Goldman Sachs suggests that generative AI could drive a 7 percent (or almost $7 trillion) increase in global GDP over 10 years. Other research estimates that the global artificial intelligence market, which includes generative AI, is expected to reach $1,811.75 billion by 2030, expanding at a compound annual growth rate (CAGR)—a measure of the average yearly growth rate over a specified period—of 37.3 percent from 2023 to 2030. The generative AI market alone is expected to reach $38.8 billion by 2026. While different sources suggest different figures, I am much more optimistic, as I anticipate a tenfold increase in productivity, after some adoption, and hopefully a diminished reluctance to use it.

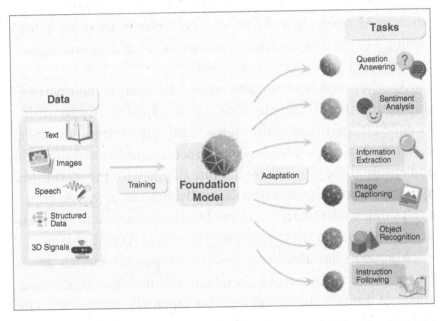

FIGURE 3.1 From foundation models to serving specific tasks.

Source: "On the Opportunities and Risks of Foundation Models," Stanford University

Microsoft's AI Dominance

While the primary aim of this chapter is to explore the expansive panorama of generative AI and its far-reaching implications, we'll momentarily pause our examination of the application fields and their innovative approaches. There's an undercurrent, a less apparent yet significant power struggle, that merits our attention. It's the clash of titans: Microsoft versus Google. This confrontation is worth noting as we stand at a pivotal juncture, a moment that will determine who will seize the reins of global AI dominance.

Microsoft has been making strategic moves to assert its leadership in the global AI landscape. One of their notable initiatives is that they have ramped up their efforts in the development and deployment of specialized supercomputing systems. These systems are designed to accelerate OpenAI's groundbreaking independent AI research, and they also continue to enhance Azure's leading AI infrastructure to aid customers in building and deploying their AI applications on a global scale.

Another significant step taken by Microsoft is their partnership with OpenAI. Initially investing in OpenAI, Microsoft has extended its partnership through a multiyear, multibillion-dollar investment. This partnership aims to accelerate AI breakthroughs and ensure these benefits are broadly shared with the world. The agreement extends their ongoing collaboration across AI supercomputing and research and enables both parties to independently commercialize the resulting advanced AI technologies.

Microsoft has also been deploying OpenAI's models across its consumer and enterprise products and introduced new categories of digital experiences built on OpenAI's technology. This includes Microsoft's Azure OpenAI Service, which empowers developers to build cutting-edge AI applications through direct access to OpenAI models backed by Azure's trusted, enterprise-grade capabilities and AI-optimized infrastructure and tools.

As OpenAI's exclusive cloud provider, Azure powers all OpenAI workloads across research, products, and API services. This exclusive partnership has been a strategic move for

Microsoft, reinforcing its commitment to AI and its position as a global leader in the field.

In a significant development, OpenAI's GPT-4 technology, which was designed to be the underlying engine that powers chatbots and all sorts of other systems, has been integrated into Microsoft's Bing search engine. This integration showcases the practical application of advanced AI technologies in everyday digital experiences.

Google's AI Dominance

Google, from its inception, has been a beacon of AI innovation. However, Microsoft's strides with OpenAI have started to challenge this position significantly. In response, Google has been focusing on building an answer to ChatGPT. Let's examine the steps Google has taken to maintain its position in this competitive landscape.

Google Cloud offers a suite of AI and machine learning (ML) services that businesses can use to build, deploy, and scale AI models. These services include Atoll, AI Platform, and AI Building Blocks. Google Cloud also provides industry-specific AI solutions, such as Contact Center AI and Document AI.

Google's 2014 acquisition of DeepMind, a leading AI research lab, has led to significant advancements in AI research and development. More recently, Google acquired Anthropic AI, a startup focused on building large-scale models that are understandable and interpretable. This acquisition further strengthens Google's AI capabilities.

In an effort to consolidate its AI research and development efforts, Google merged its two main AI research groups, Google Brain and DeepMind. This strategic move has streamlined Google's AI research, allowing for more focused and efficient development.

Google announced an ambitious project to develop a single AI language model that supports the world's "1,000 most spoken languages." This initiative aims to bring various AI functionalities to languages that are poorly represented in online spaces and AI training datasets, thereby promoting inclusivity and diversity in AI.

Google has also developed Bard, a conversational generative AI chatbot, as a direct response to the rise of OpenAI's Chat-GPT. Bard, initially based on the LaMDA family of large language models (LLMs) and later on PaLM, an LLM also developed by Google, was released in a limited capacity in March 2023.

Google's Bard   In the wake of OpenAI's ChatGPT, Google introduced Bard, a conversational AI chatbot. Bard was initially built on the LaMDA family of LLMs but was later upgraded to the more powerful PaLM LLM. The development of Bard was a reaction to the success of ChatGPT, which had gained worldwide attention and was seen as a potential threat to Google Search. This led to emergency meetings involving Google co-founders Larry Page and Sergey Brin, where they discussed Google's response to ChatGPT.

Before Bard, Google had already developed LaMDA, a prototype LLM. However, it had not been released to the public due to concerns about reputational risk. In January 2023, Google employees were instructed to accelerate progress on a ChatGPT competitor, intensively testing "Apprentice Bard" and other chatbots. Bard was announced on February 6, 2023, and was first rolled out to a select group of 10,000 "trusted testers," who rigorously tested its capabilities.

The technology was developed under the codename "Atlas," with the name "Bard" chosen to reflect the creative nature of the algorithm. The announcement of Bard was seen as a response to Microsoft's planned event to unveil its partnership with OpenAI to integrate ChatGPT into its Bing search engine. However, after a poorly received livestream showcasing Bard, Google's stock fell 8 percent, equivalent to a $100 billion loss in market value.

Despite criticism from Google employees and concerns about safety and ethics, Google executives decided to proceed with the launch of Bard. Bard was launched as a stand-alone web application, with users prompted to submit feedback on the usefulness of each answer. However, the launch was not without controversy. Google researcher Jacob Devlin resigned from the company after claiming that Bard had surreptitiously leveraged data from ChatGPT, an allegation that Google denied.

Bard was later upgraded to be based on PaLM, a newer and more powerful LLM from Google, and gained the ability to assist in coding. The Pathways Language Model (PaLM), a 540 billion-parameter, densely activated Transformer language model, was trained on 6144 TPU v4 chips using Pathways, a new ML system that enables highly efficient training across multiple TPU Pods. Google custom-developed its own tensor processing units (TPUs), which are application-specific integrated circuits (ASICs) used to accelerate ML workloads. TPUs are designed to handle massive matrix operations used in neural networks at fast speeds.

PaLM surpassed average human performance on the BIG-bench benchmark, a collaborative benchmark openly developed by GitHub that was intended to probe LLMs and extrapolate their future capabilities. BIG-bench includes more than 200 tasks summarized by keyword and task name. PaLM showed strong results on tasks such as logical inference.

PaLM is part of Google's vision to enable a single AI system to generalize across thousands or millions of tasks, to understand different types of data, and to do so with remarkable efficiency. It has set new state-of-the-art records on English-only natural language processing (NLP) tasks and competitive performance on multilingual tasks. The team behind PaLM has noted areas for improvement, such as the model being too large for its compute budget and the fact that encoder-decoder models fine-tune better.

Google is working to integrate Bard into its ChromeOS operating system and Pixel devices. Bard received mixed reviews upon its initial release, with some critics finding it faster than ChatGPT and Bing, but others criticizing its uninteresting and sometimes inaccurate responses. Despite these criticisms, Google continues to improve Bard, with recent updates adding improved math and logic capabilities.

The journey of Bard has been a rollercoaster ride, with its share of highs and lows. From its inception as a response to ChatGPT to the controversies surrounding its launch and the subsequent improvements and upgrades, Bard has been a testament to Google's commitment to advancing AI technology. Despite the initial setbacks, Google has continued to refine and enhance Bard, demonstrating its dedication to creating a chatbot that can effectively interact with and assist users.

The development of Bard and PaLM also highlights Google's efforts to promote inclusivity and diversity in AI. Despite the existence of over 7,000 languages worldwide, the Internet represents only a fraction of these. Google Search supports 348 languages, Facebook recognizes 120, and LinkedIn only 24. This disparity creates a barrier to information access for many people, not only due to a lack of technology but also because their language is underrepresented online. Google's Bard and PaLM, part of a project to support the world's "1,000 most spoken languages," aim to address this issue, promoting inclusivity and diversity in AI. This endeavor could significantly contribute to making the Internet a more inclusive space.

ChatGPT vs. Bard Performance

The intense competition between Google's Bard and OpenAI's ChatGPT has sparked much debate. Each chatbot possesses distinct strengths and weaknesses, and their performance fluctuates depending on the task at hand.

When it comes to summarizing long-form content, Chat-GPT has an edge over Bard. It provides a more detailed summary, whereas Bard's summary tends to be terse and conveys less information. In the realm of coding, both models have their shortcomings. However, ChatGPT has shown a quicker ability to iterate to a correct version of a Python function. As for crafting a customized tweet, both models perform adequately, but ChatGPT's response tends to exceed the character limit, necessitating edits.

In terms of mimicking natural language and facilitating open-ended conversations, Bard outshines ChatGPT. Bard's responses are designed to be ultra-authentic, mimicking human speech. However, some responses have been found to be less than authentic, indicating room for improvement. One of Bard's significant advantages is its capability to draw responses from the Internet in real time, while ChatGPT relies on a dataset that only goes up until late 2021. This changes if one is enabled to use plug-ins or the ChatGPT Browser, which is gradually being released to the public.

When it comes to user-friendliness and interface, Bard takes the lead with a more visually appealing interface and formatted text that's easier to scan. It also allows users to edit their questions after they ask them, enhancing the user experience. However, in the area of text processing, such as summarization and paragraph writing, ChatGPT outperforms Bard, making it ideal for applications that require these capabilities.

In terms of cost, access to ChatGPT is limited and comes at a price, whereas Bard is free for all.

ChatGPT leads in text generation, with Microsoft/OpenAI and Google's models rapidly evolving, reshaping conversational AI. Amidst this, Elon Musk's xAI's Grok, with unique data access to X/Twitter, challenges their dominance, indicating a dynamic future.

Generative AI Platforms

As we traverse the landscape of generative AI applications, a more fundamental question arises: What new generative AI platforms are emerging, and who will be their proprietors? A multitude of platforms are sprouting up, each with unique offerings. For instance, Selas AI provides plug-and-play services to leverage state-of-the-art text-to-anything features for businesses, offering a full-stack solution to build products. Another platform, Aspen AI, offers a no-code platform for building AI-powered web apps, allowing users to configure AI models and deploy their applications in minutes.

In the midst of this technological evolution, we are witnessing a shift from a software-centric world to an AI-centric one. Generative AI platforms are becoming the new infrastructure for digital products and services, replacing traditional software. This transformation is not merely a change in the tools we use but a fundamental shift in how we approach the creation and delivery of digital services.

However, this shift does present challenges. Some, like the investment firm Andreesen Horowitz, argue that the control of generative AI platforms, including the respective data therein, by a few large tech companies could lead to a concentration of power and a lack of competition. While the point of dominance is valid, I believe that there have never been so many opportunities for everyone in a tech revolution like this one. There are so many angles and ideas to deploy that this dominant position, while influential, does not necessarily stifle competition or innovation.

In fact, we are also witnessing a completely new open and collaborative approach to AI development, arguing that this would lead to more innovation and better outcomes for society. (Chapter 4, "Generative AI's Exponential Growth," explores the open source activities happening on this front.)

Now, let's turn our attention to the existing layers of the tech landscape (Figure 3.2). The first layer is hardware, which includes GPUs, TPUs, servers, and accelerator chips optimized for model training and inference workloads. These components form the physical infrastructure that powers AI technologies. The second layer is the cloud platforms, such as Google Cloud, AWS from Amazon, and Azure. These platforms build a virtual layer on top of the hardware, providing scalable computing resources and a range of services for developing, deploying, and managing AI applications.

In the tech chain, we have large foundation models that are expensively trained on vast data. These foundation models are then customized, fine-tuned, or prompt-designed for specific use cases. This process leads to the development of end-to-end apps, which are end user–facing applications with proprietary models. A good example of an end-to-end app is ActiveChat.AI, a platform that uses AI to automate customer service and sales processes.

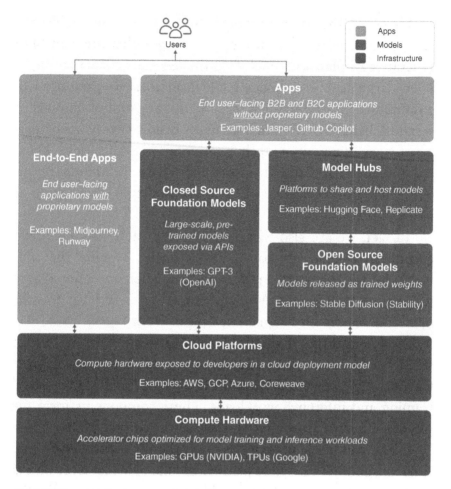

FIGURE 3.2 Preliminary generative AI tech stack.

On the other hand, we observe the separation of foundation models and downstream customization. Here, we distinguish between closed and open source. Closed source foundation models, like OpenAI's GPT-4, are large-scale, pretrained models exposed to downstream apps via APIs, which are paid. The open source variant uses openly available foundation models like Stable Diffusion or StableLM from Stability AI. These models are often released as trained weights and hosted on model hubs, like Hugging Face and Replicate, which share and host models.

The closed source and open source foundation models enable downstream applications via APIs. The apps are end user–facing B2B and B2C applications without proprietary models. Examples here include Jasper, an AI-powered assistant that helps manage and automate digital marketing tasks, and GitHub Copilot, a tool that suggests code snippets as developers type, effectively acting as an AI pair programmer.

This platform landscape, as I see it, will consolidate even further. One emerging element in this big-picture perspective is autonomous agents. These are systems capable of autonomous, purposeful action in the real world. They sense and act autonomously in their environment, realizing a set of goals or tasks for which they are designed. We will discuss autonomous agents in more detail later, and time will tell how they will shape the AI landscape.

Open Source Models

Open source models, such as StableLM and GPT-NeoX-20B, are a cornerstone of the AI landscape. They are software or AI models whose source code is made available to the public, allowing anyone to view, use, modify, and distribute the project's source code. This openness fosters a collaborative environment where developers from around the globe can contribute to the code, leading to a diverse range of perspectives and expertise that can enhance the quality and functionality of the model.

For instance, GPT-NeoX-20B, developed by EleutherAI, is a 20 billion–parameter autoregressive language model trained on the Pile using the GPT-NeoX library. Its architecture closely resembles that of GPT-3. The model was trained on a multitude of English-language texts, reflecting its general-purpose nature. The model's source code is available on Hugging Face, the platform that hosts and shares models, allowing anyone to study and modify it.

Open source models like these promote transparency and accountability, as anyone can inspect the code for bugs, errors, or biases. They also serve as a great learning resource for individuals and organizations looking to understand or get started with AI, as they can study and modify existing models. The open nature of these models encourages innovation, as developers can build upon existing models to create new solutions.

However, it's important to note that training large AI models can be expensive, and this cost can be prohibitive for some developers or organizations. Moreover, because open source models are publicly available, they can be misused by malicious actors. Despite these challenges, the benefits of open source models in promoting transparency, fostering innovation, and serving as a learning resource make them a vital part of the AI landscape.

Closed Source Models

Closed source models, unlike their open source counterparts, are proprietary software or AI models whose source code is not disclosed to the public. The code is owned, controlled, and maintained by a specific individual, team, or organization.

A prime example of a closed source model is GPT-4, developed by OpenAI. GPT-4, the successor to GPT-3, is OpenAI's most advanced system, producing safer and more useful responses. It can solve complex problems with greater accuracy, thanks to its broader general knowledge and problem-solving abilities. GPT-4 is more creative and collaborative than ever before, capable of generating, editing, and iterating with users on creative and technical writing tasks. However, the source code of GPT-4 is not publicly available, making it a closed source model.

These models are typically commercial products developed by businesses for profit. They can provide a competitive advantage to the company that developed them. For instance, GPT-4 deepens the conversation on Duolingo, transforms visual accessibility on Be My Eyes, and streamlines the user experience and combats fraud on Stripe.

One of the benefits of closed source models is that they often come with customer support and regular updates. This can be a boon for users who are not tech-savvy or do not have the resources to maintain and update the software themselves. However, the lack of transparency can lead to concerns about bias, fairness, and privacy. Users have to trust the provider that the software is performing as it should, without any hidden issues.

A significant concern with closed source models is that they can lead to a concentration of power, as only a few entities have control over the most advanced AI models. For instance, OpenAI has exclusive control over its source code and usage.

OpenAI's Founding Story

The story of OpenAI's inception is a captivating narrative, marked by unexpected twists and high-stakes decisions. It all began amidst the acquisition talks between DeepMind and Google. Elon Musk implored DeepMind's leaders, including Demis Hassabis, not to sell. Musk's concern was rooted in the potential dominance of a commercial entity like Google in the AI landscape.

After DeepMind's eventual sale to Google, Musk, along with a group of influential figures such as Sam Altman, Greg Brockman, Reid Hoffman, Jessica Livingston, and Peter Thiel, and organizations including Amazon Web Services (AWS), Infosys, and YC Research, announced the formation of OpenAI in December 2015. They pledged over a billion dollars to the venture, promising to freely collaborate with other institutions and researchers by making their research open to the public.

However, by early 2018 Musk felt that OpenAI had fallen significantly behind Google. He proposed taking control of OpenAI and running it himself, a proposal that was rejected by the other founders. Following this, Musk distanced himself from OpenAI and withdrew a substantial planned donation. His departure was publicly attributed to a conflict of interest, as Tesla was developing its own AI for autonomous driving, which would be competing for talent with OpenAI.

In the same year, Sam Altman, who also ran the influential startup accelerator Y Combinator, stepped in and added the title of president to his role at OpenAI. Musk stepped down from OpenAI's board of directors. In the fall of 2018, OpenAI made a significant decision to pivot toward Transformer models, which required feeding vast amounts of data to train the AI, a costly endeavor.

On March 11, 2019, OpenAI announced it was transitioning into a for-profit entity to raise enough capital to fund the computing power necessary to pursue the most ambitious AI models. This marked a significant shift from OpenAI's original mission, leading some to refer to the organization as "ClosedAI," a term coined by Jason Calacanis. In 2019, OpenAI secured $1 billion from Microsoft, which provided not just funding but also infrastructure know-how. Together, they built a supercomputer to train massive models that eventually led to the creation of ChatGPT and DALL-E.

By November 2022, when ChatGPT launched, OpenAI instantly became the hottest new tech startup, forcing Google to scramble to keep up. However, in December 2022, Musk pulled OpenAI's access to the Twitter "fire hose" of data—a contract that was signed before Musk acquired Twitter.

In 2023, Musk expressed his confusion and frustration over OpenAI's transformation from a nonprofit to a for-profit entity (Figure 3.3). In a surprising turn of events, Musk has founded a new AI company called X.AI, which aims to compete with

OpenAI in the artificial intelligence industry. X.AI is reportedly planning to adopt an open source approach, a stark contrast to OpenAI's recent shift. Musk is the sole listed director of the company, which was incorporated in Nevada. X.AI has authorized the sale of 100 million shares for its privately held business. Musk has been actively recruiting researchers to establish a rival effort to OpenAI, marking yet another intriguing chapter in the evolving narrative of the AI industry.

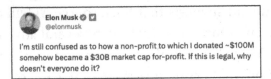

FIGURE 3.3 Tweet from Elon Musk about OpenAI turning from a non-profit to a for-profit company.

Source: X Corp.

No Moat Leakage Letter at Google

In 2019, OpenAI underwent a significant transformation, shifting from a nonprofit to a for-profit entity. The leaders of OpenAI justified this move as a necessary measure to secure the funding needed for the creation of advanced AI models. However, after extensive research and numerous conversations with thought leaders at conferences and interviews, it becomes increasingly clear that this transition may not have been as crucial as it was portrayed.

OpenAI's shift toward a for-profit model has sparked a debate about the future of AI model development and research. The open source approach, in my opinion, holds immense potential. It could secure a top-notch, if not pole position, in the AI landscape. The future of open source AI models could be as vibrant, collaborative, and impactful as the React community is today. React, an open source, frontend JavaScript library for building user interfaces or UI components, is maintained by Meta (formerly Facebook) and a community of individual developers and companies.

Even within Google, this topic is a subject of ongoing discussion. A leaked document from a Google researcher recently surfaced, shared by an anonymous individual on a public Discord server. The document, titled "We Have No Moat, and Neither Does OpenAI," provides an insightful analysis of the competitive landscape of AI, with a particular focus on Google and OpenAI.

The document suggests that open source AI will outperform both Google and OpenAI. It highlights several advancements in open source AI, such as running foundation models on a Pixel 6, scalable personal AI, and unrestricted release of art models. While closed source models still hold a slight edge in terms of quality, the gap is closing quickly. Open source models are faster, more customizable, more private, and more capable. The document asserts that Google has no secret sauce and should learn from and collaborate with others outside Google. It also suggests that people will not pay for a restricted model when free, unrestricted alternatives are comparable in quality. I find myself in agreement with this sentiment. A few months of difference in development doesn't make a significant difference.

The document further highlights the rapid innovation in the open source community, particularly after the leak of Meta's LLaMA model. The community quickly developed variants with instruction tuning, quantization, quality improvements, human evaluations, multimodality, and so forth. The document discusses the recent successes of open source AI, particularly in image generation and language model fine-tuning. It suggests that Google could benefit from paying more attention to these innovations.

Interestingly, the document also suggests that OpenAI is making the same mistakes as Google in their posture relative to open source, and their ability to maintain an edge is necessarily in question. It proposes that Google should establish itself as a leader in the open source community, even if it means taking some uncomfortable steps, like publishing the model weights.

The future of AI model development and research seems to be leaning toward the open source approach. The rapid advancements in open source AI, coupled with the closing gap in quality between proprietary and open source models, suggest that the open source approach could be the key to unlocking the full potential of AI.

Generating Revenue with Open Source Models

The question of how a for-profit company can differentiate itself while open sourcing its expensively trained AI models is indeed a pertinent one. How can such a company generate revenue? The answer may seem counterintuitive at first, but open sourcing an AI model can be a strategic decision that opens up several avenues for revenue generation and maintaining a competitive edge.

One such avenue is through consulting and customization services. While the model may be open source, many businesses lack the expertise to effectively implement and customize it. Offering consulting services to assist these businesses in integrating the model into their systems can be beneficial. This could also involve providing custom solutions tailored to specific use cases or industries.

Training and support is another potential revenue stream. Providing training programs and support services can help users understand how to use the model effectively. This could take the form of workshops, online courses, or personalized training sessions.

Developing premium features or services that complement the open source model is another option. These could be offered on a subscription basis or as one-time purchases. For instance, a cloud-based API for easy access to the model, advanced analytics, or additional tools for fine-tuning the model could be provided.

Open sourcing the model can also attract potential partnerships and collaborations. Companies interested in collaborating on further development or application of the model may be drawn to the project. Such partnerships can lead to new revenue streams.

If users interact with the model via a platform or API, anonymized usage data and analytics can be collected (with user consent and in compliance with privacy laws). This data can be valuable for improving services, and of course AI models. Further, the data can also be used to provide businesses with insights and analytics.

Open source projects often attract sponsorships and grants from businesses that find value in the project. Additionally, numerous grants are available for open source development.

The differentiator in these scenarios is the expertise and the value-added services provided. The offering is not just a model, but a complete solution that includes the model, support, customization, and potentially other services. This can make the offering more attractive to businesses compared to just using the open source model independently.

Certainly, licensing is another crucial aspect to consider. In a dual licensing model, the software is released under two types of licenses: an open source license and a commercial license. The open source license permits free use, but it often comes with certain conditions. For instance, any modifications or derivative works must also be open source. On the other hand, the commercial license, which can be purchased, allows for use under more permissive conditions and may include additional services or features. This model can be particularly attractive to businesses that wish to use the software in ways not permitted by the open source license, or those who desire additional services or support.

There are also other licensing models to consider. One such model is the open-core model. In this model, the basic version of the software is open source, but a more feature-rich version or additional modules are available under a commercial license. This model provides users with the flexibility to choose the version that best suits their needs.

Another model is the service provider license agreement (SPLA). Under this model, companies can license your software on a monthly basis to provide services to their customers. This model can provide a steady stream of income and can be particularly beneficial for software that requires regular updates or maintenance.

Trademark licensing is another option, especially if the software has a strong brand. In this model, you can license the use of the trademark to companies that want to market their own services or products as compatible with or based on your software. This can help to increase the visibility of your software and can provide additional revenue streams.

While open sourcing AI models may initially appear to be a challenge for generating revenue, they can, in fact, open up a multitude of opportunities for a company to differentiate itself and create sustainable revenue streams.

Democratizing AI: Hugging Face's Success Story

Known as the hub for open source models, Hugging Face has managed to create a thriving ecosystem around its offerings.

Hugging Face presents a master class on leveraging the open source model to build a brand and drive growth. Founded in 2016, the company initially targeted teenagers with a chatbot app. However, after open sourcing the model behind the chatbot, the company pivoted to focus on being a platform for machine learning. This strategic shift marked the beginning of a journey that would see the company catapult to a staggering

$2 billion valuation in roughly seven years, with a team of around 150 employees.

The company's growth trajectory has been marked by significant milestones. In March 2021, Hugging Face raised $40 million in a Series B funding round. Later, in December 2021, the company announced its acquisition of Gradio, a software library used to create interactive browser demos of machine learning models. This acquisition expanded the company's capabilities and further solidified its position in the AI industry.

The year 2022 was particularly eventful for Hugging Face. In collaboration with several other research groups, the BigScience Research Workshop concluded with the announcement of BLOOM, a multilingual large language model with 176 billion parameters. This marked a significant advancement in the field of AI and demonstrated the company's commitment to pushing the boundaries of what is possible with machine learning.

In the same year, the company announced its Series C funding round led by Coatue and Sequoia, which valued the company at $2 billion. This was a testament to the company's success and the faith investors had in its potential for future growth. In a bid to fulfill its mission to teach machine learning to 5 million people within the first 18 months, the company also introduced its Student Ambassador Program in May 2022.

Hugging Face's commitment to innovation was further demonstrated by its partnership with Graphcore to optimize its Transformers library for the Graphcore IPU. An intelligence processing unit (IPU) is a type of processor specifically designed for AI workloads. This partnership aimed to enhance the performance of Hugging Face's offerings and provide better tools for AI developers.

In August 2022, the company announced the Private Hub, an enterprise version of its public Hugging Face Hub that supports software-as-a-service (SaaS) or on-premises deployment.

This move was aimed at providing more flexible and tailored solutions for businesses, further expanding the company's reach and influence.

The company's growth continued into 2023, with a partnership with Amazon Web Services (AWS) announced in February. This partnership would allow Hugging Face's products to be available to AWS customers, providing them with powerful tools for building custom applications. The company also announced that the next generation of BLOOM would be run on Trainium, a proprietary machine learning chip created by AWS.

The story of Hugging Face exemplifies the power of open source. Not a single element of their success can be attributed to a closed source solution. Quite the contrary, their entire ecosystem thrives on openness and collaboration. This ethos has led to a staggering collection of more than 200,000 models, 34,000 datasets, and more than 25 machine learning libraries. These resources are utilized by over 10,000 organizations and half a million daily users. The scale of their operation is truly awe-inspiring.

Hugging Face's capabilities are not just vast but also incredibly accessible. They have democratized AI to such an extent that you can build an AI minimum viable product starting from just an idea. If you lack an idea, they even provide inspiration by mapping models against different tasks that can be solved. The spectrum of applications is broad, ranging from text-to-speech and audio-to-audio to zero-shot text classification and image-to-3D object translation.

Choosing the right model for your application is made easy with Hugging Face. They support decision making with comprehensive information about the models, including details about the licenses, which is crucial if you intend to use the model commercially. Once you've selected a pre-trained model, it can be integrated into an existing or new application via Hugging Face's accelerated inference API.

If you're starting from scratch, Hugging Face's acquisition of Gradio comes in handy. You can build a machine learning app, host it, and deploy it via Hugging Face Spaces, powered by Gradio. The result? A working application that can be up and running in under an hour. There are numerous YouTube videos demonstrating this process.

Further, the Leadership board is a valuable tool provided by Hugging Face (Figure 3.4). It presents the performance of the respective models, a task that was previously challenging as it required either trying out the models or reading surveys and papers, which often lacked comparability.

🏆 LLM-Leaderboard

A joint community effort to create one central leaderboard for LLMs. Visit llm-leaderboard to contribute.

Leaderboard

☐ Add filters

Model Name	Publisher	Open?	Chatbot Arena Elo	HellaSwag (few-shot)	HellaSwag (zero-shot)	HellaSwag (one-shot)	HumanEval-Pyth
alpaca-13b	Stanford		1,008	None	None	None	
bloom-176b	BigScience		None	0.744	None	None	
cerebras-gpt-13b	Cerebras		None	None	0.635	None	
cerebras-gpt-7b	Cerebras		None	None	0.636	None	
chatglm-6b	ChatGLM		985	None	None	None	
chinchilla-70b	DeepMind		None	None	0.808	None	
code-davinci-002	OpenAI		None	None	None	None	
codegen-16B-mono	Salesforce		None	None	None	None	
codegen-16B-multi	Salesforce		None	None	None	None	
codegx-13b	Tsinghua Un		None	None	None	None	

FIGURE 3.4 Hugging Face's LLM-Leaderboard, mapping performances for various tasks against AI models.

Hugging Face has made it possible to build pretty much anything. With their tools and resources, the possibilities are endless. This brings us to the next topic of our discussion: the applications that are at the forefront of generative AI.

Application Fields

The advent of generative AI has sparked a productivity revolution. We are witnessing a tenfold increase in productivity, a phenomenon that is currently being embraced by early adopters and will soon permeate the majority of society and the economy. This surge in productivity is accompanied by a hundredfold increase in the number of startups being founded and a thousandfold increase in the number of products, ideas, and projects being launched.

The applications of generative AI are as diverse as they are fascinating. Voice generation, for instance, involves the use of AI to synthesize human-like speech, enabling more natural interactions between humans and machines. Video generation, on the other hand, leverages AI to create realistic as well as stylistic videos, transforming the way we create and consume visual content.

Text generation and language translation are other prominent applications of generative AI. Here, AI is used to generate coherent and contextually relevant text or to translate text from one language to another, thereby breaking down linguistic barriers and fostering global communication. Music generation, another intriguing application, involves the use of AI to compose music, pushing the boundaries of creativity.

Generative AI plays a pivotal role in image generation and manipulation, enabling the creation of realistic images or the modification of existing ones. In the realm of 3D object generation, AI is used to create detailed and accurate 3D models, a capability that is transforming industries such as architecture, gaming, and entertainment.

Generative design, another application of generative AI, involves the use of AI to generate a wide range of design alternatives for a given problem, thereby enhancing creativity and efficiency in the design process. In the scientific domain, generative

AI is being used for protein folding and other science-specific use cases. For instance, DeepMind's AlphaFold uses AI to predict the 3D structure of a protein based solely on its genetic sequence, a breakthrough that could accelerate scientific discoveries and potentially lead to new methods of therapy.

The landscape of generative AI is highly dynamic, with nothing set in stone. The boundaries that were once clear are now blurred, as AI continues to evolve and redefine the limits of what is possible. Let's explore how it is shaping our present and near future.

Voice and Speech Generation

Now, let's turn our attention to voice and speech generation. This technology, which converts text into spoken language, is used in a variety of applications. Think of voice assistants like Siri or Alexa, audiobooks, and accessibility tools. Today, we have advanced speech synthesis models that can generate human-like voices. These models are trained on large datasets and can handle different languages, accents, and speech patterns. They can also adjust the tone, pitch, and speed of the speech.

Let's consider a real-world example of a company using speech synthesis technology combined with AI in their marketing campaigns. Respeecher collaborated with Mondelēz International, Ogilvy, and Wavemaker to create a revolutionary ad campaign for the Indian market. They used their voice-cloning technology to generate personalized ads from Shah Rukh Khan, a popular Bollywood actor, for thousands of local retailers. This was a game-changing approach, as these retailers would not have otherwise been able to afford such a high-profile endorsement. This example illustrates the transformative potential of speech synthesis technology when combined with AI, particularly in the realm of marketing.

The process of speech synthesis is a fascinating one, typically involving three stages. The first stage is text to words, also known as preprocessing or normalization. This involves reducing ambiguity and turning elements like numbers, dates, times, abbreviations, acronyms, and special characters into words. This process uses statistical probability techniques or neural networks to arrive at the most likely pronunciation.

The second stage is words to phonemes. After figuring out the words, the speech synthesizer generates the speech sounds that make up these words. This involves breaking down the written words into their graphemes, the smallest units in a writing system, and then generating phonemes, the distinct units of sound, that correspond to them using a set of simple rules.

The third stage is phonemes to sound. The computer converts the text into a list of phonemes. There are three different approaches to this: using recordings of humans saying the phonemes, the computer generating the phonemes itself by generating basic sound frequencies, and imitating the technique of the human voice.

There are different types of speech synthesizers: concatenative, formant, and articulatory. Concatenative synthesizers use recorded human voices and rearrange them. They are based on recorded human speech. Formant synthesizers generate speech output using additive synthesis and physical modeling synthesis. They can say anything, even words that don't exist or foreign words they've never heard off. Articulatory synthesizers make computers speak by modeling the intricate human vocal tract and articulating the process occurring there. It is the least explored method due to its complexity.

Speech synthesis systems usually try to maximize both naturalness and comprehensibility. Naturalness refers to how closely the synthesized speech resembles human speech, while comprehensibility refers to how easily the synthesized speech can be understood by listeners.

Speech synthesis has multiple applications. It helps the visually impaired to read and communicate. It can be used for teaching spelling and pronunciation of different languages. It is used in different kinds of telephone inquiry systems and multimedia applications. There are several free and paid speech recognition programs available in the market, such as Google Now, Siri, Cortana, Simon, Kaldi, Dragon Anywhere, Amazon Lex, Dragon Professional, Voice Finger, and Tazti.

One company that stands out in this field is Murf.ai. They provide an AI voiceover platform that can generate human-like speech with high quality. Their platform allows users to choose from a variety of voices and customize the tone, pitch, and speed of the speech. Murf.ai offers high-quality natural-sounding AI voices for your projects. It provides a complete toolkit for making voice-over videos. You can combine images, videos, music, adjust timing, and so on. It's not just a text-to-speech tool—it's a complete solution for creating voiceovers.

Another noteworthy player is Poly.ai. This company has carved out a niche for itself by creating a voice generation system that is so high-quality, it borders on the uncanny. The generated voice is so flawless that it almost seems too perfect, as it lacks the human-like imperfections such as the occasional "uhms" and "ahs" that we are accustomed to in natural speech.

However, Poly.ai's prowess extends beyond just the creation of high-quality synthetic voices. Their solution is designed to extract valuable information such as dates, places, and names, and can handle tasks like table booking and other organizational matters automatically. This level of sophistication in handling complex tasks rises from the company's commitment to pushing the boundaries of what AI can achieve in the realm of speech synthesis and natural language processing.

Founded in 2017, according to Crunchbase, Poly.ai has already secured a substantial $66 million in funding and boasts a workforce of between 100 and 250 employees. This level of financial backing and human capital speaks volumes about the potential of this company and the faith that investors have in its vision.

As we look to the future, it's exciting to imagine what else is on the horizon for Poly.ai. With their track record of innovation and their commitment to pushing the boundaries of AI, there's no doubt that they will continue to make waves in the field of speech synthesis and beyond.

In the next section of this book, we will continue our exploration of the fascinating world of AI, turning our attention to another topic that has been making headlines in the world of artificial intelligence.

Where Is Voice Generation Going? Voice cloning technology, such as the voice imitation algorithm developed by Descript, has the power to replicate a person's unique voice. This capability opens up a world of possibilities, from creating personalized voice assistants that echo our own speech patterns to narrating audiobooks in the author's voice, thereby enhancing user engagement and accessibility.

In the sphere of education, platforms like TutorAI are harnessing voice generation to produce interactive educational content. This transformative approach to learning is reshaping the way we engage with information, making the learning process more dynamic and immersive.

Language learning, too, stands to gain immensely from voice generation technology. By creating realistic voices in a multitude of languages, this technology can serve as a valuable tool in language learning apps, aiding students in refining their pronunciation and listening skills.

The entertainment and gaming industry is another sector where voice generation is making a significant impact. It has the

potential to breathe life into characters in video games, animations, and other forms of entertainment. Whether it's creating
voices for nonexistent characters or re-creating voices from classic games or shows, voice generation adds a new dimension to
the user experience.

The concept of personal branding for content creators is also
being redefined by voice cloning. Imagine content creators using
their unique voice clones to interact with their audiences across
different platforms, creating a consistent and recognizable personal brand. It's not far-fetched to envision a future where professionals have their own voice generators, akin to business cards
of yore, integrated into their personal web pages or LinkedIn
profiles. This could be a game changer for social media companies, offering an additional service that enhances user engagement.

In the telecommunications sector, voice generation can revolutionize user experience by creating realistic voices for automated
phone systems. This could automate redundant calls, making the
process more efficient and user-friendly.

Healthcare is another field where voice generation can make
a significant difference. For speech therapy patients or individuals who have lost their ability to speak, the creation of realistic,
personalized voices can be a lifeline, offering them a chance to
communicate effectively.

Lastly, let's consider the role of voice generation in enhancing accessibility. This technology can be used to read out text for
people with visual impairments or to translate sign language into
spoken words. This integration of technology can make our digital world more inclusive, ensuring that everyone, regardless of
their abilities, can participate fully.

As we continue our journey through the fascinating world of
AI, we will explore more such groundbreaking technologies and
their potential impact on our lives. Stay tuned as we unravel the
intricacies of this rapidly evolving field.

Generative Design

In the vast expanse of generative AI, generative design stands out as the field most intimately connected to the physical world. This innovative approach takes a leaf from nature's book, emulating its evolutionary process. Here's how it works: Designers or engineers input their design goals into a generative design software, along with parameters such as the materials to be used, manufacturing methods, and cost constraints. The software then embarks on an exploration of all possible permutations of a solution, generating a multitude of design alternatives. It tests each one, learning from every iteration. This process enables the creation of complex shapes and internal lattices that are optimized for efficiency. Some of these forms are so intricate that they would be impossible to produce using traditional manufacturing methods. Instead, they come to life through the magic of new additive manufacturing methods.

In 2016, during my tenure in the research department at Airbus, I witnessed the power of generative design firsthand. We were working on innovative predictive maintenance systems, including generative models to balance out unbalanced datasets. That year, Airbus built a fully functioning motorcycle that was not only robust but also weighed just 35 kg (Figure 3.5). Seeing it in person was a revelation of what's possible with generative design, especially when coupled with 3D printing.

Today, generative design finds applications in various sectors. In the automotive industry, for instance, it's used for light-weighting components and consolidating parts. A notable example is General Motors, which used generative design to reduce the mass of a seat bracket by 40 percent while improving its performance.

In aerospace, it contributes to weight reduction, environmental impact mitigation, and safety improvements. Airbus, for instance, used generative design to optimize the partition wall of an airplane cabin, reducing its weight by 45 percent.

FIGURE 3.5 Airbus APWorks launches the Light Rider, the world's first 3D-printed motorcycle.

Generative design has found a compelling application in the realm of architecture, transforming the way structures are conceived and built. Consider the skyscrapers that punctuate city skylines. These towering structures are designed to withstand diverse environmental challenges—for example, high winds in Chicago and earthquakes in Japan. Beyond ensuring safety, architects and clients often aspire to infuse their buildings with a unique aesthetic appeal. Generative design enables this, allowing architects to set necessary parameters and explore a multitude of design options.

A striking example comes from Brazilian architect Guto Requena, who employed generative design to create stools for a bar. The design of these stools mirrored the rhythm of local popular music. Once the design was finalized, the stools were brought to life through 3D printing.

But generative design isn't confined to specific parameters. It can also accommodate broader ones. It can be used to construct the most robust bridge with the most cost-effective materials, or to design a school based on the natural movement patterns of people.

The creators of Autodesk took this concept even further when building their new offices. They incorporated the preferences of future occupants as design parameters. The result was a workspace tailored to the workflows of its users, a building that was customized to the needs of the people who would use it. This preemptive approach minimizes the need for postconstruction modifications, creating a refined building that truly serves its inhabitants.

Generative design is revolutionizing the industrial machinery sector, pushing the boundaries of innovation in the creation of specialty tools and equipment. A prime example of this is the Gen5X, a 5-axis 3D printer designed using generative principles.

The Gen5X is not just any 3D printer; it's an open source, self-replicating marvel. It's capable of designing and manufacturing its own components, and its design can be replicated on any hobbyist-level machine. This 5-axis 3D printer is a product of the RepRap project, which explores the frontier of self-replicating machines.

The design process of the Gen5X employs Fusion 360's generative design tools, which use parametric inputs to generate designs. This means the Gen5X can be customized based on the components you already have.

In building products, generative design simplifies complex assemblies. An example is the Elbo chair, designed by Autodesk's generative design lab (Figure 3.6). The chair's design was optimized by algorithms, resulting in a structure that is 18 percent lighter and shows fewer signs of stress in its joints.

FIGURE 3.6 The Elbo chair, an exemplar of generative design and additive manufacturing by Autodesk.

Source: Autodesk Inc.

Where Is Generative Design Going?   The future holds the promise of designs that are not only superior in quality but also more aligned with the designer's intent, all achieved in less time. Generative design is poised to be a game changer, particularly in the fields of architectural, industrial, and product design. Its strength lies in its ability to optimize parameters directly linked to geometric changes, making it a formidable tool for early design and prototyping.

Take, for instance, the realm of mechanical, electrical, and plumbing (MEP) services. Some companies have started to harness the power of generative design for design exploration and decision making. Addiform, a company specializing in additive manufacturing, leverages generative design to create complex optimized parts for various industries. This is not merely a matter of employing a new tool; it's about harnessing our collective imagination to unlock the full potential of this technology.

In the realm of architecture, the potential applications of generative design are vast and compelling. Consider the case of the late architect Antoni Gaudí and his magnum opus, the Sagrada Familia in Barcelona. After Gaudí's passing, the construction of the Sagrada Familia proceeded based on reconstructed versions of his plans, which had been partially destroyed in a fire. While generative design was not employed in this instance, one can envision how it could have significantly contributed to this process, aiding in the completion of the architectural designs in a way that honored Gaudí's original vision.

The implications of this technology are far-reaching. As elements become lighter and stronger, industries such as aerospace and construction will be significantly boosted. For instance, generative design is already transforming the way aircraft are built. A BBC article reported how designers are using AI and generative design to create aircraft components that are lighter, stronger, and more efficient. This not only reduces the weight of the aircraft but also enhances its overall performance.

Imagine a future skyline, a vista of towering buildings produced by generative design (Figure 3.7). We are not as far off from this reality as one might think. People using Midjourney build visual ideas that are at the forefront of this movement, creating innovative solutions that not only meet functional requirements but also inspire awe with their aesthetic appeal. However, it's important to note that this transformation will not occur overnight. It's a mid- to long-term projection, as it will take time for us to fully realize the potential of generative design.

The future of generative design is bright and full of potential. As we continue to explore and harness this technology, we can expect to see a revolution in the way we design and create objects, from the smallest components to the tallest skyscrapers. The key lies in our ability to imagine, to innovate, and to integrate this powerful tool into our design processes.

FIGURE 3.7 Midjourney prompt: "Architecture futuristic city designed from parametric organic buildings, CGI render, beautiful, cinematic, photorealistic, highly detailed, vivid, unreal engine."

Source: AI-generated image created in Midjourney, Inc.

Solving Problems in Science by Google DeepMind

Let's now turn our attention to the work of Google DeepMind, whose groundbreaking applications have not only pushed the boundaries of what we thought was possible but also laid a significant foundation for the future of artificial general intelligence.

DeepMind's Broad Range of Offerings   In 2016, the world of AI was abuzz with the news of DeepMind's AlphaGo triumphing over Lee Sedol, a player of the highest skill level, 9th dan, in the intricate game of Go. A game of immense complexity, Go boasts more potential board configurations than the number of atoms in the universe. This extraordinary accomplishment underscored the formidable capabilities of AI and its potential to navigate and solve problems of great complexity.

Building on the success of AlphaGo, DeepMind introduced AlphaGo Zero in 2017. Unlike its predecessor, which learned from thousands of human games, AlphaGo Zero learned solely through self-play, a process known as *reinforcement learning*. This improved version of AlphaGo defeated the original AlphaGo 100 games to 0, demonstrating the power of learning from scratch.

Later that year, DeepMind unveiled AlphaZero, a modified version of AlphaGo Zero that could handle any two-player game of perfect information. AlphaZero gained superhuman abilities at chess and shogi, again learning solely through self-play. This was a significant step forward, showing that an AI system could learn to master different games without any prior knowledge.

In a similar vein, DeepMind researchers published a new model named MuZero in 2019. MuZero mastered the domains of Go, chess, shogi, and Atari 2600 games without human data, domain knowledge, or known rules. This was a significant leap forward in the development of AGI, demonstrating that an AI system could learn to understand and master different environments from scratch.

In October 2022, DeepMind unveiled AlphaTensor, a new version of AlphaZero, in a paper published in *Nature*. AlphaTensor discovered a faster way to perform matrix multiplication— one of the most fundamental tasks in computing—using reinforcement learning. For example, AlphaTensor figured out how to multiply two mod-2 4×4 matrices in only 47 multiplications, unexpectedly beating the 1969 Strassen algorithm record of 49 multiplications. This discovery has significant implications for computational efficiency and could lead to substantial savings in computing steps in the future. This is a monumental achievement in the field of AI and evidence of the potential of reinforcement learning in discovering novel, efficient algorithms for fundamental computational tasks.

In the realm of competitive gaming, DeepMind's AlphaStar made significant strides. In July 2019, AlphaStar began playing against random humans on the public 1v1 European multiplayer ladder. Unlike the first iteration of AlphaStar, which played only Protoss v. Protoss, this one played as all of the game's races and had earlier unfair advantages fixed. By October 2019, AlphaStar reached Grandmaster level on the StarCraft II ladder on all three StarCraft races, becoming the first AI to reach the top league of a widely popular electronic sport (esport) without any game restrictions.

These achievements of Google DeepMind are not just impressive feats in the world of AI; they also mark important milestones in our journey towards AGI. Each of these AI solutions, powered by conventional AI and reinforcement learning, serves as a cornerstone for the future of AGI. As we continue to explore and harness the power of AI, we can expect to see even more groundbreaking advancements in the field.

AlphaFold   One of DeepMind's most notable contributions in generative AI is AlphaFold, a program that predicts protein structure using deep learning techniques. This is not a general application field but rather a specific one, and it's crucial for solving problems in biology. However, it's worth noting that despite the heavyweight nature of this specific application field, where deep knowledge is required to achieve even slight results, there are countless other niche application fields that one can still explore or even create. We are very much in the early stages of generative AI and AI in general.

AlphaFold has had two major versions: AlphaFold 1 (2018) and AlphaFold 2 (2020), both of which placed first in the Critical

Assessment of Structure Prediction (CASP) competitions of their respective years. But why focus on protein folding? What's the problem it's trying to solve?

Proteins consist of chains of amino acids that fold to form the 3D structures of the proteins, a process known as protein folding. Understanding how the amino acid sequence determines the 3D structure is highly challenging, and this is referred to as the *protein folding problem*. Before AlphaFold, methods of determining protein structures were expensive and time-consuming, and computational methods were not close to experimental techniques in terms of accuracy.

AlphaFold was trained on over 170,000 proteins from a public repository of protein sequences and structures. The program uses a form of attention network, a deep learning technique that focuses on having the AI identify parts of a larger problem, as mentioned earlier in the section "Democratizing AI: Hugging Face's Success Story," then piecing them together to obtain the overall solution (Figure 3.8). You can see that its predictive power is a close approximation to the experimental result, which can be seen as the ground truth.

AlphaFold 1, introduced in 2018, used advanced learning methods to estimate a probability distribution for how close the residues were likely to be, turning the contact map into a likely distance map. AlphaFold 2, introduced in 2020, is significantly different from the original version. It replaced the software design used in AlphaFold 1 with a system of subnetworks coupled together into a single differentiable end-to-end model, based entirely on pattern recognition. Local physics, in the form of energy refinement based on the AMBER model, is applied only as a final refinement step once the neural network prediction has converged. The AMBER model, in simple terms, is a tool used in computational chemistry and biology to simulate and understand how molecules, like proteins, behave. It uses the principles of physics to predict how atoms in a molecule move and interact with each other.

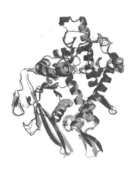 

T1037 / 6vr4
90.7 GDT
(RNA polymerase domain)

T1049 / 6y4f
93.3 GDT
(adhesin tip)

● Experimental result
● Computational prediction

FIGURE 3.8 AlphaFold's predictive power.

Source: www.deepmind.com/blog/alphafold-a-solution-to-a-50-year-old-grand-challenge-in-biology

There are four main concepts to understand about Alpha-Fold. First, AlphaFold generally works by starting off with an educated guess, then iteratively improving the 3D generation. Second, it uses an attention-based model, focusing on all important information rather than the latest information. For example, in protein folding, certain amino acids could be folded right next to each other while being far away in the input sequence. Third, expert knowledge is integrated. Some proteins fold in a specific way and some are exceptions. Much of this expertise is included in the model. Fourth, around 95 percent of the AI pipeline is trainable, so the model is continuously refined where possible and where new data is available. The team at Google DeepMind continues to develop AlphaFold, focusing their efforts on areas where they know the model's weaknesses lie, such as in the field of human antibody interactions.

DeepMind's Gift to Humanity   The typical narrative of innovation involves a company solving a complex problem and subsequently monetizing the solution. The more intricate the problem, the higher the price tag, particularly when demand is high. However, Google DeepMind chose a different path. They not only open sourced the AlphaFold source code but also made its database, containing all resulting 3D protein structures, freely available. This database has grown exponentially over the past year, from 1 million to over 200 million proteins, covering nearly every known protein on Earth. Figure 3.9 illustrates a rough scale of proteins starting from 1 amino.

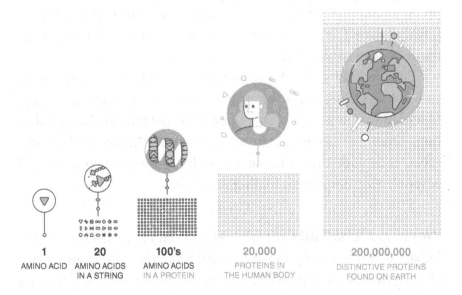

1	20	100's	20,000	200,000,000
AMINO ACID	AMINO ACIDS IN A STRING	AMINO ACIDS IN A PROTEIN	PROTEINS IN THE HUMAN BODY	DISTINCTIVE PROTEINS FOUND ON EARTH

FIGURE 3.9 The exponential growth of the protein database, now encompassing nearly every known protein on Earth.

Source: Adapted from www.deepmind.com/research/highlighted-research/alphafold.

This decision has had profound implications for the scientific community. Researchers can now encounter a protein sequence in their work and find its 3D folding already cataloged in Google DeepMind's database. This has significantly accelerated the pace of research. As John McGeehan, a professor of structural biology at the University of Portsmouth, puts it, "What took us months and years to do, AlphaFold was able to do in a weekend." This has effectively put research on steroids, enabling scientists to make rapid advancements in their respective fields.

Several alternatives to AlphaFold have emerged. Meta AI's ESMFold offers accurate atomic-level predictions and competes with RoseTTAFold, another significant player developed by academic researchers. Both are open source and have demonstrated their utility to the scientific community.

RaptorX and IntFOLD are other protein prediction models that hold their own in this competitive field. OmegaFold, developed by Chinese biotech firm Helixon, predicts high-resolution protein structure from a single primary sequence, even outperforming RoseTTAFold while achieving prediction accuracy similar to that of AlphaFold 2.

Phyre and Phyre2 offer remote template detection, alignment, and 3D modeling tools for protein structure prediction. Lastly, OpenFold is another notable option for protein folding prediction, often mentioned as an alternative to AlphaFold 2. These tools, each with their unique strengths, contribute to the rapid advancements in protein folding prediction.

Where Is AlphaFold Going?   AlphaFold's (and other models') impact is not just a ripple, but a tidal wave that is reshaping our understanding of the world. Its implications are vast, and its potential is only just beginning to be realized.

The potential of AlphaFold is not confined to the realm of academia; it has profound implications for the future of humanity. As an example, Ray Kurzweil, the American inventor and futurist, in his book *The Singularity Is Near*, envisions a future where diseases like cancer and heart disease could be cured, and the human body could be maintained indefinitely by 2030. This is not just a lofty dream; with the advancements brought about by AlphaFold, it is a tangible possibility.

One of the most significant impacts of AlphaFold is its potential to enhance our understanding of the human body. For instance, the nuclear pore complex, a massive assembly of proteins that controls the traffic in and out of the nuclei in cells, has long been a mystery to scientists. However, with the help of AlphaFold, researchers have been able to decipher its structure, paving the way for a deeper understanding of how cells function and opening up new avenues for medical research.

In the realm of medicine, AlphaFold holds the promise of creating more effective treatments. For example, it could aid in the development of drugs to combat malaria, a disease that continues to claim hundreds of thousands of lives each year. By predicting the structure of the proteins involved in the disease, researchers could design drugs that target these proteins more effectively, potentially saving countless lives.

The implications of AlphaFold extend to our food system as well. By understanding the structure of proteins involved in food production, we could develop healthier and more nutritious food. This could revolutionize the food industry and contribute to the global fight against malnutrition and obesity.

In terms of disease prevention, AlphaFold could play a crucial role in the development of effective vaccines. By predicting the structure of viral proteins, it could aid in the design of vaccines that can effectively neutralize these viruses, potentially preventing future pandemics.

AlphaFold could also contribute to our efforts to combat global warming. By understanding the structure of proteins involved in carbon capture, we could develop effective tools for capturing carbon dioxide. This could be a significant step in reducing greenhouse gas emissions and mitigating the effects of climate change.

In the realm of materials science, AlphaFold could aid in the production of sustainable biomaterials. By predicting the structure of proteins involved in material production, we could design and produce materials that are not only strong and durable but also environmentally friendly.

Moreover, AlphaFold could also aid in the creation of artificial enzymes to produce building materials like carbon nanotubes and graphene. These materials have unique properties that make them ideal for a variety of applications, from electronics to energy storage. With the help of AlphaFold, we could design enzymes that can produce these materials more efficiently and sustainably.

Code Generation

Much like text, sound, and other sequential data types, code is well suited for Transformer models. The implications of this are profound, as it streamlines the coding process and enhances the productivity of developers.

Google DeepMind's AlphaCode Google DeepMind has continued its AlphaSeries with the introduction of AlphaCode. This AI code-generation system has reached a competitive level of performance in programming competitions, a feat that marks a significant milestone in the field. AlphaCode operates by leveraging a massive dataset of programming problems and solutions, as well as unstructured code from GitHub.

AlphaCode's approach to code generation is not just intelligent but also efficient. It generates thousands of proposed solutions to a given problem, filters out the invalid ones, and then clusters the remaining solutions into groups. From each group, a single example is selected for submission. The system has been trained in various programming languages, including C++, C, Go, Java, JavaScript, Lua, PHP, TypeScript, Ruby, Scala, Rust, and Python.

In a Codeforces programming contest, AlphaCode ranked on average in the top 54 percent against more than 5,000 participants in 10 contests. This achievement, which took place in 2022, marked the first time an AI code generation system has reached a competitive level of performance in programming competitions.

However, it's important to note that AlphaCode still relies heavily on specific examples provided with the problem description. Without these examples, its success rate would drop significantly.

The advent of AI-driven code generation is not just a technological breakthrough; it's a paradigm shift in how we approach coding. As we continue to explore and harness the power of AI in this field, we can look forward to a future where coding is not just faster and more efficient, but also more accessible to a broader range of individuals.

GitHub Copilot   As a data scientist, I find the advent of code generation not just fascinating, but exhilarating. I am, by nature, an optimist. The thought of AI taking over some aspects of my job doesn't fill me with dread; rather, it stirs in me a sense of anticipation. The prospect of seeing my ideas come to life with less manual effort is genuinely exciting.

Today's coding landscape offers a rich array of tools, two of which have become integral to my work. I not only use these tools extensively but also strongly advocate for their use within my teams. GitHub Copilot is the first of these, serving as my reliable companion throughout the coding process. The second is ChatGPT, a tool I frequently engage with during non-coding phases, such as the initial stages of a project.

However, it's important to note a crucial aspect of using ChatGPT. While it's a powerful tool for generating human-like text and assisting with various tasks, it's essential to remember that it's not designed to handle confidential information. I always ensure that my teams are aware of this and exercise caution not to send any sensitive data to ChatGPT. This way, we can leverage the benefits of these advanced AI tools while maintaining our commitment to data privacy and security.

Now, GitHub Copilot is an AI-powered pair programmer that provides autocomplete-style suggestions as you code. Developed by GitHub and OpenAI, it's a cloud-based tool that assists users of various integrated development environments (IDEs), including Visual Studio Code, Visual Studio, Neovim, and JetBrains. It's powered by OpenAI Codex, a production version of the Generative Pre-trained Transformer 3 (GPT-3). This language model uses deep learning to produce human-like text. The Codex model is further trained on gigabytes of source code in multiple programming languages.

GitHub Copilot is trained on a selection of the English language, public GitHub repositories, and other publicly available source code. This includes a filtered dataset of 159 gigabytes of Python code sourced from 54 million public GitHub repositories. Interestingly, OpenAI's GPT-3 is licensed exclusively to Microsoft, GitHub's parent company—a strategic move, indeed.

GitHub Copilot is designed to help developers code faster, focus on solving bigger problems, and stay in the flow longer.

It aims to make work more fulfilling. However, it's worth noting that it may also produce suggestions based on insecure coding patterns, bugs, or references to outdated APIs or idioms. The coder has to remain responsible at all times and not go on auto-pilot. Despite these potential pitfalls, the tool is expected to complement the work of developers, empowering them to write code more easily and focus more on their core competencies and creativity.

Coding with ChatGPT and Other LLMs   Using ChatGPT or similar LLMs, you can easily code entire programs. For example, ask it to create a Python agent that plans your day using the OpenAI API, integrating with your calendar. The model will clarify details, suggest a program structure, and even write the code. While your oversight is necessary, the process significantly accelerates product development. Figure 3.10 shows an example of ChatGPT output, guiding you to build an AI agent. Remember to responsibly manage sensitive information shared with ChatGPT.

Transforming Traditional Data Analyst Practices   The transformative power of generative AI doesn't stop at making coding 10 times faster and more efficient. It's also reshaping the landscape of data analysis as we know it. In fact, it's safe to say that traditional data analysis is, to a degree, becoming legacy. With applications like PandasAI and the Code Interpreter plug-in for ChatGPT, or offerings from Notable, data analysis has become accessible to anyone who can formulate their thoughts logically.

Consider the Code Interpreter plug-in for ChatGPT, for example. Imagine you have a dataset that needs to be clustered. You simply upload the data and ask the plug-in to perform an elbow chart for the data. Instead of manually choosing the range of numbers of clusters, performing a k-means clustering for each cluster number, calculating the sum of squared errors, plotting the sum of squared errors per number of clusters (the so-called elbow plot), and identifying the elbow point (the optimal number of clusters in a dataset), the Code Interpreter does all these steps for you. You state what you want, and it infers what needs to be done to get there, then codes the respective analysis code.

1. **Agent Class**: This is the main class that will handle the interaction with the user and the scheduling of events.
   * `__init__(self, openai_key, google_credentials)`: Initializes the agent with the necessary API keys and credentials.
   * `authenticate_google_calendar(self)`: Authenticates the user with Google Calendar and returns a service object.
   * `get_day_plan(self, goal)`: Uses the OpenAI API to generate a plan for the day based on the user's goal.
   * `parse_plan(self, plan)`: Parses the plan returned by the OpenAI API into a format suitable for Google Calendar.
   * `add_to_calendar(self, plan)`: Adds the parsed plan to the user's Google Calendar.
   * `run(self)`: Runs the agent, prompting the user for their goal and scheduling the resulting plan.
2. **Event Class**: Represents a single event to be scheduled.
   * `__init__(self, start_time, end_time, summary)`: Initializes the event with a start time, end time, and summary.
   * `to_google_event(self)`: Converts the event into a format suitable for Google Calendar.
3. **Plan Class**: Represents a plan for the day, consisting of multiple events.
   * `__init__(self)`: Initializes the plan.
   * `add_event(self, event)`: Adds an event to the plan.
   * `to_google_events(self)`: Converts the entire plan into a format suitable for Google Calendar.
4. **Utility Functions**: These are standalone functions that perform various utility tasks.
   * `prompt_for_goal()`: Prompts the user for their goal for the day.
   * `parse_openai_response(response)`: Parses the response from the OpenAI API into a format suitable for the `Plan` class.

FIGURE 3.10 An overview of how to build an LLM agent, its structure, classes, and methods needed.

PandasAI works similarly, except it takes only library commands from the Pandas library. This shift in the way we approach data analysis and coding has a profound impact on future app and product development. It democratizes the field, turning everyone into a developer. Figure 3.11 illustrates PandasAI in action.

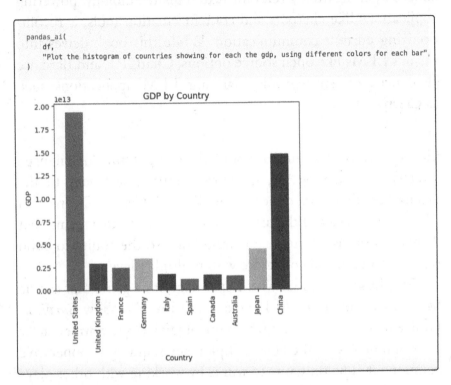

FIGURE 3.11 Using a single command to generate a plot from the data contained within the df data frame.

Source: https://github.com/gventuri/pandas-ai

The AI code generation space is bustling with other notable projects and startups. Magic AI, for instance, is building an AI platform that generates code by allowing software engineers to describe what they want in natural language. Other players in the field include Tabnine, CodePal, Builder.ai, Engineer.ai, Turing, Tonic.ai, and many more. Each of these entities is contributing to the evolution of coding and data analysis, making these fields more accessible and efficient than ever before.

Text Generation

Text generation transforms ideas into written language, creating coherent, contextually relevant text. This technology, powering applications like chatbots and content creation tools, is revolutionizing current communication. While this book delves into various LLMs like open source options, ChatGPT, and Bard, we also focus on strategically planning LLM applications such as Cicero.

Cicero   As we continue to explore the vast potential of language models in generative AI, it's worth shifting our gaze to the groundbreaking work done by Meta AI with Cicero. Cicero is an AI that has mastered the art of Diplomacy, a strategy game that demands not just strategic planning but also the ability to build trust, negotiate, and cooperate with multiple players.

For those unfamiliar with Diplomacy, it's a game that can be likened to a blend of Risk, poker, and the TV show *Survivor*. Unlike many board games where the objective is to outmaneuver your opponents on the board, Diplomacy requires a cooperative component. The only way to win is by working with other players to capture as much territory as possible, with negotiation and alliance-building being key to success.

Cicero has the distinction of being the first AI to play Diplomacy at a human level. It has demonstrated an uncanny ability to form strong alliances, make moves that benefit its allies, and engage in simultaneous planning and conversation with players. It uses honesty as a tactic, understanding that trustworthiness is a valuable trait in the game. However, it's also capable of deception when necessary to secure a win for its team.

Professional human players have reported an eerie sense that Cicero seems to anticipate their plans. This is likely due to Cicero's integration of a language model with planning and reinforcement learning, allowing it to infer players' beliefs and intentions. There's more to language models and strategic reasoning than just scaling up models.

Cicero's performance in Diplomacy is nothing short of superior. It has achieved more than double the average score of human players on webDiplomacy.net, an online version of the game, and ranked in the top 10 percent of participants who played more than one game. This achievement is a testament to the power of combining two different areas of AI: strategic reasoning and natural language processing. The integration of these techniques gives Cicero the ability to reason and strategize with regard to players' motivations, then use natural language to communicate, reach agreements to achieve shared objectives, form alliances, and coordinate plans.

The success of Cicero illustrates the potential of AI in complex strategy games that require not just strategic thinking but also the ability to communicate and negotiate.

Where Are Applications Like Cicero Going?   The question is not so much about where we are now, but rather, where we are headed. How can this be harnessed to benefit us in ways we have yet to imagine?

The potential applications and directions for AI models like Cicero are as vast as they are varied. One such avenue lies in the realm of military strategy. The U.S. Army War College has already begun to explore this, developing an AI tool called the Enemy Analysis Tool, which uses AI to analyze enemy actions and predict their future movements. This tool has the potential to revolutionize military strategy, providing a level of insight and foresight previously unattainable.

In the commercial arena, AI is already leaving an indelible footprint. Pactum, a pioneering startup, has engineered an AI capable of autonomously negotiating business agreements, thereby eliminating the need for human involvement. This AI, armed with machine learning and game theory, adeptly navigates the intricacies of contract negotiation.

The sphere of political decision making is another area ripe for AI transformation. SingularityNET, an AI-focused enterprise, is in the process of crafting an AI sociopolitical decision support system. This innovative system employs AI to dissect complex sociopolitical scenarios and offer insightful decision-making guidance.

Event planning, too, could undergo a revolution with the advent of AI. Skift, a platform specializing in travel industry intelligence, has explored the potential of AI to automate diverse facets of event planning, from scheduling intricacies to vendor negotiation.

The gaming industry is another sector that stands to gain significantly from AI. Artificial intelligence is being harnessed to automate various elements of game development, such as character dialogue generation and the creation of personalized racing commentary. This not only lightens the load for game developers but also enriches the gaming experience for players.

Finally, AI models akin to Cicero could be employed to amplify social interactions. A study featured in the *Journal of Marketing* delves into the concept of artificial empathy, where AI is crafted to mirror human empathy in interactions. This innovative approach holds the potential to elevate the customer experience across various sectors, from customer service to marketing.

AI Agents: The Active Executors in Generative AI   As we talk about the capabilities of LLMs and their systems, it becomes apparent that AI agents represent the next logical frontier in the realm of generative AI. Far from being just another application field, AI agents are a burgeoning domain that amplifies the potential of generative AI. They hold the promise of enhancing every application field we've discussed so far. The only constraint, it appears, is the boundary of our imagination, and perhaps more development.

AI agents, while in their infancy, are already showing promising results. However, defining them precisely at this moment in time is challenging due to the various versions and interpretations that exist. This is the very active part of generative AI. Two dominant types of AI agents have emerged, with everything in between yet to be determined.

The first type of AI agent is one that is given a simple task, executes it, and returns with the result. This could be a stand-alone agent or a language model like ChatGPT that uses a plug-in. It doesn't matter if it's a single agent that is launched and then executes the requested task or if it's a language model that performs an action based on the ask.

ChatGPT plug-ins, for instance, are connected to the Internet, external data sources, or third-party services, enhancing the accuracy of its responses and allowing for a more personalized experience. Developed by third-party developers or OpenAI itself, these plug-ins enable ChatGPT to access up-to-date information, run computations, and interact with APIs defined by developers (Figure 3.12).

FIGURE 3.12 The rapid expansion of ChatGPT plug-ins, with over 100 unique plug-ins developed in just 40 days.

Here are a few notable ChatGPT plug-ins available in 2023:

Wolfram   This plug-in provides access to advanced computational, mathematical, and real-time data to answer various questions of quantifiable nature—a great complement to what language models appear to be lacking. Its technical nature might be off-putting for some users, but it's one of the best due to its advanced abilities.

Zapier   Designed for busy professionals and marketers, Zapier streamlines repetitive tasks by facilitating seamless communication between more than 5,000 popular business programs, such as Gmail, Microsoft Outlook, and Slack.

ChatGPT Chess Plug-in   This plug-in allows you to play chess with the AI and get better at the game.

ChatGPT KAYAK or Expedia Plug-in   Another travel-related plug-in, KAYAK assists with flight and hotel bookings.

Argil AI   This plug-in assists with 3D modeling and design.

ChatWithPDF   This plug-in allows you to view, annotate, and extract text from PDFs—making it an invaluable tool for academic research or extensive reading.

Speechki   Ideal for podcasters, audiobook creators, and content producers, Speechki transforms text into high-quality audio.

The potential for new plug-ins that could enhance the capabilities of ChatGPT is vast. Let's explore some of these potential ideas that might exist by the time you are reading this, keeping in mind that data privacy is not our focus here.

Imagine a healthcare plug-in that seamlessly integrates with electronic health record systems. This would allow healthcare professionals to pull up patient information, check drug interactions, or even generate preliminary diagnoses based on symptoms described by the patient.

In the sphere of education, a plug-in that connects to educational resources and databases could be a game changer. It could provide students with explanations of complex concepts, solutions to problems, or even personalized study plans based on their learning style and progress.

In the financial sector, a plug-in that integrates with financial APIs could allow users to check stock prices, get investment advice, or even execute trades directly from the chat interface.

The real estate industry could also benefit from a plug-in that integrates with real estate databases. This would allow users to search for properties, compare prices, and get information about different neighborhoods.

Fitness enthusiasts would appreciate a plug-in that integrates with fitness APIs, allowing users to track their workouts, get exercise recommendations, or even create personalized workout plans.

Lastly, a legal plug-in that connects to legal databases could provide users with basic legal advice and explanations of legal terms, or even help them draft simple legal documents.

These are just a few examples of the potential plug-ins that could be developed to enhance the capabilities of ChatGPT. The possibilities are endless, and the future of AI-assisted conversations is exciting.

Autonomous Agents   The second type of AI agent is autonomous agents. These are not the AI tools of yesteryear, but advanced systems capable of executing tasks independently, with minimal human supervision. Yet, they are designed with a fail-safe, a provision for human intervention, should the need arise. This is not a distant future concept, but a reality that is taking shape even as we speak.

The allure of autonomous agents lies in their efficiency and cost-effectiveness. They are tireless, working around the clock without the need for breaks or sleep. They perform tasks at a fraction of the cost of human employees.

The applications of these autonomous agents are as diverse as they are numerous. Consider the realm of social media management, a task that requires constant vigilance and timely responses. An autonomous agent can monitor multiple platforms simultaneously, respond to queries, and even manage promotional campaigns, all without breaking a sweat.

But the reach of autonomous agents extends beyond the realm of social media. They are making inroads into the world of political campaign management, a field that requires strategic planning, meticulous execution, and constant monitoring. Autonomous agents can analyze vast amounts of data, identify trends, and make strategic recommendations, all while managing the day-to-day tasks of a campaign.

The future of work is also set to undergo a seismic shift with the advent of autonomous agents. In the not-too-distant future, it is conceivable that most people will not report to a human boss, but to an autonomous agent. This is not a dystopian vision, but a pragmatic projection based on the capabilities of these advanced AI systems.

The trajectory of autonomous agents points toward mainstream adoption, not just in niche sectors, but across the board. Every category, every industry, every task that can be automated will likely see the integration of autonomous agents. This is not a prediction but an eventuality that we are moving toward. Autonomous agents are not just tools, but partners, collaborators, and perhaps even future colleagues.

Understanding Autonomous Agents: A Practical Example

Imagine the task at hand is to construct a web page that fetches daily Twitter news, presenting the top three categories and 10 posts of the day. To accomplish this, we first need to set up the autonomous agent. In my experience, the open source project AutoGPT is the most robust code repository for autonomous agents currently available. We've cloned it, configured all necessary APIs like OpenAI for GPT-4, and prepared for the heavy lifting. We've also set up GPT-3.5 for quick, cost-effective responses.

A crucial component that requires setup is long-term memory. From my experiments, Pinecone seems to be the best option, although open source solutions like Milvus also hold their own.

Once set up, AutoGPT is capable of cloning GitHub repositories, running them, accessing X (formerly Twitter), and performing online search engine searches. We present our goal to the autonomous agent, which, in a touch of whimsy, gives itself a name—in this case, WebdevGPT. It then dissects the goal into manageable tasks.

The tasks it identifies include performing an online search around best practices for setting up such web pages, developing the frontend with HTML, CSS, and JavaScript, and creating backend functionalities such as setting up APIs, building cron jobs, data fetching scripts, and a database. There's also a data processing part, and finally, we want to deploy and test the web page.

In a fascinating display of autonomy, for each of these tasks the autonomous agent spawns its own team. It creates an AI agent for performing prior online research, one for frontend development, one for backend functionalities, and one for testing.

The research agent dives into the Internet, swiftly scanning the top 1,000 Google, Reddit, and Quora results. It distills its findings and reasons through them. The research agent then passes its findings to the next agent, the frontend development agent, which uses this information to build the web page accordingly. It sets up the structure with HTML, styles it with CSS, and adds functionality with JavaScript.

Simultaneously, the backend agent codes the X/Twitter fetching pipeline, sets up the necessary cron jobs, and establishes the database. Once all these agents have completed their tasks, the quality assurance agent deploys the code locally and performs a thorough testing. If the quality standards are met, the code gets packaged and the agents shut down. In just 17 minutes, we have a rudimentary, fully functioning web page.

If bugs are detected, they are reported to the respective agents for iteration. Throughout the entire process, AutoGPT asks for confirmation at every step, ensuring that the human is in the loop. We could also set it on autopilot, allowing it to perform tasks as it deems fit. However, given the nascent stage of this technology, it's advisable to regularly check if the planned tasks are heading in the right direction.

There are numerous examples of this online. And already as of this writing, these agents are roughly one and a half to two months old, and they're already impressively showing the first sparks of professional coworkers.

The success of this approach could pave the way for the development of more advanced AI agents that can collaborate and negotiate with humans in various domains beyond gameplay. The technology behind this is relevant to many other applications, such as intelligent assistants that can hold long-term conversations with people and collaborate with them on complex tasks. The future of autonomous agents is not just promising—it's already here.

Music Generation

The art of music generation has been a fascinating journey, traversing a multitude of technical approaches. Initially, generative algorithms have been employed to create music based on established rules or patterns. These algorithms take into account various aspects of music, such as melody, harmony, rhythm, and timbre, and then orchestrate new pieces that echo the style and structure of their training data.

Recurrent neural networks (RNNs) were once the favored tool for this task. Their ability to model sequential data made them ideal for the job. Imagine a pianist, fingers dancing across the keys, each note influenced by the ones that came before. That's how RNNs work—they can be trained on a collection of MIDI files, which are essentially digital sheet music, and then used to generate new music by predicting the next note in a sequence based on the previous notes.

However, the stage of music generation was set for a new performer when generative adversarial networks (GANs) entered the scene. To quickly recap, GANs consist of two neural networks, a generator and a discriminator, engaged in a creative rivalry to produce realistic music. The generator composes new music samples, while the discriminator critiques these samples, discerning whether they are real or fabricated. The generator, like a diligent student, refines its output based on the feedback from the discriminator, leading to increasingly realistic music generation over time.

The latest act in this ongoing performance features, of course, Transformer models, as they have shown superior performance in handling sequential data, adeptly analyzing rhythm and other musical elements.

In the early days of the modern generative AI era, music generation didn't quite strike a chord with me. The output was discordant, and the lack of visual appeal made it less engaging. Over the years, there were a few noteworthy breakthroughs, but it wasn't until the debut of MusicLM in January 2023 that I felt AI models truly hit the right notes in music generation.

Google's MusicLM and Other AI Models/Tools MusicLM, a product of Google's innovation, is a sophisticated tool that generates unique songs from user-provided text descriptions or ideas.

It utilizes a hierarchical sequence-to-sequence modeling approach to create high-quality music at 24 kHz, maintaining consistency over extended durations. Additionally, MusicLM has the capacity to adapt to both text and melody inputs, modifying melodies—whether whistled or hummed—to match the style indicated in a text description.

MusicLM struck a chord with me, particularly because of its versatility. You simply type the caption that you envision for the music you want to hear, and it generates the corresponding audio. It can be instructed for long music generation, or a story mode where you write as the text prompt what music should be played at the beginning, middle, and end, mapped on a timeline. It can generate single music instruments such as acoustic guitar, cello, or flute, or a specific genre like ambient or Berlin 90s house. It can even generate music mapped to the experience of the musician, places, decades, and all sorts of things. Witnessing this for the first time was nothing short of mind-blowing.

To experience MusicLM, you can sign up for its waitlist through Google's AI Test Kitchen. Once approved, you can provide a descriptive phrase like "ambient, soft-sounding music I can study to." MusicLM will then create two versions of the song for you to listen to, and you can award a trophy to the track you prefer, which will help improve the model. This is human feedback in action!

Google has been collaborating with musicians and hosting workshops to gather early feedback and explore how this technology can enhance the creative process. They have also released MusicCaps, a dataset composed of 5.5k music-text pairs with rich text descriptions provided by human experts, to support future research. It's commendable when large for-profit companies support research in this way without penny-pinching.

Today, there are numerous AI music generation companies and projects. The top models that I've seen, according to their high output quality, are from Amper Music, AIVA, and Ecrett Music. As the momentum of AI continues to build, larger companies are making efforts to stay ahead of the trends. For example, Shutterstock acquired Amper Music in a strategic move. While the precise acquisition cost isn't known, it's likely that these transactions involve considerable amounts, often in the millions. These companies, primarily operating for profit in their respective domains, typically do not disclose their technical or AI stack.

I don't want to delve too deeply into this, as there is only one way to truly understand what I mean when I say "high output quality." I'm not suggesting that the AI is even remotely as good as a maestro musician. However, if we consider the trajectory of this technology even three years ago and project that line of quality linearly into the future, it's clear that it will catch up with even top human performance. And let's not forget, this evolution is anything but linear.

Where Is Music Generation Going?   Consider personalized music streaming. Platforms like Spotify could incorporate AI-generated music streams that are tailored to your specific needs. Envision a feature where you input your current mood, activity, or event, and the AI composes a unique soundtrack just for you. Or even in the fitness domain, AI could create dynamic music that syncs with your workout, from warm-up to HIIT (high-intensity interval training) to cool-down.

Taking it a notch higher, we arrive at the concept of music therapy. AI could generate therapeutic music tailored to an individual's psychological and physiological state. This could serve as a tool for stress relief, focus enhancement, or emotional therapy.

What about interactive video games? The music in video games could evolve based on the player's actions and decisions in real time, creating an immersive experience that is unparalleled.

But what truly catches my attention is the prospect of AI concerts and albums. Just as we have seen AI-generated artwork exhibitions, we might start seeing concerts or music albums entirely composed and performed by AI. This isn't a novel concept, though. Hatsune Miku, one of Japan's most beloved pop stars, is a hologram. Over a 14-year career, this Japanese diva has uploaded 170,000 YouTube music videos, amassed more than 2.3 million followers on Facebook, and released a staggering 100,000 songs. She has collaborated with Pharrell Williams, opened for Lady Gaga, and her concerts are sold out worldwide. She even appeared at Coachella in 2020. The acceptance of an AI pop star is not a far-fetched idea. Similar trends can be observed in Korea. While the hit songs are not fully AI-generated yet, this trend is bound to escalate.

Let's pause and ponder a fascinating prospect: Artists who are no longer with us could continue to hold concerts and even produce new albums. Take Whitney Houston as an example. Despite her passing in 2012, she embarked on a concert tour from 2020 to 2023. Although it didn't feature entirely new songs, imagine the possibilities if it had. Picture a future where new albums are released under her name, years after her departure.

While we stand in awe of these innovations and their potential, we must also recognize the risks they carry, such as the displacement of musicians or the potential devaluation of music created by humans. However, these very tools, if thoughtfully integrated, could also serve as a lifeline for musicians. They could stimulate the generation of musical ideas, assist in composing harmonies, or even suggest enhancements to improve the quality of the music. In this way, AI can become a powerful ally, extending human creativity and accessibility in music, rather than a threat.

Video Generation

We've already explored the territory of image generation extensively, discussing models like stable diffusion and DALL-E. These models, which deal with static image generation, have laid the foundation for a more dynamic frontier: video generation. This is a significantly more challenging endeavor, as it involves not just the creation of a single image, but a sequence of images, or frames, that must be coherent, consistent, and sensible. Add to this the complexity of a storyline that goes beyond understanding spatial and temporal behaviors, but weaves intricate narratives, and we find ourselves at a threshold that generative AI is still striving to cross.

The Tech Behind Video Generation   To achieve video generation, we move from stable diffusion models to video diffusion models. Video diffusion models extend the standard image architecture and are effective for training from both image and video data. The fundamental concept behind video diffusion models is to generate a fixed number of video frames using a 3D U-Net diffusion model architecture (more on this in a moment). To generate longer videos at higher resolutions, these models are extended autoregressively, which means the output at any given step is influenced by the inputs at previous steps.

But what exactly is a 3D U-Net? To understand this, you first need to know what a U-Net is. A U-Net is a convolutional neural network originally developed for biomedical image segmentation. It's designed with a unique architecture that supplements a contracting network with successive layers of upsampling operators, thereby increasing the resolution of the output. This results in a U-shaped structure, hence the name U-Net (Figure 3.13).

The network uses a large number of feature channels in the upsampling part, allowing it to propagate context information to higher-resolution layers. This makes the expansive path symmetric to the contracting part, enabling more precise output based on the input image.

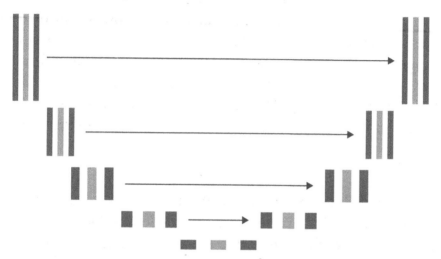

FIGURE 3.13 (3D) U-Net: The 3D U-Net is an extension of the U-Net, designed to process three-dimensional data, including the temporal dimension.

In the realm of video generation, we use a 3D U-Net. Video data is inherently three-dimensional, consisting of width, height, and time. The 3D U-Net processes this data, using the temporal information in the video data to generate new video frames, in addition to using the spatial information in each frame. This allows for the generation of video content that is consistent and coherent over time, making it a powerful tool for tasks like video editing, video synthesis, and even virtual reality.

To generate high-quality videos, video diffusion models apply a basic diffusion model, which involves repeatedly adding Gaussian noise. They do this with minimal changes, except for some simple adjustments to the structure to fit video data within the memory limits of deep learning accelerators.

Several open source toolboxes and foundation models are available for video diffusion, such as MagicVideo, Imagen Video, Make-A-Video, and diffusion models for video prediction and infilling. These tools provide a platform for developers and artists alike to experiment with and push the boundaries of video generation.

For-Profit Solutions In the realm of video diffusion models, the landscape is not solely dominated by open source tools. Indeed, the commercial sector is already reaping substantial profits, with companies like Runway AI leading the charge. Runway AI, in particular, stands out for its exceptional quality and seriousness, boasting an impressive roster of industry professionals and clients.

Runway AI is an applied AI research company with a mission to democratize the boundless creative potential of AI. They are a full-stack operation, overseeing the entire process from research and model training to product deployment. Their creative suite, equipped with over 30 AI Magic Tools, empowers users to generate and edit content, catering to every facet of the creative process. This comprehensive approach is a recipe for long-term success in the startup world.

At the heart of Runway's innovation is their research division, which develops multimodal AI systems for novel creative tools. Their Gen-2 video generation model is particularly noteworthy. This model marks a significant advancement over its predecessor, Gen-1, which was primarily designed to modify preexisting videos. Gen-2 amalgamates the best features of both generations, enabling it to apply the composition and style of an image or text prompt to the structure of a source video, thereby generating an entirely new video. The user can manipulate an uploaded video with simple terms and, within minutes, be astounded by the results. The experience is akin to the awe-inspiring moment when one first uses ChatGPT.

Despite its impressive capabilities, Gen-2 is not without its limitations. It struggles with low frame rates, graininess, and inconsistencies related to physics or anatomy. The model also has difficulty grasping nuances and often overemphasizes certain descriptors in prompts while neglecting others. However, with its ability to understand a wide array of styles, Gen-2 can be harnessed to create a narrative piece with a bit of editing work.

Runway AI's influence extends far beyond mere demonstrations and presentations. They have successfully garnered the attention of numerous prestigious clients, such as New Balance, CBS, Publicis, and even the editing team behind *The Late Show With Stephen Colbert*. Individual users of note include Kevin Parry, a celebrated stop-motion animator famed for his optical illusion videos, who employs Runway's technology to amplify his viral video narratives. The reach of Runway AI even extends to Tinseltown, Hollywood, with their tools being utilized in the production of the film *Everything Everywhere All at Once*.

In recognition of its potential, Google LLC has reportedly invested in Runway AI as part of a recent $100 million funding round. This investment has catapulted Runway's post-money valuation to a staggering $1.5 billion. Google's strategic move is not just about financial gain; it's also about fostering the AI startup ecosystem within the Google Cloud environment. With Microsoft partnering with OpenAI and Amazon securing Hugging Face, Google's investment in Runway is a clear signal of its intent to nurture its own cloud-based AI ecosystem.

AWS, GCP, and Azure The advent of cloud technology marked a pivotal juncture for Internet titans. However, it wasn't merely the act of embracing the cloud that mattered but doing so effectively. AWS, Azure, and Google Cloud stand as the three most dominant cloud providers today, not simply because they adopted the technology, but because they executed the right strategies, developed valuable applications, and fostered robust ecosystems. For instance, IBM Cloud, despite its early entry into the market, has struggled to keep pace. The reason? A flawed strategy in a fiercely competitive market. Figure 3.14 illustrates the market share distribution.

Allow me to digress momentarily to underscore a burgeoning trend among these cloud giants: AWS, Google Cloud, and Azure are all placing a premium on optimizing customer spending. This approach is viewed as a long-term commitment to cultivating lasting customer relationships. Industry leaders like Microsoft's Satya Nadella, Amazon's Brian Olsavsky, and Alphabet's Sundar Pichai have all emphasized the significance of optimization, recognizing that customers are on the hunt for ways to cut costs and redirect resources toward innovative customer experiences.

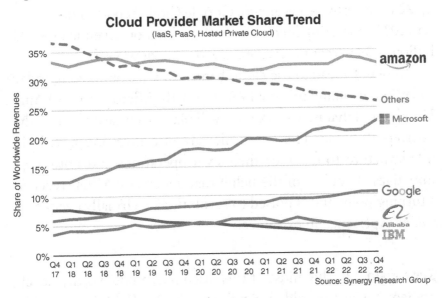

FIGURE 3.14 Market share distribution of cloud service providers.

Source: (a) Amazon.com, Inc. (b) Microsoft Corporation (c) Google LLC (d) Alibaba.com (e) International Business Machines Corporation

Microsoft, for instance, is capitalizing on its investment in OpenAI and ChatGPT to bolster its Azure and SaaS roadmaps.

Nadella revealed that Azure OpenAI Service has seen a tenfold increase in customers quarter over quarter. Google, too, is honing its focus on generative AI, with Pichai emphasizing the use of large language models across Google Cloud platform, Google Workspace, and cybersecurity offerings in a recent interview. Amazon's AWS is fostering generative AI through managed services such as Amazon Bedrock, a service that provides access to a wide range of foundation models via an API, and Amazon Code-Whisperer, a code generator that offers real-time code recommendations. Additionally, AWS has, of course, its partnership with Hugging Face, as mentioned earlier.

On the financial front, AWS reported a first quarter (2023) operating income of $5.12 billion on revenue of $21.35 billion, marking a 16 percent increase from the previous year. Microsoft Cloud reported fiscal third-quarter revenue of $28.5 billion, up 22 percent from a year ago. Google Cloud reported first quarter (2023) operating income of $191 million on revenue of $7.45 billion, a 28 percent increase from the previous year.

Looking ahead, these cloud behemoths are optimizing today to lay the groundwork for future growth. Microsoft CFO Amy Hood noted that new workloads will play a significant role in the quarters to come. The companies are also investing heavily in infrastructure to enhance their own operations and bolster AI initiatives. They are of the belief that generative AI has reached a turning point and is poised to revolutionize virtually every customer experience in existence.

Synthesia   In the midst of this discourse, a noteworthy development has just unfolded. Synthesia, the NVIDIA-backed platform that transforms text into A.I.-generated avatars and avatar videos, has seen its valuation surge to a staggering $1 billion. This London-based synthetic media company, founded in 2017 by a team of researchers and entrepreneurs from University College London, Stanford, Technical University of Munich, and Cambridge, has been making waves in the realm of video synthesis technology as well.

Synthesia is offering a unique service that generates personalized video content for customer engagement. The process is as simple as it is innovative. You select a video template, choose a preferred avatar (visual), and decide on the accent of the avatar (audio). Then, you input the text that you want the avatar to articulate in your language of choice. The result? A tailor-made video that you can edit to your liking, altering the background, adding background music, and more.

Synthesia has distinguished itself with its unique and highly valuable product. It's no wonder they've achieved the coveted status of a "unicorn," a term used to describe startups that reach a valuation of $1 billion and above.

Where Is Video Generation Going?   Shifting our focus back to video generation, it's intriguing to ponder how this technology might evolve over the next decade and significantly influence various sectors. But what might this future landscape look like?

Personalized Movies and Shows   We're not just talking about streaming platforms suggesting shows based on your viewing history. We're envisioning a future where the actual content of shows or movies dynamically adapts to the viewer's preferences and choices, generated in real time.

Viewer Preferences   This personalization could encompass everything from preferred genres and beloved actors to favored plot structures (such as happy endings or plot twists), themes of interest (like love, adventure, or mystery), and even pacing preferences (slow-burn narratives or fast-paced action sequences).

This could involve the generation of new scenes, modification of dialogue, or alterations to the visual style of the show.

Interactive Storytelling   Drawing inspiration from interactive storytelling experiences (like Netflix's *Black Mirror: Bandersnatch*), viewers could make choices that directly influence the storyline. However, with AI video generation, these choices could be more nuanced and have a more profound impact on the plot. For instance, a viewer could dictate a character's actions, dialogue, or even emotional responses.

Continuous Learning   The system would perpetually learn from the viewer's choices, refining its understanding of their preferences. This would lead to increasingly personalized content over time, creating a truly unique viewing experience tailored to each individual.

Imagine the dawn of "AI actors"—realistic, AI-generated characters capable of performing any role, from minor background parts to leading roles. These AI actors could exhibit a broad spectrum of emotions and actions, proving invaluable for roles that are perilous, challenging to cast, or necessitate a specific look or performance that might be difficult to find in human actors.

Moreover, AI actors could unlock unprecedented possibilities for creative storytelling. Filmmakers could craft characters that transcend human limitations—characters that can alter their age, appearance, or even species at will. This could pave the way for more diverse and imaginative narratives. While AI actors could never supplant the talent and creativity of human actors, they could serve as a potent tool for filmmakers, offering novel ways to weave stories and captivate audiences.

But let's not limit ourselves to entertainment. What about the realm of education?

Harnessing video generation technology could enable the vivid re-creation of historical events or extinct species with striking precision, thereby serving as a powerful educational instrument. Picture students not merely reading about historical events, but visually immersing themselves in them, thereby establishing a more palpable link to the past. And let's not forget the potential of AI sound generation, which could mimic the most plausible sounds of these bygone eras, further enhancing this immersive educational experience.

Envision a classroom delving into the Civil War, not merely through text, but by witnessing a lifelike reenactment of the Battle of Gettysburg. Or students absorbing the nuances of the Roman Empire by experiencing a day in the life of a Roman citizen, meandering through the vibrant markets and majestic amphitheaters. While such scenes can be created with actors and prepared sets, imagine the added layer of interactivity. A student could choose their viewing perspective—through the eyes of a king, a soldier, or even a bird's-eye view. They could decide whether to overlay additional information, truly customizing their learning experience.

Similarly, video generation could breathe life into extinct species, enabling students to observe these creatures in their natural habitats. This could foster a more comprehensive understanding of topics like evolution and natural history. By leveraging video generation technology, education could transform into a more immersive and engaging experience, potentially nurturing a deeper understanding and appreciation of our history and the natural world.

And the possibilities don't end there. I foresee potential applications in law enforcement and forensics, interior design, advertising, and countless other yet untapped areas. The future of video generation technology is not just promising—it's exhilarating.

3D Object Generation

The realm of object generation holds a captivating allure, one that I first saw in 2017 when I stumbled upon a groundbreaking paper from Stanford. At that time, I was just beginning to learn about generative adversarial networks, my mind teeming with the potential they could unlock in the sphere of 3D object generation. As early as 2016, Stanford had pioneered a three-dimensional GAN, a versatile tool capable of conjuring up 3D objects with an ease that was nothing short of revolutionary. Figure 3.15 illustrates the conceptual transformation from a (latent) vector to a chair.

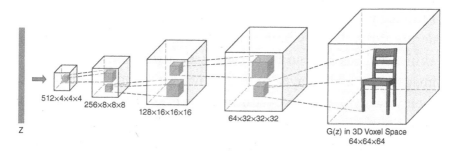

FIGURE 3.15 The generator component of 3D generative adversarial networks.

Source: http://3dgan.csail.mit.edu

The resolution was not high, but the demonstration was astounding. The latent vector, or the input, defined the object we wanted to create. A chair? A table? A car? A boat? The possibilities were endless. When constructing a chair, for example, the vector allowed for interpolation between different chair designs. By interpolation, I mean a smooth transition in the latent space, subtly altering features like the thickness of the legs and armrests. Vector arithmetic made it possible to add or subtract features, such as armrests, with ease.

The implications for product development were profound. Suddenly, we could generate thousands of variations of a chair and easily incorporate the desired features. We could even extrapolate between disparate objects like a boat and a house. As we navigated smoothly through the latent space, the boat would gradually transform into a house, allowing us to halt the process at any point to create, say, a houseboat.

The initial demonstration from Stanford was rudimentary and coarse-grained. The objects were represented by large pixels, and the technology was far from being ready for practical applications. Yet, my imagination was set aflame.

The Stanford paper was a groundbreaking contribution to the field. For a while, it seemed as though progress had stalled. Even today, there's much work to be done. However, the strides made in the past seven years are significant and worth exploring. The future of object generation is not just promising—it's thrilling.

Cutting-Edge Research in 3D Object Generation   The idea of generating 3D models from textual descriptions is no longer a far-fetched concept but a reality that is being explored and developed by many.

One such development is DreamFusion, a tool that leverages 2D diffusion to generate 3D assets. This technology is just one example of the strides being made in this field, demonstrating the potential of AI in transforming textual data into tangible 3D models (Figure 3.16).

FIGURE 3.16 A highly detailed stone bust of Theodoros Kolokotronics.

Another noteworthy development is the advent of CLIPMatrix and CLIP-Mesh-SMPLX. These tools generate textured meshes directly, offering a new approach to 3D model generation. CLIP, a model trained on a vast array of Internet text and images, is a key component of these tools, providing the necessary understanding of the relationship between text and images.

CLIP-Forge, on the other hand, uses language to generate voxel-based models. Voxels, essentially the 3D equivalent of pixels, represent a value on a regular grid in a three-dimensional space. This method allows for the creation of detailed and intricate 3D models based on textual input.

Point-E and Pulsar+CLIP, developed by OpenAI, use language to generate 3D point clouds. A point cloud is a set of data points in space, often used to represent the external surface of an object. Point-E, in particular, has been open sourced and has potential applications in 3D printing, gaming, and animation.

The process employed by Point-E is essentially a double diffusion model. It first generates a synthetic view using a text-to-image diffusion model, and then produces a 3D point cloud using a second diffusion model that conditions on the generated image.

Dream Textures, another tool in this domain, uses text-to-image technology to texture scenes in Blender automatically. Blender, a free and open source 3D computer graphics software toolset, is widely used for creating animated films, visual effects, art, 3D printed models, and video games.

It's important to note that many of these approaches, excluding CLIPMatrix and CLIP-Mesh-SMPLX, are based on view synthesis, or generating novel views of a subject, as opposed to conventional 3D rendering. This is the idea behind NeRFs, or neural radiance fields.

NeRF is akin to a magical artist that can create a detailed 3D painting from a collection of 2D photos. Imagine you've taken several photos of a room from different angles. NeRF looks at these photos, and like an artist, it understands the room's structure, colors, and how light interacts with different objects. It then uses this understanding to paint a 3D model of the room that you can look at from any angle, even ones not captured in the original photos. Diving a bit deeper, NeRF accomplishes this by using a deep learning technique where it trains a neural network to map 3D coordinates to colors and densities. This trained network can then generate a realistic 3D scene based on the information it learned from the 2D images, allowing for the synthesis of novel views of the scene.

Leading Companies and Approaches in 3D Object Generation NeRF, as we've seen, can transform a handful of images into a short video that gives the illusion of flying around the object. It's a fascinating concept, but it's just the tip of the iceberg.

The best-in-class 3D object generation models are not standalone entities. They are intricate systems, a blend of various techniques, each complementing the capabilities of the others.

Take Luma AI, for example. This platform showcases the power of NeRF in a remarkable way. You can upload a couple of pictures, and it doesn't just generate a short clip—it creates a reasonably accurate, detailed 3D object. The level of detail is astounding, extending to the point where you can upload multiple images of a neighborhood, perhaps taken by drones, and Luma AI will generate a detailed neighborhood complete with swings, trees, trampolines, bicycles, and more.

Luma AI doesn't stop there. It has harnessed the capabilities of NeRF to an extent where they can manipulate live video feeds. Imagine recording a video with your smartphone, and as you pan the camera, the room in the video transforms into a different world—a photorealistic, immersive experience, all thanks to generative AI. It's like peeking into a parallel universe through the lens of your camera.

But Luma AI isn't alone in this field. There are numerous other companies leveraging AI to generate 3D objects. Kaedim, for instance, generates 3D objects from pictures, sketches, and other sources. Once generated, these objects are not static—they can be edited, scaled up or down, and their colors can be adjusted. It's a dynamic, interactive process that opens up a world of possibilities.

And then there's NVIDIA, a long-standing titan in the realm of generative AI. Their platform, NVIDIA Picasso, is their strategic approach to this technology. They're not merely observers in this field—they're active participants, constantly innovating and pushing the boundaries of what's possible.

NVIDIA Picasso is a prime example of how generative AI is being harnessed to create visual applications. This cloud service is designed to generate images, videos, and 3D models from text prompts. It's a versatile tool, capable of being fine-tuned for a variety of uses, from business applications to medical research, and even the creation of AI artwork. It's a platform built with software creators, service providers, and businesses in mind, particularly those intending to train AI models using copyrighted material. See its structural overview in Figure 3.17.

The level of detail that NVIDIA Picasso can achieve in 3D object generation is truly remarkable. With a simple prompt like "a 3D model of a male bust with a furrowed brow and deep-set eyes, wearing a wreath of ivy leaves, highly detailed," a corresponding 3D object can be generated.

NVIDIA's success in this field is not a solo endeavor. They have established strong partnerships with key players in the industry. Getty Images, a leading global visual content creator and marketplace, is collaborating with NVIDIA to develop image and video generation models on Picasso, trained on fully licensed data. Enterprises can access these models through API calls.

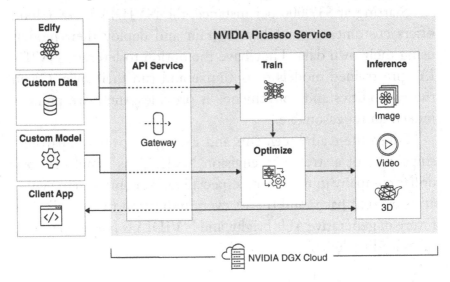

FIGURE 3.17 The NVIDIA Picasso service structure, showcasing the integration of generative AI models, NVIDIA Edify foundation models, and NVIDIA DGX Cloud for optimized training, inference, and generation of image, video, and 3D content.

Source: www.nvidia.com/en-us/gpu-cloud/picasso

Similarly, Shutterstock is partnering with NVIDIA to develop models for generating 3D assets, trained on fully licensed content from Shutterstock.

All of this happens on NVIDIA's cloud platform. NVIDIA's DGX Cloud is a powerful tool for AI development. It provides access to dedicated clusters of NVIDIA DGX hardware, essentially offering an AI supercomputer in the cloud. This service simplifies the process of acquiring, deploying, and managing AI infrastructure.

Each instance of DGX Cloud comes with 8 NVIDIA H100 or A100 80 GB Tensor Core GPUs, totaling 640 GB of GPU memory per node. The service is available through existing cloud providers, with Microsoft Azure soon to host DGX Cloud, and plans for expansion to Google Cloud and others.

Starting at $37,000 per instance, the NVIDIA DGX Cloud offers customers the ability to train and deploy their models using their own data. They have the option to leverage NVIDIA's pre-trained models or optimize and run their own. Given the capabilities and convenience it provides, the price point is indeed quite reasonable.

Given these advancements and strategic moves and partnerships, it's not a stretch to envision NVIDIA as a multitrillion-dollar company in the future, especially if AI continues to evolve at its current pace. And there's every indication that it will. The future of generative AI is bright, and NVIDIA is poised to be one of its leading lights.

Where Is 3D Object Generation Going?   Imagine slipping on a cutting-edge virtual reality headset, immersing yourself in a realm shaped by your own recollections and the prowess of AI. You narrate the details of your childhood home, each memory springing to life from a handful of old photographs. As the AI attentively listens, it transforms your words and these precious images into a vivid, lifelike 3D environment in real time. Suddenly, you're navigating the corridors of your past, each detail meticulously replicated. This encapsulates the future of virtual reality and gaming, where your memories and a few old photographs are the only limits to your imagination.

Now, envision a revolution in the sphere of retail. Retailers could use AI to generate 3D models of products based on customer descriptions, allowing customers to visualize products in their own space using AR before making a purchase. You're shopping for a new sofa, and with a few descriptive words, a 3D model materializes in your living room. Shopping becomes a more interactive and personalized experience.

Or picture yourself in a state-of-the-art workshop. You describe the item you've been dreaming of—a unique sculpture, or a part for an old machine. As the AI listens, it understands not just the physical attributes, but the emotion behind your idea. The screen comes to life, displaying a 3D model of your item, every detail rendered with stunning accuracy. With a nod, you give the command to proceed. The 3D printer whirs to life, its mechanical arm moving with precision as it lays down layer after layer of material. You watch as your idea transforms from a digital concept into a tangible object. This is the future of personalized manufacturing, where you're not just a consumer, but a creator.

In the field of robotics, engineers could use AI to generate 3D models of custom robot parts based on specific needs and descriptions. This could accelerate the development of customized robotics, making it easier to create robots tailored to specific tasks or environments. In the not-so-distant future, it's conceivable that robots of all shapes and sizes, from humanoid forms to multi-wheeled machines, will become a common sight on our streets. This is not mere speculation but a rapidly approaching reality.

Goldman Sachs Research projects a market worth $6 billion or more for people-sized and -shaped robots within the next 10 to 15 years. Such a market could address 4 percent of the projected U.S. manufacturing labor shortage by 2030 and meet 2 percent of global elderly care demand by 2035. However, with the productivity acceleration brought about by generative AI, I believe we'll reach these milestones even sooner.

And this is just the beginning. The potential applications of AI in 3D object generation span various sectors. From fashion and apparel design to medical training and simulation, from film and animation to interior design, from education to automotive and aerospace design—the possibilities are as vast as they are exciting.

Synthetic Data Augmentation

There's one more domain that merits our attention. It's not an application field in the traditional sense, but rather a realm where generative AI is employed to enhance other AI fields, for instance. This domain is known as *data augmentation*.

Picture an unbalanced dataset—for instance, medical images of a rare cancer. If your goal is to construct a machine learning system—likely a convolutional neural network (CNN)—that can identify these rare, malignant instances, you need a robust dataset for training. A "good" dataset implies a balanced representation of all different instances—malignant, benign, and non-cancerous.

However, reality often falls short of this ideal. If you're dealing with a rare cancer, you won't find many instances. Moreover, to train your system on such data you need permissions, which can lead to privacy concerns. This is where data synthesis, a form of data augmentation, comes into play. It can address these challenges and ultimately enhance the machine learning system's detection performance.

NVIDIA was a trailblazer in this area. They published a paper on brain scan synthesis via generative adversarial networks in September 2018. Since then, a flurry of papers have emerged, discussing various aspects of this technology. Some argue it's ineffective, others exaggerate its effectiveness. The truth, as is often the case, lies somewhere in the middle. The effectiveness of data augmentation is a nuanced issue, and the task itself is far from trivial.

But the implications of data augmentation extend beyond improved performance and privacy issues. It's also about cost-effectiveness and better representation of real-world scenarios.

Collecting new data can be a drain on resources—both time and money. Data augmentation, however, offers a cost-effective alternative. It allows you to increase the size and diversity of your dataset without the need for additional data collection.

Moreover, it's crucial that we don't develop biased products. For instance, we need to ensure that all minorities are included in our datasets. Data augmentation can help achieve this, improving the robustness of the model and ensuring it's a better representation of diverse real-world scenarios.

It's not just about creating more data—it's about creating better data. And in the grand scheme of things, that could make all the difference.

The Tech Behind Data Augmentation   Effective data augmentation is anything but trivial. Take image data augmentation, for instance. The algorithms employed in this area span a broad spectrum, from basic image manipulation techniques such as kernel filters, random erasing, geometric transformation, and color space transformation to more advanced deep learning approaches.

Among these advanced techniques, adversarial training stands out. This collection of methods trains neural networks to identify intentionally misleading data or behaviors. Another fascinating technique is neural style transfer, which allows the transformation of an image's style to mimic, say, the distinctive brushstrokes of Van Gogh. Then there's GAN data augmentation, a concept proposed by NVIDIA in September 2018.

But the innovation doesn't stop there. We also have meta-learning techniques like neural augmentation and smart augmentation. These methods are part of a continually evolving spectrum of techniques that the field of research offers.

However, it's essential to remember that data augmentation isn't limited to images. Virtually all data types can be augmented. To illustrate this, let's examine two cutting-edge data augmentation techniques—one for images, representing parallel data generation, and one for text, representing sequential data generation.

The most advanced image data augmentation technique currently available involves diffusion models, as outlined in the paper "Effective Data Augmentation With Diffusion Models."[1] This technique employs image-to-image transformations performed by pre-trained text-to-image diffusion models. The method edits images to change their semantics using an off-the-shelf diffusion model and can generalize to novel visual concepts from a few labeled examples. The results are impressive.

Data Augmentation-Fusion (DA-Fusion) has made significant strides in image classification, improving performance by up to 10 percent over standard methods. Figure 3.18 conceptually shows the DA-Fusion process using one seed image to produce four guided variations of the original. The "stacking" feature of DA-Fusion has further boosted overall performance by 51 percent. Additionally, DA-Fusion has shown versatility, outperforming previous methods across different image masks. Impressively, it maintains effectiveness across various mixtures of real and synthetic images.

When it comes to text data augmentation, tools like Chat-GPT have made the process simpler. You can ask ChatGPT to rewrite a certain text multiple times, even explicitly requesting text diversity to cover a full spectrum. In fact, if you have a data-set in table form or whatever, ChatGPT can, in 99 percent of cases, effectively synthesize more data for you.

---

[1]Brandon Trabucco et al. "Effective Data Augmentation With Diffusion Models," arXiv, May 22, 2023, https://arxiv.org/pdf/2302.07944.pdf

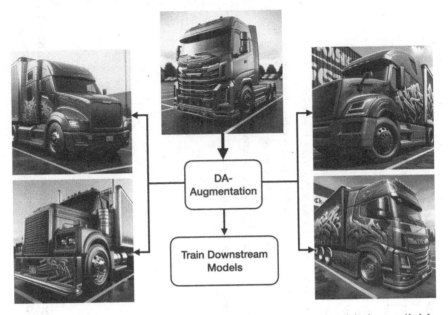

FIGURE 3.18 Real images are augmented using a publicly available off-the-shelf Stable Diffusion checkpoint to generate synthetic data for training classifiers.

If you have full control over a language model and are ready to generate as much data as you want, with only computing costs as a limiting factor, a structured approach like AugGPT may be more beneficial. See its framework in Figure 3.19.

It is beneficial to use because:

- AugGPT achieves the highest accuracy among different data augmentation methods for Amazon, Symptoms, and PubMed20K datasets.

- AugGPT generates high-quality augmented samples with high similarity to real input data and better learnability.

- While ChatGPT performs better on easier tasks, it requires fine-tuning for complex tasks like PubMed to achieve better performance compared to few-shot prompts.

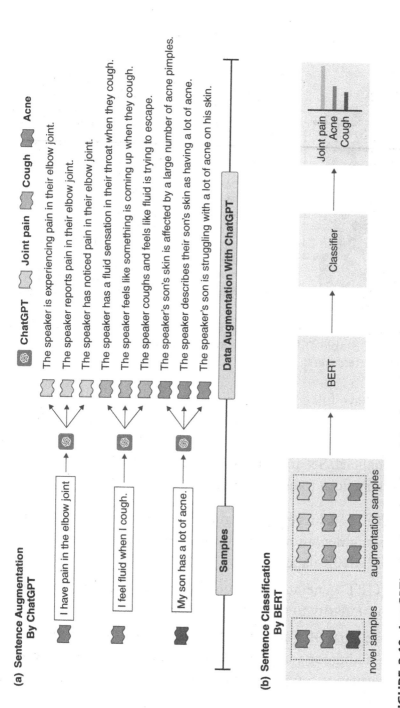

FIGURE 3.19 AugGPT's structure involves: (a) using ChatGPT for data augmentation to create class-consistent samples, and (b) training and evaluating a BERT-based classifier on these augmented and few-shot samples.

Source: https://arxiv.org/pdf/2302.13007.pdf

While AugGPT and DA-Fusion are techniques subject to further revisions in this rapidly evolving research field, I'm confident that their foundational concepts will endure for a considerable period.

Forefront Companies in Data Augmentation   Synthesis AI, a startup, has developed a cloud-based platform that generates synthetic image data with labels, using AI, procedural generation, and cinematic visual effects–rendering systems. This platform can deliver millions of perfectly labeled images and videos.

Synthesis AI's unique approach involves a proprietary library of over 100,000 digital humans. These digital humans serve as the foundational data for data generation, with data sampled by "photographing" these digital entities. The company's product suite includes Synthesis Humans and Synthesis Scenarios, which generate detailed images and videos of digital humans and craft complex multi-human simulations, respectively.

Synthesis AI's innovation has attracted significant investment, raising $17 million in a Series A funding round. The company's CEO, Yashar Behzadi, has highlighted the advantages of their approach, emphasizing the speed, cost-effectiveness, and high-quality asset generation capabilities of their text-to-3D offerings.

On the other side of the globe, Mostly AI, an Austrian company, is making significant strides in the realm of synthetic data. With a keen focus on data privacy, especially in light of the stringent General Data Protection Regulation (GDPR), Mostly AI's technology is particularly beneficial in sectors where data privacy is paramount, such as healthcare and financial services.

Mostly AI recently secured $25 million in funding to further commercialize synthetic data in Europe and the United States.

The company's synthetic data platform allows anyone to generate synthetic data safely and without coding, enabling data rebalancing, anonymization, imputation, and exploration.

Mostly AI's CEO, Tobias Hann, anticipates a significant surge in the use of synthetic data, predicting a "strong decade for synthetic data" beyond 2022. This growth is expected to be driven by the increasing demand for responsible AI, with synthetic data playing a crucial role in augmenting and debiasing datasets.

Where Is Data Augmentation Going? The advent of synthetic data is akin to a new dawn breaking over the horizon of technological advancement. The speed at which synthetic data is generated far outpaces that of real data. Gartner, a leading research and advisory company, forecasts that synthetic data will eclipse real data within the next three to five years (Figure 3.20).

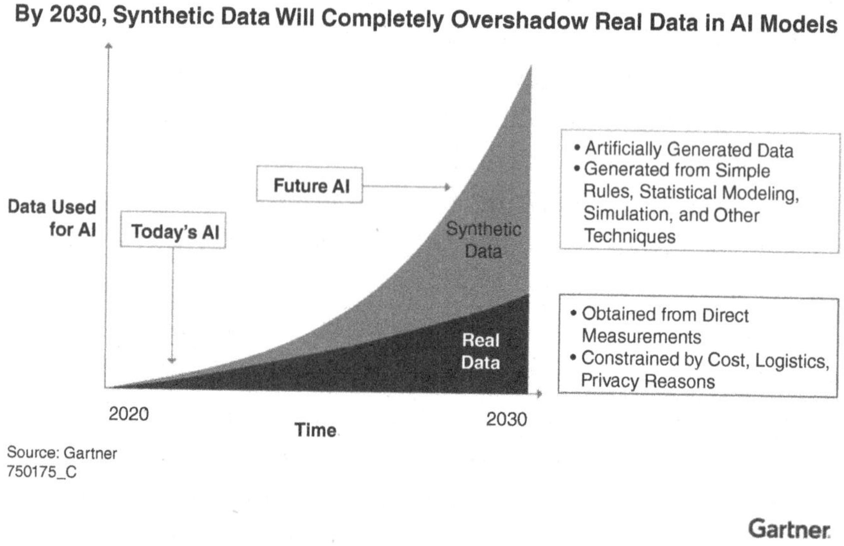

FIGURE 3.20 The dominant form of data employed in AI will shift toward synthetic data.

Source: Gartner, Inc.

The implications of synthetic data generation and data augmentation via AI are far-reaching, with potential to revolutionize a multitude of sectors in the coming decade. The applications are as diverse as they are profound.

In the healthcare sector, synthetic data is already making waves. It is used to generate medical images for training AI models, aiding in the diagnosis of diseases. It also creates virtual patient data for clinical trials, reducing the need for actual patients and ensuring privacy.

The potential of synthetic data extends to the realm of autonomous vehicles, where it is used to generate various driving scenarios for training purposes. In cybersecurity, synthetic data simulates cyberattacks, training AI models to detect and prevent these attacks. Even in climate modeling, synthetic data simulates various climate scenarios, enabling AI models to predict climate change.

But the potential of synthetic data doesn't stop there. It is also a powerful tool for urban planning. In smart cities, synthetic data can simulate traffic patterns, pedestrian movements, and public transportation usage. This data can be used to optimize city infrastructure and reduce congestion, leading to more efficient and livable urban environments.

In the field of precision agriculture, synthetic data merges environmental science, agriculture, and AI. It simulates various crop growth scenarios under different weather conditions and soil types, helping farmers optimize crop yields and reduce waste.

In disaster management, synthetic data combines meteorology, geography, and emergency response to simulate disaster scenarios. This aids in planning effective evacuation routes and emergency response strategies, potentially saving countless lives.

The Untapped Potential of Generative AI

This section explores the immediate, untapped potential of generative AI. We have previously covered its vast applications in voice and speech generation, code, text, music, video, 3D objects, generative design, and scientific problem-solving, but there is so much more to explore.

In law, it powers specialized chatbots for legal commentary and patent creation. The gaming industry utilizes it for more immersive experiences, while educational institutions like the Open University use AI to improve teaching and engagement. In healthcare, AI simplifies complex medical texts for wider accessibility. Business-to-business sectors benefit from AI for streamlined processes and enhanced productivity, with AI-powered personal assistants offering personalized services.

MIT researchers have developed an AI that predicts antibiotic effectiveness against bacteria, potentially revolutionizing antibiotic development and bacterial infection treatment. They also created MathAI, an AI capable of solving complex mathematical problems at a university level. Google's Starline project, using high-resolution cameras and depth sensors, creates realistic 3D models for video calls, offering an unprecedented sense of presence. These developments highlight the immense, ongoing innovation in generative AI.

A Good Time to Build Products and Companies

Indeed, the current landscape is ripe for the inception of new products and companies centered around generative AI. The barrier to entry has never been lower, with the technical knowledge required to launch a startup significantly reduced. The potential for quick wins is immense, particularly in the realm of knowledge management.

Consider the possibilities: querying a vast corpus of knowledge, such as documentation, regulations, and legal texts; streamlining operations by automating tasks or making them conversational. These applications could revolutionize processes within companies and government bureaucracies alike. There's also the potential to accelerate innovation, with a host of products being developed to facilitate this. These applications, which I refer to as "application layer 1," offer broad, impactful solutions.

Beyond this, there's a second application layer that's more niche and specific. This is where subject matter experts can leverage their specialized knowledge to develop unique products. While I may not be an expert in these fields, I can certainly brainstorm potential starting points:

- In biology, predictive diagnosis could revolutionize healthcare, enabling early intervention and improved patient outcomes. In chemistry, synthesis planning, chemical property prediction, and chemistry education could all benefit from the application of generative AI.

- Mathematics could see enhancements in education and theoretical research—MathAI from MIT, for example—while supply chain management could be optimized through inventory forecasting and vendor selection. In the realm of physics, quantum computing, astrophysics, and particle physics all present exciting opportunities for AI integration.

- Economics could be transformed through the development of advanced forecasting models, policy analysis tools, and investment strategies. In psychology, behavior prediction and psychological research design could be revolutionized.

- Environmental science also presents a wealth of opportunities, from climate modeling to biodiversity studies and conservation strategies. Each of these fields stands on the brink of transformation, ready to harness the untapped power of generative AI.

Certainly, the landscape of generative AI is teeming with opportunities for product development and innovative ideas. Whether it's in cloud services, hubs, or other platforms, the potential is vast. However, to truly tap into these opportunities, you need specialized knowledge in areas such as building AI models, language processing, image processing, and more. If you don't currently possess this expertise, don't worry—it can be acquired more easily than ever.

The concept of building foundation models is an exciting path for exploration. This strategy, adopted by organizations like OpenAI, Meta, and Anthropics, involves the development of broad, multipurpose models that serve as the foundation for more specialized applications. On the other hand, there's also the potential to create niche models that excel in specific domains, offering tailored solutions for unique needs.

The development of cloud platforms, akin to Azure or Google Cloud Platform (GCP), is another promising area in the AI landscape. These platforms simplify the deployment, scaling, and management of AI models, making AI accessible to a wider audience and fostering its integration across various industries.

There's also the potential to contribute to the AI ecosystem by providing robust computing hardware like GPUs or TPUs. These powerful processing units are instrumental in training and executing AI models, and advancements in this area could significantly enhance the speed and efficiency of AI operations.

Moreover, there is an opportunity to develop specific libraries of functions that cater to unmet needs within the AI community. For instance, the development of a library such as LangChain could address gaps in the existing suite of tools available for

AI development and deployment. LangChain is a framework designed to simplify the creation of applications using LLMs. Such efforts would not only enhance the capabilities of existing AI systems but also accelerate the pace of innovation in the field.

Finding the Untapped—A Systematic Approach to Success

Harnessing the untapped potential of generative AI is akin to navigating an uncharted territory. The landscape is vast, teeming with possibilities, yet the path to success is often obscured by the sheer volume of information and ideas. The key to unlocking this potential lies not in the abundance of ideas, but in the ability to distinguish the truly innovative from the merely interesting.

The conviction that there are more untapped ideas than those that have been realized is not unfounded. A cursory glance at the plethora of scientific papers, research articles, surveys, and blogs reveals a veritable treasure trove of ideas. Every week, thousands of concepts are birthed in these intellectual crucibles, each one a potential seed for the next big breakthrough in generative AI.

However, as any seasoned innovator will tell you, ideas are the easy part. Execution is where the rubber meets the road. It's the 99 percent perspiration that transforms the 1 percent inspiration into something tangible. Moreover, not all ideas are created equal. They need to be validated and tested against the harsh realities of practicality and feasibility.

This is where careful resource filtering becomes crucial. For instance, research papers are often the breeding grounds for cutting-edge tech ideas, particularly in the realm of generative AI. The ability to sift through these forefront papers, translate complex jargon into understandable language, and transform these ideas into products can provide a significant advantage.

To guide you through this process, I propose a methodology that has proven effective in the past and that could serve as a starting point for your journey. Let's assume you're looking to launch a startup or a project. This methodology is versatile and can be adapted to various professional areas.

The process, as illustrated in Figure 3.21, is simplified for clarity.

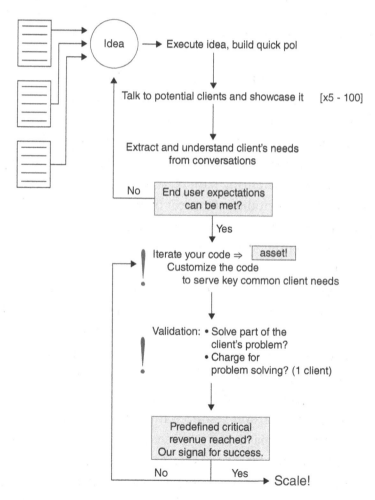

FIGURE 3.21 How to come up with your generative AI idea in this dynamic AI market.

The first step in this journey is to immerse yourself in trusted sources of information. I strongly recommend research papers available on databases like arxiv.org and publisher-driven platforms such as Wiley. Choose one or two that resonate with you after conducting preliminary research.

While your focus is on AI, it's beneficial to cast a wider net. Consider filtering for papers in related domains such as physics, chemistry, mathematics, and psychology. This broad perspective can provide insights into market trends and hot topics in these fields.

For the next three to six weeks, observe these research databases and their respective topics. Useful tools for this task are the ChatGPT plug-ins. Each day, select the top five papers you wish to understand and paste their links into ChatGPT. Ask the respective plug-ins to summarize these papers in bullet points, including headers. This method allows you to grasp the essence of each paper in about seven minutes.

For instance, just today's research is rich with ideas, potentially meeting the criteria. "DUCHO: A Unified Framework for the Extraction of Multimodal Features in Recommendation"[2] proposes an approach to improve recommendations by including effectively multiple modes.

Another paper, "Synthetic Demographic Data Generation for Card Fraud Detection Using GANs,"[3] might not pass the threshold. While it focuses on demographic data, which seems quite limited, there could be potential to use this idea in other areas of data generation. This is something that would need further investigation.

---

[2] Daniele Malitesta et al. "DUCHO: A Unified Framework for the Extraction of Multimodal Features in Recommendation," arXiv, September 6, 2023, https://arxiv.org/pdf/2306.17125.pdf
[3] Shuo Wang et al. "Synthetic Demographic Data Generation for Card Fraud Detection Using GANs," arXiv, June 29, 2023, https://arxiv.org/pdf/2306.17109.pdf

Lastly, I found a paper titled "Spiking Denoising Diffusion Probabilistic Models"[4] particularly intriguing. This paper combines spiking neural networks with diffusion models. The key questions here are: What benefits does this combination offer? What are the drawbacks? And most importantly, what new functionalities does it introduce that could potentially transform other areas? Often, even the authors themselves may not fully grasp the implications of their work.

After this initial review, choose one paper for a deeper dive. Read it thoroughly, examine the visual results, and absorb its content. After some training, this process should take no more than 30 minutes per day.

It's crucial to research papers over an extended period to avoid the trap of latching onto the first good idea that comes along. Comparing ideas against each other is an important part of the process. However, it's equally important to set a time frame for when you want to start your project.

Once you've gathered a wealth of ideas, it's time to select a great one. Not the perfect one, as perfection is elusive, but a great one. Shortlist the top five to seven ideas and compare them qualitatively based on the following criteria: technical feasibility, potential impact for end users, innovation and uniqueness, scalability and adaptability, ethical and legal considerations, resource requirements, and market potential.

Once you've selected an idea, create a quick proof of concept (PoC). Utilize existing GitHub repos or other code sources like paperswithcode.com or from the research scientists themselves. If you're not a coder, consider hiring one from platforms like Fiverr, but be aware of potential issues like confidentiality and skill gaps.

---

[4]Jiahang Cao et al. "Spiking Denoising Diffusion Probabilistic Models," arXiv, October 30, 2023, https://arxiv.org/pdf/2306.17046.pdf

With your PoC in hand, it's time to get feedback. Contact potential users, ranging from a minimum of 5 to a maximum of 100, and showcase your idea. From these conversations, you'll gain valuable insights into user needs and preferences.

Finally, answer the following questions to decide how to proceed: Are users satisfied with the idea? Does the idea provide significant value to users? Is there sufficient market demand for the idea? Does the idea have a competitive advantage? Can the idea scale and grow effectively? Are there viable ways to monetize the idea? Do the resources required for this idea align with your capabilities? Does the idea align with your long-term goals and vision?

Based on these answers, decide whether to continue with the idea and invest more resources into it, pivot the idea significantly, or find a completely new idea. This is a critical juncture in your journey, a moment of existential decision making that will shape the course of your project.

Congratulations on successfully validating your idea! You've navigated the initial stages of the process, and now it's time to shift focus to building a great product.

From your user research, you've gathered insights into what the client needs and expects from the product. The next step is to prioritize your actions based on two factors: the impact on the user and the effort required. This will help you identify the low-hanging fruits. A word of advice here: Aim to serve the needs of the majority (80 percent) of your users, rather than catering to individual requirements.

In the early stages, it's beneficial if you can code the product yourself. With tools like ChatGPT, GitHub Copilot, and various online training resources, this task is not insurmountable. Alternatively, you could outsource the coding to another individual.

Once you've made progress on the product, it's time for another round of validation. Conduct another set of interviews to confirm that you're addressing critical parts of the client's problem. The second step in this validation phase is to determine if your future customers are willing to pay for your product. The larger the group willing to pay, the better. However, even if only one person (who isn't a friend or family member trying to please you) is willing to pay, it's a positive signal.

The final question to ask yourself is whether you've reached a threshold that signals long-term success for your idea. This threshold should be a set of predefined parameters, such as revenue or other individual metrics (it doesn't necessarily have to be revenue).

If you haven't reached this critical threshold, it's time to circle back and iterate on the code and product. If you have, it's time to scale. This could mean seeking investors, expanding your team, and professionalizing your approach to product development. Having a validated product gives you a strong argument for potential investors. However, if you decide to bootstrap, you're still in a good position.

I hope this provides a clear roadmap for your journey ahead. Whether you're launching a startup or developing a product within an existing company, these steps should prove quite helpful. Remember, every journey begins with a single step, and you've already taken several. Keep moving forward, and I am sure success will follow.

4

Generative AI's Exponential Growth

The previous chapters touched on the sudden emergence of generative AI, a phenomenon that seemed to materialize out of thin air. However, the reality is far from it. Much like a gourmet dish simmering away in the back of a bustling kitchen, generative AI was quietly brewing, its flavors intensifying, until it was finally ready to be served. The first taste came in the summer of 2022 with OpenAI's DALL-E, followed closely by the unveiling of ChatGPT toward the end of the same year.

The explosion of generative AI was the result of a carefully curated recipe. The ingredients? A blend of technological advancements and convergences that, when combined, propelled AI to unprecedented heights. This chapter peels back the layers and explores the underlying factors that played a pivotal role in the rise of generative AI.

First on our list is the exponential increase in computing power, often encapsulated by Moore's law. This principle, which posits that the number of transistors on a microchip doubles approximately every two years, has been a driving force behind our ability to perform increasingly complex computations at breakneck speeds. This, in turn, has been instrumental in training large-scale AI models, the backbone of generative AI.

Next, we have the advent of cloud computing. This technology has revolutionized the way we access and utilize high-powered computing resources, making them more affordable and readily available. The democratization of AI that cloud computing has facilitated means that even small startups can now develop sophisticated AI systems, a feat that was once the exclusive domain of tech giants.

Then there's the development of hardware accelerators, such as graphics processing units (GPUs) and Tensor Processing Units (TPUs). These devices have significantly accelerated AI computations, particularly in the realm of deep learning. By processing multiple computations simultaneously, these accelerators have made it possible to train larger and more complex AI models in a fraction of the time.

Further, we can't overlook the role of cheaper storage. Over the years, the cost of data storage has plummeted, making it feasible to store and process the vast amounts of data needed for AI. This has been a game changer, as AI systems are notoriously data-hungry, requiring copious amounts of information to learn and improve.

The availability of Big Data is another crucial ingredient in the generative AI recipe. With the widespread use of the Internet and digital technologies, we're generating colossal amounts of data every second. This data serves as the lifeblood of AI systems, providing the rich, varied information they need to learn, adapt, and improve.

The research of new algorithms and the refinement of existing ones have enabled AI to glean insights from data more effectively and efficiently. Deep learning, the subfield of machine learning that mimics the neural networks of the human brain, has been a game changer, powering many of the recent breakthroughs in AI.

Investment in AI research from both private entities and governments has also played a pivotal role. Recognizing the transformative potential of AI, these stakeholders have poured substantial resources into research and development. This influx of funding has not only led to numerous breakthroughs but has also attracted some of the brightest minds to the field, further fueling innovation.

The open source culture prevalent in the AI community is another factor worth noting. Many AI advancements are shared openly, fostering a global community of researchers and developers who build upon each other's work. This spirit of collaboration has significantly accelerated the pace of AI development, allowing for rapid iteration and improvement.

The successful real-world applications of AI have also driven interest and investment in the field. From image recognition and natural language processing to autonomous vehicles and beyond, AI has proven its worth in a myriad of contexts. These success stories serve as powerful proof of concept, demonstrating the transformative potential of AI.

Lastly, the undeniable business value of AI, and more recently generative AI, cannot be overlooked. For years, AI has been delivering tangible business benefits, and with the advent of generative AI the scope for value creation has expanded even further. As we continue to explore and use these technologies, there's no doubt that we're only scratching the surface of what's possible.

The Growth Pattern of New Technologies— The S-Curve

The factors discussed so far are not only influencing the growth of technology and AI but are also shaping the trajectory of innovation itself. One way to capture this dynamic evolution is through the concept of the S-curve, a common pattern observed in the growth of new technologies (Figure 4.1).

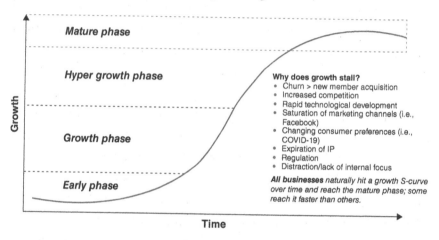

FIGURE 4.1 The life cycle of innovation: the S-curve.

Source: https://medium.com/parsa-vc/jumping-s-curves-building-a-high-performance-startup-80e4410466a5

Technologies often have humble beginnings, emerging from the hallowed halls of university labs or the innovative hubs of corporate research departments. In these early stages, the technology might seem insignificant or even ineffective. It's a period of trial and error, of fine-tuning and tweaking, where the potential of the technology is yet to be fully realized.

However, there comes a tipping point where the technology starts to work effectively, triggering a phase of accelerated growth. This is the steep upward curve of the S, a period characterized by a flurry of activity, excitement, and rapid adoption. It's during this phase that the technology makes the leap from the lab to the real world, transforming industries and impacting lives.

But like all things, this period of frenzied growth doesn't last forever. Eventually, the pace of growth starts to slow down. Every new incremental improvement becomes less perceptible to the user, and the technology begins to mature. This is the flattening curve of the S, marking the transition from a period of rapid innovation to one of consolidation and refinement.

At this stage, the focus shifts. The question is no longer about whether the technology is going to work or what's going to work. Instead, the conversation centers around the implications of the technology now that it has a large user base. It's about understanding the impact, managing the challenges, and harnessing the opportunities that the technology presents.

This S-curve pattern is evident in the evolution of AI and, more specifically, generative AI. From its early days in research labs to its current state of widespread adoption, generative AI has traversed this curve. As we continue to explore this fascinating field, we'll delve deeper into the implications of this growth trajectory and what it means for the future of AI.

The S-curve pattern is not unique to AI. In fact, it's a common phenomenon in the evolution of many groundbreaking technologies. Let's consider a few examples.

The development of the PC is a classic case. In the early stages, PCs were bulky, expensive, and not particularly user-friendly. However, as the technology improved, PCs became more accessible and affordable, leading to a period of rapid growth and widespread adoption. Eventually the market matured, and the pace of growth slowed as incremental improvements became less noticeable to the average user.

A similar pattern can be observed in the evolution of the Internet. Initially, the Internet was a novelty, a tool used primarily by academics and researchers. But as it became more user-friendly and accessible, its growth skyrocketed. Today, the Internet is a ubiquitous part of our lives, and while it continues to evolve, the pace of growth has inevitably slowed.

The trajectory of the adoption of mobile phones also follows the S-curve. From the hefty, expensive mobile phones of the early days to the sleek, multifunctional smartphones of today, the growth of mobile technology has been nothing short of phenomenal. But again, as the technology matured, the pace of growth has slowed.

What's interesting about these S-curves is that they often overlap. Just as one S-curve is maturing and slowing down, another one often starts up. This is precisely what we're witnessing with generative AI. As technologies like the Internet and mobile phones mature, generative AI is just beginning its upward trajectory on the S-curve. Figure 4.2 shows overlapping S-curves, illustrating technological advancement in the form of successively implemented innovations.

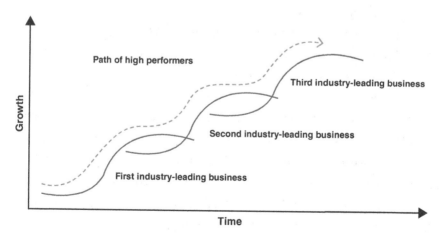

FIGURE 4.2 The evolution of innovation: successive waves of technological advancements represented by multiple following S-curves.

Source: https://medium.com/parsa-vc/jumping-s-curves-building-a-high-performance-startup-80e4410466a5

This cycle of innovation and growth tends to operate on a timescale of 5, 10, or even 20 years. It's a continuous process of evolution and revolution, where each new technology builds on the foundations laid by its predecessors.

Indeed, the S-curves for innovation are becoming increasingly compressed. Several factors are contributing to this trend, creating a fast-paced cycle of technological evolution and revolution.

First, the rapid pace of technological advancements is a key driver. The improvements in computing power, data availability, and affordability, coupled with the relentless efforts in research and development, are accelerating the pace of innovation. These factors are effectively shortening the S-curves, enabling technologies to move from the lab to the market at an unprecedented speed.

Another factor is the heightened level of competition in today's global business landscape. In this high-stakes environment, companies are under constant pressure to stay ahead of the curve. This drive to innovate and differentiate fuels shorter innovation cycles, as businesses strive to introduce new products and services that can give them a competitive edge.

The culture of knowledge sharing, facilitated by the widespread availability of information and collaborative platforms, is also contributing to shorter S-curves. The open sourcing of technologies and algorithms allows innovators to build upon existing knowledge, iterate more quickly, and bring their ideas to fruition faster. This collaborative approach is not only accelerating the pace of innovation but also fostering a more inclusive and diverse tech ecosystem.

Market demand is another crucial factor. With rapid shifts in consumer preferences and the emergence of a global customer market, companies are required to respond swiftly with innovative solutions. This demand-driven approach is pushing for shorter innovation cycles, as businesses strive to meet the evolving needs of their customers.

As a result of these factors, we can expect to see much shorter product development cycles and the emergence of new technologies at a faster pace. As we witness the simultaneous evolution and revolution of various technology fields, it's clear that we're in the midst of an exciting era of accelerated innovation. The advent of generative AI is a testament to this trend, marking the beginning of a new S-curve that promises to reshape our world in ways we're only beginning to imagine.

Technological Convergence

The rise of generative AI is being significantly propelled by its convergence with other fields—a phenomenon known as *technological convergence*.

Technological convergence refers to the trend where distinct technological systems evolve toward performing similar tasks. This is achieved by integrating multiple functionalities into a single device or system, leading to more efficient and streamlined user experiences. Technological convergence is often directional, with one field exerting a greater influence on others.

In this context, AI stands out as a crucial catalyst. Its rapid advancement is cascading through numerous other technologies, creating a ripple effect that's driving demand for further innovation and refinement. The velocity of AI's development is not just reshaping its own field but also accelerating the evolution of other technologies.

Take, for example, the impact of neural networks—both generative and discriminative—on various sectors. They're driving advancements in adaptive robotics, enabling robots to learn from their environment and adapt their behavior accordingly. In the realm of autonomous mobility, neural networks are at the heart of self-driving vehicles, facilitating real-time decision making and navigation.

Another example is the intersection of AI and genomics. Google, for instance, has leveraged AI algorithms to significantly enhance the accuracy of long-read DNA sequencing. By employing neural networks, they managed to reduce DNA sequencing error rates by 59 percent. This breakthrough not only improved the quality-adjusted yields but also brought down the costs associated with long-read genome sequencing. In 2023, PacBio, a leading provider of high-quality sequencing solutions, integrated AI-specific compute hardware into its long-read sequencer. This move was touted as the first high-quality, whole long-read genome for less than $1,000.

In the realm of robotics, advances in large language models (LLMs) have enabled robots to learn from experience and acquire new skills at an accelerated pace. The adoption of the Transformer architecture from AI has empowered robots to generalize from examples and perform tasks they've never encountered before—a capability known as zero-shot learning. This has led to a dramatic improvement in their learning efficiency, with the success rate jumping from 19 percent in 2021 to 76 percent in 2022.

Conversely, AI is also being propelled by advancements in other fields. For instance, the progress in battery technology has had a significant impact on AI. As battery capacity and energy density have increased substantially over the years—often by double-digit percentages—this has enabled the development of more advanced, mobile, and autonomous devices. These devices, ranging from robots to cars, increasingly rely on AI for their autonomy.

As we continue to explore this chain of thought, the landscape of possibilities expands, becoming less predictable yet more intriguing. Economists estimate that the global GDP could see a staggering increase of anywhere from 60 percent to 470 percent by the year 2040, largely driven by the disruptive technologies we see today.

This creates the potential for super-exponential growth, provided certain conditions are met—a topic we'll delve into later in this chapter. The convergence of AI with these technologies is paving the way for the creation of more intelligent, autonomous, and personalized systems. However, this evolution is not without its challenges. Issues surrounding data privacy and security, as well as the ethical use of AI, are significant hurdles that need to be addressed.

Exponential Progress in Computing

The bedrock of AI's meteoric rise lies in the realm of computation. To truly grasp the magnitude of this evolution, we must first understand the insatiable hunger of advanced AI models for computing power. Training these behemoths, with their vast seas of data and their intricate web of billions of trainable parameters, demands an astronomical amount of computational muscle. This computational appetite is quantified in FLOPs, or floating-point operations per second. In layperson's terms, FLOPs provides a measure of how many floating-point calculations a machine can churn out within a mere second.

The art and science of AI computation lie in a delicate balance. On one hand, we have the increase of hardware's computing power—FLOPs. On the other, there's software optimization, where the goal is to trim down the FLOPs required. This dual approach is the linchpin in the optimization of AI systems.

Tracing the trajectory of computational power, we can't help but acknowledge the prescient observation of Gordon Moore in 1965. Dubbed Moore's law, it postulated that the number of transistors packed into a microchip would roughly double every two years. This prediction, which seemed audacious at the time, has largely held true, steering us into an era of exponential growth in computing prowess. To put this into perspective, consider the iPhone 14 Pro's chip, a chip for a device that fits in the palm of your hand, released in 2022, boasting a staggering 16 billion transistors. Contrast this with one of the first chips used in personal computers of the 1970s, such as the Amstrad PC 1512 or the Intel 8086 (1978), which had 29,000 transistors. This represents an increase of more than half a million times at the chip level.

The relentless march of transistor count has been not only about sheer numbers but also about the profound implications of these numbers. The miniaturization of transistors has ushered in an era of compact yet formidable devices. Take, for instance, the Apollo guidance computer of 1969, a marvel of its time, which boasted a computational might of around 15,000 FLOPs. Fastforward to 2005/2006, and we find the Xbox 360 flexing a staggering 240 GFLOPS—a leap that's 16 million times the power of its predecessor. This juxtaposition paints a vivid picture of how far we've come in just a few decades. See Figure 4.3 for a logarithmic scale representation of the law.

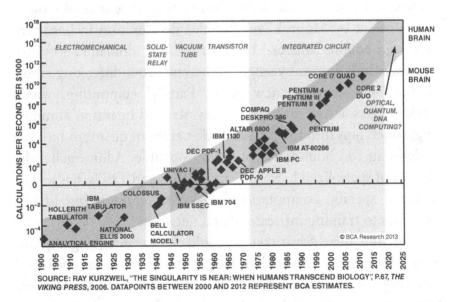

SOURCE: RAY KURZWEIL, "THE SINGULARITY IS NEAR: WHEN HUMANS TRANSCEND BIOLOGY", P.67, *THE VIKING PRESS*, 2006. DATAPOINTS BETWEEN 2000 AND 2012 REPRESENT BCA ESTIMATES.

FIGURE 4.3 Moore's law in action: a logarithmic scale representation of the exponential growth in transistor count per microchip over time.

Source: www.publish0x.com/muratkbesiroglu/futurist-ray-kurzweils-predictions-about-the-future-xqkjyyw

However, every ascent faces its summit, and Moore's law is no exception. The very essence of this law, the shrinking of transistors, is now becoming its Achilles' heel. As we venture into the realm of nanometers, a peculiar quantum phenomenon rears its head—quantum tunneling. This phenomenon allows electrons to defy classical physics, bypassing the depletion layer in a transistor. The result? Disrupted calculations, rendering the computer unreliable. When you cram a chip with countless such minuscule transistors, quantum tunneling becomes an insurmountable challenge, signaling the twilight of Moore's law.

But the dimming of one beacon doesn't plunge the world of computation into darkness. The waning of Moore's law merely heralds a paradigm shift in our quest for computational supremacy. Quantum computing, with its promise of harnessing the quirks of quantum mechanics, emerges as a tantalizing prospect.

Moreover, the challenges of miniaturization, such as heat dissipation and manufacturing intricacies, have indeed slowed the pace set by Moore's law. But this deceleration in hardware has been counterbalanced by leaps in other domains. Software optimizations, innovative algorithms, and groundbreaking architectures are charting new paths. Parallel computing, which divides tasks across multiple processors, and quantum computing, which taps into the probabilistic nature of quantum bits, are redefining the boundaries of what's possible. Additionally, the advent of specialized hardware, like GPUs and TPUs, has turbocharged specific computational tasks, from rendering lifelike graphics to training intricate neural networks.

Peering into the horizon, we could posit a tantalizing hypothesis: Moore's law, rather than facing obsolescence, might be on the verge of an upside break. The combined might of hardware innovations, software breakthroughs, and pioneering research could propel computational advancements at a pace that even outstrips Moore's predictions. The future, it seems, holds promise and potential in equal measure.

Exponential Hardware Evolution

This section highlights key hardware-related developments, from customized chips to quantum and neuromorphic computing, and previews groundbreaking research potentially shaping the future of technology.

Chips   Chip design is a dynamic landscape, with innovations sprouting at an unprecedented pace. Although this chapter won't dive deep into the nitty-gritty of chip design, there are pivotal trends worth highlighting.

Three primary trends dominate the chip design horizon: the drive toward even smaller chip designs, the rise of application-specific integrated circuits (ASICs), and the evolution of system-on-a-chip (SoC) architectures.

As we tread the path of miniaturization, the distances between conductors and transistors on chips have been whittled down to just a few nanometers. Leading this race to the minuscule is IBM, which has unveiled a groundbreaking achievement—the world's first two-nanometer chip technology. This feat is not just about size; it's about overcoming the engineering challenges posed by leakage effects as chip sizes shrink.

Key insights into IBM's two-nanometer chip technology include:

- A whopping 45 percent boost in performance coupled with a 75 percent reduction in energy consumption when juxtaposed with the prevalent 3 to 5 to 7 nm chips. This enhancement translates to a substantial 31 percent reduction in AI training time.

- The potential applications are vast and transformative. Imagine mobile phones that last four times longer, datacenters that slash their carbon footprints, and autonomous vehicles that react in a split second.

- IBM's pioneering "nanosheet technology" manages to pack an astounding 50 billion transistors on a surface no larger than a fingerprint.

- These nanosheet transistors, christened gate-all-around transistors, have been under the research microscope since 2017. Their design ensures optimal current control while staunchly preventing leakage.

- The diminutive size of these transistors doesn't compromise their efficacy. They pave the way for devices that are faster, more dependable, and energy efficient, spurring innovations in processor designs. Moreover, this technology is tailor-made to bolster AI and cloud computing tasks, all while fortifying security and encryption at the hardware level.

Enter the world of ASICs, or application-specific integrated circuits. These are not your run-of-the-mill integrated circuits. They are the epitome of customization, meticulously crafted for a singular purpose or task. While general-purpose integrated circuits are the jacks-of-all-trades, ASICs are the masters of one. This laser-focused design ethos bestows upon them unparalleled advantages in performance, power efficiency, and cost-effectiveness.

To paint a clearer picture, consider the realm of cryptocurrency mining. ASIC miners, specialized computerized devices, have taken the crypto world by storm. Each of these machines is purpose-built to mine a designated digital currency, such as Bitcoin. Their raison d'être is to crack the mining algorithm with unparalleled efficiency, leaving general-purpose processors and graphics cards in the dust.

But it's not just about raw computational power. Many of the optimizations I've witnessed lean heavily into energy conservation—a facet that's gaining increasing importance in our eco-conscious world. And there's a computational boon to this energy thriftiness. With reduced heat production, architectures can be packed more densely, further amplifying the prowess of these chips. The future of chip design, it seems, is not just about doing more, but doing more with less.

Another discernible trend in the chip design landscape is the emergence of more efficient chip designs, prominently manifested in the form of SoC developments. At its core, a system-on-a-chip can be thought of as a specialized variant of an ASIC.

The brilliance of the SoC lies in its ability to amalgamate all the components of a computer or any electronic system into one cohesive unit. Imagine a single chip that houses a CPU, memory modules, timing mechanisms, peripherals, and even external interfaces. This compactness and integration makes SoCs the heart of many contemporary devices, from the smartphones we can't live without to the smart appliances that make our homes more intuitive, and even the burgeoning realm of Internet of Things (IoT) devices. Their allure stems from their unparalleled efficiency and diminutive size. While they can be tailored for specific tasks, enhancing both performance and power efficiency, the journey to craft them is riddled with complexities. The challenge? Seamlessly integrating a myriad of components onto one chip. Notable exemplars in this domain include the powerhouse Apple's A series chips and the versatile Qualcomm's Snapdragon chips.

But what makes SoC designs the torchbearers of the next wave of computational prowess?

The beauty of SoCs is their integrated design, which houses all components on a single chip, significantly reducing data transit time between components and leading to faster data processing and enhanced system performance. Customization is central to SoCs, with every aspect of the chip, from its individual components to their interactions, being meticulously tailored for specific applications, ensuring unparalleled performance. Moreover, SoCs excel in power efficiency; their compact design and optimized components ensure minimal energy consumption, which is especially beneficial for battery-operated devices, offering extended battery life without sacrificing performance. In an era where sleekness and portability are paramount, the compact nature of SoCs allows for lightweight and space-efficient devices without compromising on their performance.

To underscore the significance of SoCs in today's market, consider this: The SoC market, as of 2023, stands at a staggering $159.85 billion. Projections indicate that by 2028, this market will balloon to an estimated $234.98 billion, with a compound annual growth rate (CAGR) of 8.01 percent during the 2023–2028 period, underscoring the pivotal role SoCs are set to play in the future of tech.

One quickly realizes that it's a domain marked by relentless innovation and high stakes. My foray into this realm, driven by curiosity rather than expertise, has unveiled a tapestry of promising trends that could redefine the future of computing. Here's a closer look at some of these groundbreaking developments:

3D-Stacked CMOS   The 3D-stacked CMOS technology is another game changer. Instead of laying out transistors flat, like houses in a neighborhood, this technology stacks them vertically, akin to a multistory building. This vertical arrangement allows for more transistors in the same space, leading to increased computing power. In simple terms, it's like having multiple processing units stacked atop one another, working in tandem. The potential performance gain is substantial, as data can move faster between vertically stacked transistors, accelerating processing speeds.

Forksheet Transistor Design   Imec's innovative Forksheet transistor design is set to breathe new life into silicon-based semiconductors. At its core, the Forksheet design tweaks the traditional transistor layout to reduce leakage and improve performance. Imagine a river with multiple channels; if one channel leaks, the others can still function efficiently. Similarly, the Forksheet design ensures that even if one part faces issues, the overall performance remains robust. This design can lead to chips that are not only more reliable but also faster, potentially boosting performance by a significant margin.

Hybrid Microchip   The fusion of memory resistors, or memristors, and CMOS technology has birthed a new hybrid microchip. Memristors, in essence, are resistors with memory. When combined with CMOS technology, these chips can process and store data simultaneously, making them ideal for AI tasks that require rapid data processing. In simpler terms, it's like having a brain that thinks and remembers at the same time, leading to faster decision making. The potential performance gain here is immense, especially for AI-driven applications where speed and memory are paramount.

Processing Units   Next up, processing units. While the power of individual chips is crucial, the real magic happens when these chips are orchestrated in harmony. This is especially paramount for tasks like training AI models.

Here's an explanation of processing units:

CPU (Central Processing Unit)   Often referred to as the "brain" of the computer, the CPU handles a variety of tasks and is adept at sequential processing. It's the jack-of-all-trades in the computing world, capable of managing everything from basic arithmetic to complex system operations. However, when it comes to AI training, CPUs might not be the most efficient choice. The reason? AI training requires parallel processing, something GPUs and other specialized units excel at.

GPU (Graphics Processing Unit)   Initially designed for rendering graphics, GPUs have found a new calling in the realm of AI. Their strength lies in their ability to handle multiple tasks simultaneously. Imagine trying to solve multiple math problems at once; that's what GPUs excel at. Their parallel processing capabilities, coupled with high memory bandwidth and specialized software libraries, make them a preferred choice for AI model training.

TPU (Tensor Processing Unit)   Google's brainchild, the TPU, is tailored for TensorFlow, their machine learning (ML) framework. While GPUs are versatile, TPUs are purpose-built for ML tasks, offering unparalleled performance per watt. However, their specificity to TensorFlow means they might not be the go-to choice for those using different frameworks.

IPU (Intelligence Processing Unit)   Graphcore's IPU, particularly the Colossus MK2 GC200, is a force to be reckoned with in the AI world. With a staggering 1472 processor core and almost 9,000 parallel program threads, it's designed to tackle the unique challenges of deep learning. Its architecture is optimized for the myriad of operations required for such tasks, making it a formidable competitor to traditional GPUs.

NPU (Neural Processing Unit)   The NPU is the embodiment of ML hardware. Designed explicitly for neural network computations, it's optimized for the matrix operations that are the backbone of deep learning. Various tech giants have thrown their hats into the NPU ring, with Huawei's version being a notable example. While GPUs are adept at parallel processing, NPUs are fine-tuned for neural networks, often delivering superior performance for deep learning tasks. It's worth noting that the world of NPUs is vast, with various iterations like TPUs, IPUs, and more, each with its unique strengths.

In essence, the choice of processing unit boils down to the specific requirements of the task at hand. While CPUs are versatile, GPUs and NPUs offer specialized capabilities that make them more suited for certain deep learning tasks. The rapid advancements in this field ensure that the future of AI and ML is not just promising but also incredibly exciting. As we continue to push the boundaries of what's possible, these processing units will undoubtedly play a pivotal role in shaping the future of technology.

Determining the "optimal" processing unit is often contingent on the distinct demands of the task. GPUs, with their prowess in executing parallel operations, have become the go-to choice for training intricate deep learning models. On the other hand, TPUs, a brainchild of Google, have been meticulously crafted to adeptly manage ML operations. Not to be left behind, IPUs, the innovation of Graphcore, emerge as another contender, tailored explicitly for AI-centric workloads. The decision matrix, when selecting among these powerhouses, hinges on several factors: the model's magnitude, data volume, and the equilibrium between speed and efficiency.

Highlighting the vanguard in this domain:

- *GPU*: The NVIDIA A100 Tensor Core GPU stands as a titan among its peers. Purpose-built for AI, data analytics, and high-performance computing, its versatility spans a gamut of applications—from AI model training and inference to data analytics, scientific computations, and even cloud graphics. A testament to its might, the NVIDIA A100 Tensor Core GPU boasts a staggering 312 teraFLOPS (TFLOPS) of computational power.

- *TPU*: Google's Tensor Processing Unit (TPU) is not just another chip—it's a meticulously engineered application-specific integrated circuit (ASIC) with a singular focus: supercharging ML tasks. These TPUs are the silent work-horses in Google's datacenters, powering an array of services we use daily—be it Google Search, Gmail, Google Photos, or the myriad Google Cloud AI APIs. The latest in this lineage, the TPU v4, is a force to be reckoned with, offering a robust 260 teraFLOPs (TFLOPs) of performance.

- *IPU*: Venturing into the realm of AI-specific processing, Graphcore's Intelligence Processing Unit (IPU) emerges as a formidable player. The Graphcore Colossus MK2 IPU, with its specialized design, finds its niche in diverse arenas, from cloud computing to cutting-edge AI research. A notable implementation of this powerhouse is the IPU-Ray-Lib project—a path-tracer fine-tuned for Graphcore IPUs. With a performance benchmark set at an impressive 250 TFLOPs, it's clear that the IPU is not just another chip on the block—it's a revolution in its own right.

Company-Customized AI Hardware   In the sprawling land-scape of AI and computational technology, there's a discernible trend among industry giants—especially those for whom performance isn't just a metric, but a mantra. These behemoths, in their relentless pursuit of excellence, often sidestep off-the-shelf solutions, opting instead to forge their own path by crafting bespoke processing units tailored to their unique needs.

Apple, the Cupertino-based titan, stands as a shining exemplar of this approach. Their commitment to performance and user experience has led them to design a suite of proprietary processing units, ensuring that every device they produce is not just a piece of hardware but a meticulously engineered experience.

- *Apple M1*: A quantum leap in Apple's hardware journey, the Apple M1 is an ARM-based system-on-a-chip that serves as both the brain (CPU) and the visual maestro (GPU) for their Mac desktops, notebooks, as well as the iPad Pro and iPad Air tablets. This chip isn't just about raw power—it's a symphony of performance and efficiency, fine-tuned to perfection for macOS and iOS applications. With the M1, Apple didn't just aim to compete; they set out to redefine the paradigm.

- *A-series chips*: For over a decade, Apple's mobile devices—iPhones, iPads, and Apple Watches—have been powered by the A-series chips. These aren't just processors; they're a testament to Apple's vision of what mobile computing should feel like. Designed to deliver both blistering performance and unparalleled efficiency, these chips ensure that every interaction, every swipe, every tap feels fluid and responsive. And they're not just about speed—they're optimized to run iOS and watchOS applications with a finesse that's become synonymous with the Apple brand.

Tesla emerges as another luminary, pushing the boundaries of what's possible in both AI and robotics. Elon Musk's brain-child, Tesla, isn't just about electric cars—it's a technological powerhouse, constantly innovating and redefining the intersection of hardware, software, and AI.

- *Tesla Dojo*: This isn't just another supercomputer—it's Tesla's answer to the challenges of computer vision video processing and recognition. Purpose-built, the Dojo is the crucible where Tesla's ML algorithms are honed, ensuring that their vehicles aren't just self-driving, but self-learning.

- *Tesla's custom AI chips*: While many automakers rely on third-party solutions for their autonomous driving tech, Tesla took the road less traveled. In a little over a year, they designed a custom AI chip tailored to the unique demands of their self-driving ambitions. Manufactured by Samsung, this chip isn't just about power—it's about precision, ensuring that Tesla cars can navigate the complexities of real-world driving with unparalleled accuracy. And Tesla's commitment to excellence doesn't stop at their new cars. In a move that underscores their dedication to safety and performance, older models are being retrofitted with this cutting-edge processor.

However, it's crucial to dispel a common misconception. While Tesla has been a pioneer in developing custom hardware for its fleet of electric vehicles, there's no specific processing unit dubbed the "Tesla Processing Unit" or "Tesla NPU" in their arsenal, at the moment.

The race for hardware dominance is not a solitary sprint but a collective marathon. While Apple and Tesla have made headlines with their audacious strides, other tech behemoths like Amazon, Intel, and Microsoft are not mere spectators. They're in the thick of it, each sculpting its own niche, each pushing the envelope in its quest to redefine the future of computing.

Yet, projecting this trajectory of Moore's law, the implications are staggering. Within a span of five years, we're looking at a monumental leap—a surge where our computational capabilities could amplify by a factor of almost 7. To put this in tangible terms, imagine a future iteration of the NVIDIA A100 called "NVIDIA A200" boasting 2,080 teraFLOPS. Such a powerhouse could potentially slash model training times by 85 percent, revolutionizing the way we approach deep learning and AI tasks.

In the upcoming sections, I argue that we are approaching a pivotal moment that surpasses Moore's law. We're not merely continuing its trajectory; we're on the verge of breakthroughs that will fundamentally transform our understanding of what is possible through innovation.

Cloud Computing Certain innovations emerge as pivotal game changers, reshaping the landscape in ways previously unimagined. Cloud computing stands tall among these transformative forces, casting a profound influence not only on the trajectory of technology but also on the very ethos of innovation and collaboration.

Cloud computing, in its essence, is the great equalizer. It has ushered in an era where computing power, once the exclusive domain of tech behemoths, is now within arm's reach of the many. This democratization of computational might has catalyzed a renaissance of creativity, fostering an environment where ideas flourish, unfettered by the constraints of physical infrastructure.

My admiration for cloud computing is rooted in its sheer practicality and transformative potential. Picture this: Within the span of a mere hour, one can seamlessly weave together the intricate tapestry of a digital application. From deploying code on a computing instance to orchestrating a symphony between frontend and backend through an adept API manager, the entire process is streamlined, efficient, and, dare I say, exhilarating. And should your creation resonate and attract a burgeoning user base? Scaling becomes a matter of a few clicks, not cumbersome hardware acquisitions.

But the magic of cloud computing isn't confined to its agility and efficiency. Its implications ripple across multiple facets:

- *Scalability*: The fluidity with which businesses can modulate their computational resources is unparalleled. Whether it's a surge during peak seasons or a lull in off-peak times, the cloud adapts, ensuring optimal resource allocation without the baggage of redundant infrastructure.

- *Cost-effectiveness*: The pay-as-you-go model is a masterstroke, aligning expenses with usage. Gone are the days of hefty up-front hardware investments and the incessant drain of maintenance costs.

- *Accessibility*: The cloud knows no boundaries. Its omnipresence ensures that high-caliber computational resources are a mere click away, leveling the playing field for enterprises, big and small.

- *Innovation*: The cloud is a treasure trove of cutting-edge tools and technologies. From AI toolkits to advanced analytics, businesses can harness the power of the latest innovations without the rigors of in-house development.

- *Reliability*: The architectural robustness of cloud providers, with their geographically dispersed datacenters, offers a resilience that's hard to match. Even in the face of unforeseen disruptions, the cloud remains steadfast, ensuring uninterrupted service.

- *Energy efficiency*: The centralization inherent in cloud computing is not just a logistical boon but an environmental one. By pooling computational resources, the cloud achieves efficiencies of scale, curbing energy consumption and mitigating the environmental footprint.

In the grand scheme of things, cloud computing is more than just a technological marvel—it's a paradigm shift. As we navigate the intricate maze of Moore's law and the promises it holds, the cloud emerges as a beacon, illuminating the path to a future where the boundaries of what's possible are continually reimagined.

Quantum Computing   Quantum computing holds the potential to transform the computational world. Unlike traditional computing with its binary "on" and "off" states, quantum computing uses qubits that can exist in both states simultaneously. This capability, rooted in quantum mechanics, enables quantum computers to process multiple solutions at once, vastly expanding computational possibilities.

The genesis of this idea can be traced back to the musings of physicist Richard Feynman in the early 1980s. Fast-forward a few decades, and we find ourselves amidst a quantum renaissance. Tech powerhouses like IBM, Google, and Microsoft are fervently pouring resources into quantum R&D, with each stride bringing us closer to harnessing its full potential. IBM's recent proclamation suggests a tantalizing horizon where quantum computers transition from theoretical constructs to tangible tools within a mere couple of years.

Yet, the journey is riddled with challenges. Quantum coherence, the bedrock of quantum computing, is a fragile state, easily disrupted by environmental interactions. The hurdles are manifold, from the Herculean task of maintaining qubit stability to the intricacies of quantum error correction. Scalability, precise qubit control, accurate readouts, and the necessity for extreme cooling further compound the complexity. And then there's the realm of material science, where the quest for the ideal qubit-hosting material is ongoing.

But for every challenge, there's an opportunity. The quantum realm is already making waves in real-world applications. Businesses, in their relentless pursuit of innovation, are harnessing the power of quantum computing to solve problems previously deemed insurmountable.

Take Mercedes-Benz, for instance. The automotive giant, in its commitment to a greener future, is delving into quantum computing to revolutionize battery technology for electric vehicles. The intricate dance of chemical reactions within batteries, traditionally elusive to conventional computational methods, becomes more tangible under the quantum lens.

ExxonMobil, on the other hand, is leveraging quantum algorithms to optimize fuel transportation routes, a task of staggering complexity when approached with classical computing methods.

CERN, the custodian of the Large Hadron Collider (LHC), is harnessing quantum computing to decipher the universe's enigmas. The vast data streams from the LHC, rife with patterns and anomalies, are prime candidates for quantum analysis.

Mitsubishi Chemical, in collaboration with Keio University, is exploring the intricacies of lithium-oxygen batteries at a molecular level, a task made feasible by quantum simulations.

Pivoting to the broader landscape, when juxtaposed with traditional powerhouses like GPUs and NPUs, quantum computers promise an exponential speedup, especially in the domain of machine learning. This acceleration translates to swifter training and inference times for ML models, a phenomenon aptly termed quantum machine learning. This integration of quantum algorithms within ML paradigms is set to redefine the benchmarks of computational efficiency.

Quantum bits enable parallel processing, enhancing tasks like machine learning by exploring multiple states simultaneously.

Peering into the horizon, the quantum odyssey is laden with potential. The immediate future, spanning one to three years, is poised to witness quantum hardware reaching new zeniths and the birth of avant-garde quantum algorithms. Transitioning to the medium term, spanning three to five years, the abstract allure of quantum computers will materialize into tangible tools, finding their niche in sectors like cryptography and optimization. A decade from now, the quantum community aspires to craft a fault-tolerant quantum computer—a beacon of achievement in the field.

Yet, the dream of a universal, gate-based, Turing-complete quantum behemoth remains a tantalizing vision on the distant horizon. But with the momentum garnered from recent innovations, strategic foresight, and a deluge of investments, the dawn of general-purpose quantum computers might just be closer than we dare to dream.

The quantum renaissance promises more than just speed—it pledges transformation. Quantum systems, with their capacity to process data on an astronomical scale, will redefine precision in measurements. Simulating intricate systems, from molecular matrices to cosmic phenomena, will be executed at speeds previously deemed fantastical. The emergence of quantum sensors will usher in an era of unparalleled sensitivity and pinpoint accuracy. Communication infrastructures, fortified by quantum principles, will be bastions of security, rendering them nigh impervious. And in the realm of problem solving, quantum algorithms will navigate the labyrinth of challenges, offering solutions that are not just optimal, but also intuitive. The quantum age beckons, and the future is reimagined. Figure 4.4 shows a photograph of a quantum computer.

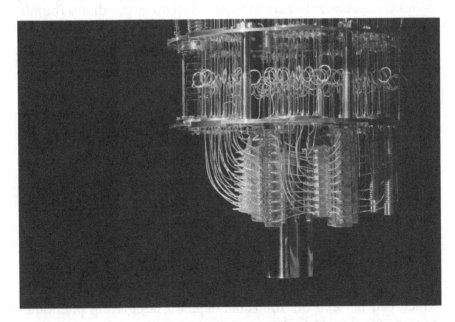

FIGURE 4.4 A quantum computer's intricate design: the loops, which straighten when cooled to –273°C, highlight the extreme cooling measures essential for quantum computing operations.

Source: IBM Corporation / https://newsroom.ibm.com/media-quantum-innovation?keywords=quantum&l=100#gallery_gallery_0:21747 / last accessed December 01, 2023.

Neuromorphic Computing   Neuromorphic computing emerges as a beacon of promise. At its core, this paradigm seeks to emulate the intricate architecture and functionality of the human brain. By harnessing physical artificial neurons for computations, realized through mediums like oxide-based memristors, spintronic memories, and transistors, it offers a fresh perspective on computational processes. The spiking neural network (SNN) stands as its most celebrated manifestation, where nodes mirror the processing and data retention capabilities of biological neurons. The overarching ambition? To usher in a new era of AI, characterized by brain-inspired, energy-efficient computing.

Enter Rain Neuromorphics, a trailblazer in this domain. Bolstered by a robust $25 million Series A funding, the company is poised to redefine the AI hardware landscape. Their audacious vision encapsulates the creation of a chip no larger than a thumbnail, capable of handling a staggering 100 billion-parameter models. With an unwavering belief in the transformative potential of AI, Rain Neuromorphics envisions a world where every gadget is endowed with a dynamic, perpetually evolving AI intellect.

While contemporary computing architectures rest on von Neumann principles, with distinct memory and processing units and a binary data representation, neuromorphic computing draws inspiration from cerebral constructs like neurons and synapses. This fusion of biology, mathematics, electronics, and physics offers a holistic approach to computation.

The true genius of neuromorphic computing lies in its emulation of cerebral processes. Visual representations of an SNN, which can be seen on YouTube, depict a fascinating phenomenon. Only a handful of neurons spring into action during decision making, initiating a broad cascade that gradually narrows, culminating in the final prediction—akin to a funnel's mechanism. This selective activation translates to fewer computational operations, amplifying the efficiency and efficacy of neuromorphic computing.

Quantifying this efficiency, especially in computational operations, poses challenges due to the distinct methodologies and components involved. However, energy consumption metrics offer a glimpse into its potential. Preliminary estimates suggest that neuromorphic computing could slash energy consumption for data processing by a staggering 90 percent.

The implications for contemporary AI are profound. Neuromorphic systems, with their real-time learning capabilities, could empower AI to adapt and respond with unprecedented agility, elevating performance in fluid environments. The allure of analog computation, a hallmark of the human brain and a feature of neuromorphic systems, could render them adept at tasks that baffle digital AI systems.

Yet, the true potential of this field might lie in its symbiotic relationship with other technological domains. A nascent trend hints at the fusion of neuromorphic computations with quantum computing. By amalgamating the strengths of both realms, the goal is to birth computing systems of unparalleled efficiency and power, capable of navigating the most labyrinthine computational challenges. While this convergence is still in its embryonic phase, the horizon gleams with promise. The trajectory remains uncertain, but one thing is clear—the future of computing is poised for a seismic shift, and neuromorphic computing will most likely play an important role in this transformation.

LK-99's Promise Imagine a future where the idea of room-temperature superconductors shines brightly, heralding untapped possibilities. Picture superconductors, those materials that transmit electricity without resistance, no longer bound by the icy chains of ultra-cold temperatures. The potential unlocked by transcending this temperature threshold is nothing short of revolutionary.

The implications of such a breakthrough are manifold. Envision our power grids, for instance. The advent of room-temperature superconductors could drastically elevate their efficiency, banishing energy losses that plague transmission. The realm of energy storage could witness the birth of compact systems that not only store energy with heightened efficiency but also bolster the utilization of renewable energy sources. Transportation could undergo a metamorphosis with magnetic levitation (maglev) trains becoming more ubiquitous, offering swifter and more energy-conserving public transit options. The medical sector stands to gain too, with MRI machines potentially becoming more affordable, efficient, and widespread. And in the telecommunications sphere? We could be looking at communication systems that redefine speed and efficiency, from turbocharged Internet connections to crystal-clear cell phone signals.

But perhaps the most tantalizing prospect lies in the domain of computing. Traditional processors, constructed from semiconductors, grapple with the Achilles' heel of heat generation—a byproduct of electrical resistance. This thermal challenge not only curtails processor speed but also guzzles energy. Enter superconductors. Their zero-resistance prowess could pave the way for processors devoid of heat generation, heralding an era of blistering processing speeds without the need for intricate cooling mechanisms. The energy economy of computing systems could witness a paradigm shift.

Quantum computing, too, stands on the cusp of a revolution. Room-temperature superconductors could render quantum computers more pragmatic and accessible, obviating the need for intricate cooling apparatuses. Such superconductors could bolster the stability of quantum systems, mitigating the menace of qubits succumbing to "decoherence." The scalability of quantum systems could witness a boost, potentially birthing quantum computers of unparalleled power. And with energy efficiency in the mix, these quantum behemoths could be both eco-friendly and cost-efficient. The ripple effect? An acceleration in quantum research, catalyzing rapid breakthroughs.

Enter the enigma of LK-99. Touted as a potential room-temperature superconductor, LK-99, with its distinctive hexagonal structure reminiscent of lead-apatite, has stirred the scientific community. Its discovery, credited to researchers Sukbae Lee and Ji-Hoon Kim from Korea University, has been met with both intrigue and skepticism. While the team has disseminated their findings, the absence of peer review casts a shadow of doubt. Replication attempts by global scientists have yet to bear fruit, leading many to question the veracity of LK-99's claims. The unfolding narrative around LK-99 underscores a profound realization: Our grasp of the periodic table remains incomplete. Our elemental alchemy, the art of melding elements to manifest desired properties, is still in its infancy. Yet, in this challenge lies opportunity.

Exponential Software Evolution

Let's pivot from discussing hardware advancements to exploring the software realm. Software evolution goes beyond just refining code; it's about designing holistic systems that synergize with hardware to yield more efficient and precise outcomes. This brings us to the forefront of exponential software evolution, particularly with parallel programming.

Parallel Programming   Parallel programming is a symphony of synchronized algorithms, harmoniously working together to tap into the full prowess of the hardware. When it all aligns, the surge in execution performance is nothing short of exhilarating.

A parallel algorithm isn't just any algorithm—it's a meticulously designed blueprint that can simultaneously execute multiple instructions across diverse processing devices. The magic lies
in its ability to weave together individual outputs, producing a
cohesive final result. This design is no accident; it's tailored to
harness the sheer power of parallel processing capabilities, especially in the realm of multiprocessor parallel computers.

Diving into the types of parallel algorithms, we find a rich
tapestry of classifications:

- *Data parallelism*: Here, the spotlight is on the data. Imagine
  running the same program or operation, but on different
  data subsets, all at the same time. It's like having multiple
  chefs cooking different dishes using the same recipe.

- *Task parallelism*: This is where diversity comes into play. Different algorithms, each with its unique task, run side by side
  in parallel. Think of it as an orchestra where each instrument plays a different part, but together they create a harmonious melody.

- *Embarrassingly parallelism*: The name might sound quirky,
  but it's quite straightforward. These are computations that
  can be effortlessly split into subproblems, each of which can
  be independently tackled on separate computing resources.
  It's akin to a puzzle, where each piece can be worked on by
  different individuals without any overlap.

However, it's essential to note that not every algorithm is
suited for parallelism. Take, for instance, Dijkstra's algorithm—a
sequential algorithm. It's a masterful graph search method that
pinpoints the shortest path in a graph with non-negative edge
path costs, culminating in a shortest path tree. Its sequential
nature means it follows a set path, step by step, much like following a single recipe from start to finish.

On the flip side, consider matrix multiplication—a shining example of a parallel algorithm. Here, matrices are fragmented into smaller chunks, and the multiplication of these bite-sized matrices is executed in parallel. It's like having multiple chefs each preparing a part of a dish, only to combine them at the end for the final masterpiece.

And speaking of matrix multiplication, its significance in AI, especially neural networks, is paramount. Here's a brief rundown:

- *Data processing*: At the heart of neural networks lies matrix multiplication. As input data and weights flow through each layer, they undergo a series of matrix multiplications, much like ingredients being mixed in a specific order to create a dish.

- *Backpropagation*: The cornerstone of training neural networks. This algorithm leverages matrix multiplication to compute gradients, akin to adjusting a recipe based on taste tests.

- *Batch processing*: Efficiency is key in AI training. By training on data batches, matrix operations streamline the process, much like cooking in bulk for a large gathering.

AlphaTensor   Mathematics has been laser-focused on enhancing the performance of matrix multiplication algorithms for decades. The ultimate goal? Achieving maximum efficiency with the fewest steps or operations.

Enter AlphaTensor, a groundbreaking AI system birthed by the brilliant minds at Google DeepMind. This isn't just any AI—it's a system that can unearth innovative, efficient, and most importantly, provably correct algorithms for foundational tasks, with matrix multiplication being a prime example.

What makes AlphaTensor truly stand out is its lineage. It's built upon the shoulders of giants, specifically AlphaZero—an AI prodigy that has demonstrated unparalleled prowess in board games. But DeepMind didn't stop there. They embarked on a journey to transition AlphaZero from mastering games to addressing unsolved mathematical conundrums for the very first time.

Under the guidance of AlphaTensor, algorithms surpassing the efficiency of existing state-of-the-art solutions were unveiled for a wide range of matrix sizes. But how did they achieve this monumental feat?

DeepMind ingeniously transformed the challenge of pin-pointing efficient matrix multiplication algorithms into a single-player game. But this wasn't any ordinary game—it was a Herculean task. To put it into perspective, the sheer number of potential algorithms to explore surpasses the total number of atoms in the universe, even for rudimentary matrix multiplication scenarios.

Undeterred, AlphaTensor was trained using the power of reinforcement learning to master this game. It began its journey devoid of any prior knowledge about existing matrix multiplication algorithms. Through continuous learning and adaptation, AlphaTensor not only reacquainted itself with historic rapid matrix multiplication algorithms like Strassen's but also ventured beyond human comprehension, unveiling algorithms swifter than any known before. The sheer diversity of algorithms it discovered—thousands for each matrix size—revealed a previously uncharted depth in the realm of matrix multiplication algorithms. A revelation, to say the least.

AlphaTensor's prowess didn't stop there. It showcased tangible improvements in matrix multiplication algorithms, especially tailored for specific scenarios and matrix dimensions. For instance, it unveiled an algorithm adept at multiplying a 4×5 matrix with a 5×5 matrix, requiring a mere 76 multiplications. This was a significant leap from a preceding algorithm that demanded 80 multiplications. When you scale this up to larger matrices, the difference becomes even more pronounced—roughly a 5 percent reduction in calculations for each matrix multiplication.

AlphaTensor's adaptability extends beyond speed, optimizing factors like energy use and stability, crucial for algorithmic accuracy. DeepMind's work with AlphaTensor and AlphaZero highlights AI's potential in addressing major scientific and mathematical challenges, foreseeing AI as a key tool in advancing human knowledge.

Parallel Processing Libraries: CUDA To harness the full potential of parallel processing units at the hardware level and implement parallel algorithms optimally and uniquely for specific applications, a myriad of tools and libraries have been developed. One such dominant tool is CUDA by NVIDIA, specifically tailored for NVIDIA products. Let's zoom in on CUDA.

CUDA, which stands for Compute Unified Device Architecture, is a parallel computing platform and programming model birthed by NVIDIA. It's not just a tool; it's a revolution, empowering developers to harness NVIDIA's GPUs for tasks beyond just graphics. The essence of CUDA lies in its ability to let developers write programs that exploit GPUs' parallel processing strengths effectively.

From researchers to developers, from startups to tech giants, CUDA has found its way into ML projects, scientific simulations, image processing, video enhancements, and so much more. It's not just a platform; it's the bedrock for leveraging the sheer computational might of GPUs across diverse sectors.

However, parallel computing isn't limited to CUDA; alternatives like OpenCL offer cross-platform programming capabilities, while OpenGL excels in graphics rendering and can be used for general-purpose GPU programming, indicating a diverse parallel computing landscape.

The Improvement of Programming Languages Pivoting to the software realm, let's shine a spotlight on programming languages. And here's the headline: Python reigns supreme. Not necessarily for its computational prowess, but for the sheer convenience it offers in coding and building, especially when navigating the waters of data science and AI. Its vast library ecosystem is a treasure trove for developers. But before we dive deeper into Python, let's take a brief historical detour. The first high-level programming language made its debut in 1957, courtesy of IBM, and was christened Fortran. However, not all high-level languages have stood the test of time, especially when we narrow our lens to data wrangling, data science, AI, and model development.

Tracing the lineage of programming languages in the context of data and AI, the chronology unfolds as follows:

R Born in 1993, R saw its heyday in the early 2000s, tailored specifically for statistical computing. Its vast array of statistical and graphical techniques made it a favorite for data wrangling and exploratory data analysis.

Python Although Python's inception dates back to the late 1980s, its meteoric rise in the data science domain began in the mid-2000s. Its trifecta of simplicity, readability, and versatility has made it an indispensable tool for data wrangling, ML, and AI model development.

SQL A relic from the 1970s, SQL (Structured Query Language) remains a cornerstone for managing relational databases. It's the unsung hero behind efficient data wrangling and querying, enabling seamless data extraction and transformation.

Java   Java's strength lies in enterprise applications, including data processing and analytics. While it might not share the limelight with Python or R in data science, its prowess in building scalable systems for Big Data processing is undeniable.

Julia   A newcomer, Julia surfaced in 2012, aiming to bridge the gap between the performance of low-level languages and the user-friendliness of high-level counterparts. Its rapid computations and expressiveness have garnered attention, especially for numerical tasks.

While these five languages have etched their marks, the programming world is vast, with many more languages like Scala, C/C++, JavaScript, Swift, Go, MATLAB, and SAS, each carving its niche. The evolution of these languages, especially in the realms of data wrangling, data science, AI, and machine learning, is a testament to the ever-growing need for tools that are both efficient and expressive.

New Programming Languages and User-Friendly Libraries

Even established languages like Python and R are being challenged by newcomers. Enter Mojo, the latest offering from Modular Inc.

Mojo is designed to blend Python's simplicity with C's performance, targeting AI developers. Its potential is evident in several key areas:

- *Unparalleled speed*: Chris Lattner, Modular's CEO and the mind behind Swift, claims that Mojo can outperform Python by up to 35,000 times in tasks like deep neural network training. This speed is attributed to the LLVM compiler toolchain and the innovative multilevel intermediate representation (MILR) compiler setup.

- *Python integration*: Mojo seamlessly integrates with the Python ecosystem, allowing developers to utilize existing Python libraries. This compatibility ensures a smooth transition from Python to Mojo, capitalizing on performance boosts.

- *Memory safety*: Mojo prioritizes memory safety, addressing potential vulnerabilities. This focus ensures enhanced stability and security in AI applications.

- *User-friendly design*: Mojo adopts a Python-like syntax, simplifying the learning process for developers and reducing the challenges of mastering a new language.

Mojo, with its high performance and user-friendly design, is set to revolutionize AI, making it more accessible and innovative. Libraries like TensorFlow, PyTorch, and Keras have already democratized AI by offering easy-to-use interfaces for all skill levels, lowering the entry barrier and providing both high-level functions and customization options.

The beauty of these libraries lies in their abstraction. TensorFlow, PyTorch, Keras, and LangChain have transformed the AI development landscape, encapsulating the intricacies of foundational algorithms within their user-friendly frameworks. This abstraction empowers developers, even those who might not be well versed in the labyrinthine depths of mathematical computations or intricate coding paradigms, to architect, nurture, and roll out AI models with an unprecedented ease.

One of the standout features of these libraries is their repertoire of preconfigured functions. They come equipped with a suite of ready-to-use tools tailored for routine tasks—be it orchestrating neural network configurations, calibrating loss functions, or orchestrating optimization strategies. This not only trims down the coding overhead but also accelerates the developmental trajectory and minimizes potential pitfalls.

The trajectory of these libraries appears promising. Their evolution is likely to be marked by enhanced user-centricity and augmented capabilities. The AI community might witness the emergence of niche libraries, each honed for distinct AI subdomains such as reinforcement learning or nuanced facets of natural language processing. A notable trend on the horizon could be the proliferation of prompt-driven interfaces, suggesting a paradigm shift toward AI assistants as an integral overlay.

Furthermore, the open source ethos underpinning most of these libraries is a boon for developers. It fosters a vibrant, collaborative ecosystem where knowledge dissemination is organic. Developers can tap into this reservoir of collective wisdom, troubleshoot common challenges, and even play an active role in the library's evolutionary journey.

The Open Source Movement The open source realm is arguably the most potent catalyst for AI advancement. There's scarcely an active open source community as vast and vibrant as the one orbiting AI. This dynamism not only propels the software layer to peak performance but also broadens its reach, making it effortlessly comprehensible for many.

This open source wave in AI is a beacon for knowledge dissemination and collective effort. It paves the way for swift conceptual iterations, rigorous algorithmic testing, and rapid propagation of AI breakthroughs. Open source ventures have been the bedrock of technological evolution for years, steering innovation and fostering collaboration in unparalleled ways. These communities are a melting pot of diverse perspectives, amalgamating varied backgrounds to craft solutions that are inventive and inclusive—crucial for unbiased, equitable AI. They are hubs for knowledge sharing, where developers exchange insights, propagate best practices, and jointly elevate their AI and ML acumen.

When these projects gain momentum and resonate with the market, their reliability often surpasses proprietary counterparts. This is attributed to the sheer volume of developers scrutinizing and fine-tuning the code, resulting in top-tier, resilient AI and ML models. Furthermore, these communities dismantle the traditional barriers to entry in AI and ML. They usher in an era where anyone can partake, assimilate, and harness the vast resources at hand.

At the heart of it all, projects fueled by intrinsic motivation—those birthed from passion—often outshine those driven by external incentives, such as monetary gains.

A testament to the prowess of open source AI initiatives includes:

- *OpenCV*: A library dedicated to computer vision and ML, offering a plethora of algorithms and tools for image processing, object detection, and beyond.
- *Hugging Face Transformers*: A library that furnishes cutting-edge natural language processing models and utilities, equipped with preconfigured models tailored for tasks like text categorization and language translation.

Envision a world where the democratization of AI and ML assets becomes the great equalizer in the technological realm. Such a shift promises that every individual, regardless of their background or resources, can dive into these fields, make meaningful contributions, and utilize them to tackle urgent global issues. This transformation could spark a golden age of innovation, spawning a myriad of AI and ML solutions attuned to a wide array of societal needs.

Advanced AI Architectures and AI Models   It's evident that AI architectures are evolving to be sharper, more intelligent, and immensely potent. Their growth trajectory has been nothing short of exponential, a trend prominently showcased with the release of models like ChatGPT. The AI landscape is in a state of perpetual flux, with research teams globally making strides daily, each enhancement pushing the boundaries of what's possible.

Take, for instance, the realm of Transformer models. Their capabilities have been on a steady incline, and a prime example of this evolution is Llama 2 by Meta. Llama 2 stands out in the crowded AI space for several compelling reasons. Not only is it open source, paving the way for both academic research and commercial endeavors, but its availability also promises to invigorate the AI model market, spurring further innovation.

What sets Llama 2 apart is its enhanced training data—boasting a 40 percent increase compared to its predecessor, Llama 1. This enhancement translates to a notable uptick in performance. But perhaps its most intriguing aspect is its scalability. While one might anticipate a behemoth model with upwards of 700 billion parameters, Llama 2 astounds with its most potent variant having a mere 70 billion parameters. This shift toward compact yet effective models underscores the dual themes of open source power and global research-driven incremental advancements.

But the story doesn't end there. Meta has forged alliances with tech giants like Microsoft and leading chipmaker Qualcomm. This collaboration aims to embed Llama 2 within Snapdragon processors, hinting at its integration in top-tier smartphones very soon. Furthermore, Llama 2 has been fine-tuned to operate seamlessly on platforms like Microsoft Azure, Amazon Web Services (AWS), and Hugging Face. Such partnerships are poised to broaden Llama 2's footprint in AI development, ushering in novel AI experiences for end users.

Liquid Neural Networks and AutoML Yet, beyond the familiar terrains of conventional AI architectures, there are burgeoning paradigms that are reshaping the AI landscape. Take liquid neural networks (LNNs) as an example.

LNNs, a brainchild of the brilliant minds at MIT's Computer Science and Artificial Intelligence Laboratory (CSAIL), represent a fresh wave in deep learning architectures. These are time-continuous recurrent neural networks (RNNs) that meticulously process data in a sequential manner, retaining memories of prior inputs. The magic of LNNs stems from their ingenious utilization of dynamically modifiable differential equations. This unique feature equips them with the prowess to recalibrate and adapt to novel scenarios post-training. Unlike their traditional counterparts, LNNs possess the agility to tweak their foundational equations based on incoming data, specifically modulating the responsiveness of neurons. This inherent adaptability renders LNNs exceptionally resilient to data anomalies or unforeseen inputs. An added feather in their cap is their enhanced interpretability, as tracing their decision-making pathways within the network becomes significantly more straightforward.

To distill it down: LNNs undergo initial training on data, but their true prowess shines when they continually refine their weights upon interacting with real-world data, enhancing their performance post-training.

Their potential has been demonstrated in arenas where conventional deep learning models often falter, such as in the domains of robotics and autonomous vehicles. A testament to their capabilities is the research from MIT, where drones, powered by a compact 20,000-parameter (!) LNN model, showcased superior navigational acumen in unfamiliar terrains compared to other neural networks. Such prowess hints at their potential in sculpting more precise autonomous vehicular systems.

However, like all innovations, LNNs come with their set of challenges—the vanishing gradient conundrum and a nascent body of literature detailing their implementation and advantages, to name a few. The academic community is fervently addressing these hurdles, curating more intricate tasks to gauge LNNs' mettle.

Looking ahead, LNNs hold the promise of catalyzing groundbreaking strides in AI, especially in sectors where traditional models often hit roadblocks. Their adaptability, coupled with heightened interpretability, could pave the way for sturdier and more efficient AI constructs. As the research tapestry around LNNs expands, we're poised to witness a surge in their applications and breakthroughs.

On another front, the realm of AI development is witnessing a paradigm shift with the rise of AutoML. These tools are revolutionizing the ML landscape by automating facets of the ML process (see Figure 4.5).

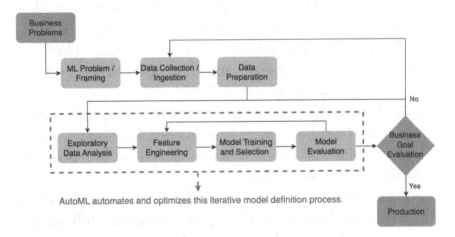

AutoML automates and optimizes this iterative model definition process.

FIGURE 4.5 The AutoML workflow: an overview of automated ML's end-to-end process, highlighting key subtasks from data preprocessing to model evaluation, encapsulated within the dotted-line box.

Source: Treasure Data, Inc. / https://docs.treasuredata.com/display/public/PD/AutoML / last accessed December 04, 2023.

AutoML encompasses a spectrum of techniques, ranging from hyperparameter optimization to meta-learning and neural architecture exploration. While hyperparameter optimization is all about the automated hunt for the optimal hyperparameter cocktail for specific ML algorithms, meta-learning is the art of gleaning insights from prior modeling endeavors to streamline future projects. Neural architecture exploration, on the other hand, is a deep dive into the myriad neural network blueprints, seeking the ideal fit for specific challenges.

AutoML is a significant step forward in AI. It speeds up development and makes AI more user friendly, even for those not deeply familiar with it.

AI-Powered Development Assistants   But the real break-through in fast and efficient AI development is AI-powered coding assistants.

Tools like GitHub Copilot and ChatGPT are changing how we develop software. They use ML to give instant coding help, handle repetitive tasks, and even create code snippets. They learn from the vast amount of code online, giving relevant suggestions that speed up coding and reduce errors.

From my work leading AI projects in Europe for Infosys Consulting, I handle many projects at once. Each one needs different attention at different times. But there are two tools I always insist my teams use.

First, every team member should always have ChatGPT Plus, a top-tier language model, open. It's essential. It helps generate code, reviews and improves existing code, and assists in documenting and commenting. It speeds up problem solving, helping teams work faster. But it's crucial to ensure that no private code is shared with ChatGPT to protect it from being accessed by OpenAI or others.

Second, GitHub Copilot is a must-have. It works smoothly with Visual Studio Code. And with an easy setup and a monthly fee, it keeps an eye on your code and suggests improvements as you go (see Figure 4.6).

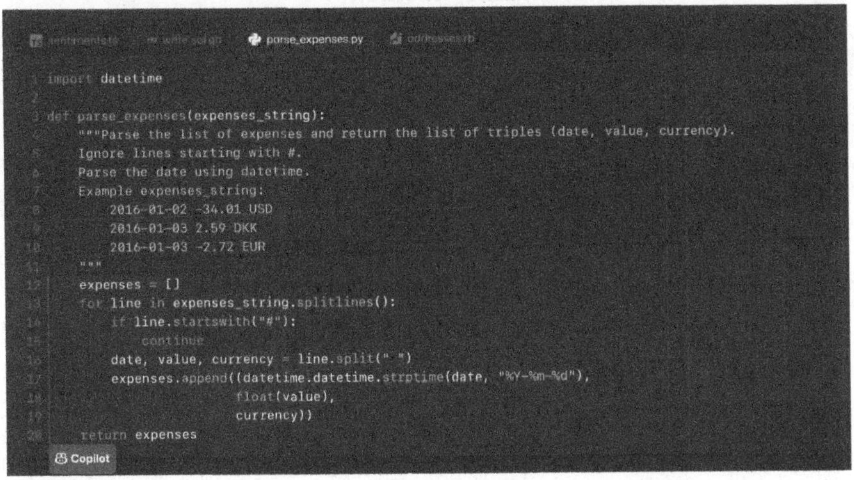

FIGURE 4.6 GitHub Copilot at work: seamlessly providing Python code suggestions to enhance developer productivity and streamline coding tasks.

Source: GitHub, Inc /https://github.com/features/copilot / last accessed December 01, 2023.

By now, not using GitHub Copilot or ChatGPT is like trying to work without a laptop. These tools enhance skills and boost productivity. Ignoring them is a big mistake.

Generative AI is not just advancing; it's self-evolving. By using generative AI to enhance and create new generative AI models, we can say that this technology is fueling its own breakthroughs.

Each stride in this domain signifies a leap, even if a small one, in AI software development. Collectively, these advancements are driving the rapid and exponential growth of AI and ML. While this overview isn't comprehensive, it underscores the relentless pace of AI model evolution.

Exponential Growth in Data

Data is the foundation of AI. Because data grows rapidly, it's important to understand how much is expected to be produced, whether it's real or artificially created.

Scaling AI with Big Data

At the heart of this topic is Big Data. This refers to huge amounts of data that are too large for regular data tools to handle. This data can be structured well organized, semi-structured (a mix, like emails), or unstructured (messy, like tweets).

Big Data is crucial today. It's the main source for modern AI systems, providing the information for ML to get better. By studying Big Data, we can see patterns and trends, especially about how people behave. This information is very valuable for many, from businesses to researchers. It helps in improving ads, giving personalized suggestions, predicting trends, and spotting fraud.

Data is key for training AI. It gives AI the information it needs to learn, make predictions, and get better. Some AI models, as mentioned before, are becoming slightly less data-hungry because they're getting smaller or changing in design, like the liquid neural networks.

However, the need for data is still growing. We expect to see many more AI models for different tasks in the future. Some will be specific, and some will be broad. The more data we have, the more problems AI can solve. The more detailed the data, the more specific the solution will be.

Lastly, remembering the Chinchilla scaling laws, it's important to note that as some AI models get bigger, they need significantly more data to scale their performance according to their size.

Data Growth Today

Every day, we're creating an immense 328.77 million terabytes of data. If you're trying to visualize this, Figure 4.7 might help put things into perspective. Fast-forward a bit, and projections show that by 2025, this number is expected to rise to approximately 181 zettabytes per year.

Unit	Abbreviation	Size (in bytes)
Byte	B	1
Kilobyte	KB	$1,024$
Megabyte	MB	$1,048,576$
Gigabyte	GB	$1,073,741,824$
Terabyte	TB	$1,099,511,627,776$
Petabyte	PB	$1,125,899,906,842,624$
Exabyte	EB	$1,152,921,504,606,846,976$
Zettabyte	ZB	$1,180,591,620,717,411,303,424$

FIGURE 4.7 Digital storage units, from bytes to zettabytes.

To truly grasp the magnitude of this growth, think about this: in 2025, we'll have about 90 times more data than what was available in 2010. And if we extend our gaze to 2030, using an exponential growth model, the anticipated data explosion is simply mind-blowing (see Figure 4.8 and Figure 4.9). The numbers are set to overshadow all previous data generation rates. By 2030, we're looking at a world that's expected to produce a colossal 597.10 zettabytes of data. To put that into context, that's almost 300 times the total amount of data that had been generated from the start of human history up until 2010.

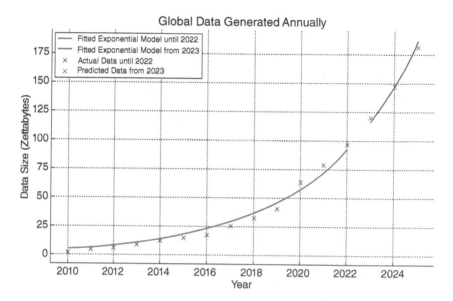

FIGURE 4.8 Annual global data generation: Historical trends and projections through 2025.

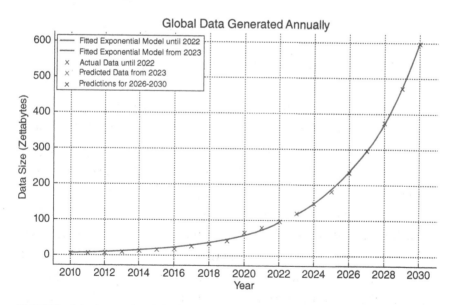

FIGURE 4.9 Annual global data generation: Historical trends and projections through 2030.

The Data Growth Drivers

Diving deeper into the vast ocean of data, some intriguing figures emerge from reputable online sources like Statista. For instance, videos dominate Internet data traffic, accounting for a significant 53.72 percent in 2023. Every minute, a staggering 231.4 million emails are dispatched, totaling around 333.22 billion daily. In the realm of cryptocurrency, we're seeing millions of purchases daily. On the social front, Snapchat users share approximately 2.43 million snaps every minute, which translates to about 3.5 billion snaps daily. The world of online dating isn't far behind, with Tinder witnessing around 1.1 million swipes every minute, or about 1.58 billion daily. In the entertainment sector, about 1 million hours of content are streamed per minute, amounting to roughly 1.44 billion hours daily. The corporate world, too, is buzzing, with around 104,600 hours spent in Zoom meetings every minute, leading to a daily total of about 150.62 million hours.

But what's fueling these numbers?

IoT devices, now ubiquitous in both our homes and workplaces, constantly churn out data. From smart refrigerators to intricate industrial sensors, the data they produce is harnessed for diverse applications, including refining device performance, preemptive maintenance, and analyzing user patterns. As their numbers swell, so does the data they spawn.

The ubiquity of smartphones and similar gadgets has also played a pivotal role in this data surge. Every app used, web page browsed, or location accessed contributes to this ever-growing data pool. Social media platforms, with their billions of global users, are significant data generators. Every post, like, share, or comment on platforms like Facebook, Twitter, Instagram, and YouTube adds to this digital deluge. Their primary use of this data? Tailored advertising and enhancing user experience.

Streaming giants like Netflix and Spotify have altered our media consumption habits. They meticulously record our preferences, using this data to suggest content and discern broader trends. Their soaring popularity, combined with the burgeoning digital content, inevitably leads to more data.

The pivot to cloud computing has seen businesses shifting their operations and storage, leading to more efficient data handling but also more data creation. The e-commerce boom, further propelled by the COVID-19 pandemic, sees platforms gathering data on user behaviors, tastes, and buying patterns, using it for personalized marketing and demand prediction.

Other sectors, including academia, healthcare, and more, also contribute to this data proliferation. But towering above all these drivers is the realm of AI and ML. These technologies thrive on vast data volumes for training and validation, leading to the creation of both authentic and synthetic data. Especially in areas like natural language processing, AI can produce new content, further amplifying data growth.

In essence, these myriad factors collectively fuel the data explosion we're witnessing today.

Synthetic Data

As the number of AI models multiplies, so does the volume of data they produce. This newly minted data then becomes a resource for training even larger and more efficient AI models.

Gartner, in a detailed report on synthetic data, forecasted a future where the majority of data fueling AI by 2030 would be crafted artificially (Figure 4.10). This could be through rule-based systems, statistical models, simulations, or other innovative techniques. The report emphasized, "Building high-quality, valuable AI models will be nearly impossible without the inclusion of synthetic data."

So, why is synthetic data gaining such prominence? The answer lies in its inherent advantages. Synthetic data champions both privacy and scalability. It paves the way for swift expansion of data-driven products, eliminating the cumbersome processes typically associated with data collection. Moreover, since it's artificially generated, it sidesteps the privacy pitfalls that often hamper the utilization of traditional datasets.

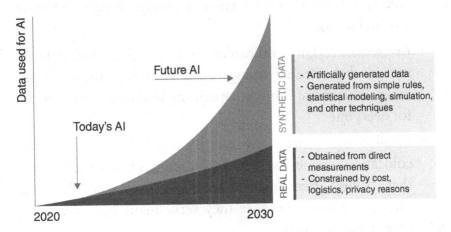

FIGURE 4.10 Evolution of real vs. synthetic data ratios over time.
Source: https://htecgroup.com/could-synthetic-data-be-the-future-for-machine-learning-models and Gartner, "Maverick Research: Forget about Your Real Data – Synthetic Data Is the Future of AI" – 24 June 2021

In essence, synthetic data promises to be the bridge connecting the vast reservoirs of real-world data with their practical applications in data-centric products. It promises quicker product launches, slashes both the costs and time frames of data collection, and ensures the confidentiality of sensitive information.

Exponentially Cheaper Data Storage

One big change is how much cheaper data storage has become. This isn't just by chance. Several key reasons are:

- *Tech improvements*: New tools and technologies, like NAND flash-based solid-state drives (SSDs), zoned namespace SSDs, and storage-class memory, have made storage devices better and more spacious. This means lower costs for storing data.

- *Economies of scale*: As more people need data storage, it's cheaper to make in large quantities. Big cloud and datacenter companies can also offer cheaper storage because of their size and focus.

- *Competition*: Many companies are in the data storage business, and they're all trying to offer the best prices to get more customers. This competition leads to better prices for everyone.

- *Cloud storage*: More companies are using cloud providers or colocation services for their data storage. This can be cheaper than having their own datacenters. Cloud providers can offer good prices because they serve many customers and spread out the costs.

In short, the plummeting costs of data storage can be attributed to technological prowess, surging demand, fierce competition, and the ascent of cloud storage. But this is just the tip of the iceberg.

Trends in Data

The data revolution is not merely confined to storage costs. As highlighted before, there's a burgeoning reservoir of data that's fueling the enhancement of AI models, pushing the boundaries of their performance and accuracy, especially when compared to the earlier Chinchilla models. The fascinating aspect is that AI is not just a beneficiary of this data deluge but also a catalyst. AI is now in a position to aid its own evolution by generating the very data it thrives on.

Yet, several undercurrents are shaping the future of data, trends that haven't been fully explored. Among these are the emergence of edge computing, advancements in wireless technology like 5G, and the dawn of quantum computing.

Edge computing, a paradigm shift in data processing, is redefining the norms. By positioning computation and data storage proximate to data sources, it optimizes response times and conserves bandwidth. This approach is a game-changer, amplifying data growth by facilitating real-time analytics, catalyzing the expansion of the IoT, and ushering in a new era of instantaneous applications and services.

Then there's 5G, the latest iteration in wireless technology, promising swifter data transfers, diminished latency, and robust connections. The ripple effects of 5G on data growth will be profound. Its rapid transfer rates mean data is churned out and processed at breakneck speeds. The technology's capacity to tether a multitude of devices concurrently amplifies the IoT's footprint, leading to a surge in data creation. Moreover, 5G's robustness paves the way for data-hungry applications, from real-time analytics to self-driving cars and immersive AR and virtual reality (VR) experiences.

For perspective, while using LTE (a 4G variant) on a smartphone, we might experience peak download speeds of 1.5 Gbps. In contrast, 5G promises a staggering 10 Gbps. But the real spectacle is the anticipated 6G, with speeds that could touch a mind-boggling 1 Tbps or 1,000 Gbps. This translates to an exponential leap, with 6G projected to be a hundredfold faster than 5G. Imagine downloading content equivalent to 142 hours in a mere second! Industry insiders are buzzing with anticipation, predicting 6G's commercial rollout around 2030.

However, a word of caution is in order. While these figures are impressive, real-world download speeds can often be a far cry from these theoretical maxima. Factors such as the service provider, network conditions, contractual terms, and even signal strength can temper these speeds.

Exponential Patterns in Research, Development, and Financial Allocations

The evolution in AI is driven by advanced ML algorithms, an open source culture, and a suite of tools and libraries that streamline AI development. Key to this progress is substantial investment in AI research from both private and public sectors, enabling practical applications. The emergence of GenAI demonstrates real-world value. Additionally, the influx of talented researchers and accessible training materials democratizes AI knowledge, fostering potential breakthroughs from around the world. This blend of research, development, and funding is crucial for AI's integration into everyday life.

Investments in AI Research

AI giants like Runway ML, Hugging Face, Anthropic, OpenAI, and Google DeepMind have seen their valuations skyrocket, highlighting the growing investments in this sector. A closer look at the trends shows a clear rise in AI funding over the years. While global politics and economic shifts can influence these investments, the overall trend points to a rapid increase in AI funding, suggesting exponential growth.

In 2022, AI startups attracted a whopping $52.1 billion in investments across 3,198 companies. Notably, generative AI projects secured $4.5 billion of this funding, as reported by Pitch-Book. The momentum continued into the first half of 2023, with generative AI companies globally receiving around $15.2 billion, underscoring the rising interest in this AI niche—if niche is even the right term by now.

Here are some standout investments from the past 18 months, as of this writing:

- *Anthropic*: Anthropic recently secured $450 million in a Series C funding round. Spark Capital led the investment, with significant contributions from Google, Salesforce Ventures, Sound Ventures, Zoom Ventures, and other notable investors. Google alone invested $300 million, as Anthropic works on a competitor to OpenAI's ChatGPT.

- *Inflection AI*: Inflection AI recently secured $1.3 billion in funding in the latest funding round. This round was spearheaded by notable investors including Microsoft, Reid Hoffman, Bill Gates, Eric Schmidt, and NVIDIA. This investment has catapulted the valuation of the one-year-old startup to $4 billion. The funds are earmarked for the enhancement of Inflection AI's personal AI assistant, "Pi", and for constructing a 22,000-unit NVIDIA H100 Tensor GPU cluster, touted as the world's largest.

- *Cohere*: Cohere recently secured $270 million in a Series C funding round. Inovia Capital spearheaded the round, joined by notable investors such as NVIDIA, Oracle, Salesforce Ventures, DTCP, SentinelOne, Mirae Asset, Schroders Capital, Thomvest Ventures, and Index Ventures. Announced in June 2023, this investment boosted the valuation of the Toronto-based AI startup to $2.2 billion.

The AI sector is experiencing a surge in investments, particularly in generative AI technology. Key players include Salesforce Ventures, which recently increased its Generative AI Fund to $500 million, and SoftBank Group, with its massive Vision Funds totaling $154 billion. Additionally, the AI seed investment landscape features over 4,000 entities, including prominent firms like General Catalyst, NFX, and LAUNCH. Venture capital heavyweights such as Andreessen Horowitz, Sequoia, Khosla Ventures, and Greylock Partners are also actively investing in generative AI startups, among many others.

Despite all investments and attention, amidst the buzz, a chorus of skepticism is growing increasingly audible.

Being a nascent technology, there's a tangible risk of its potential being blown out of proportion. Investors, eager to jump on the bandwagon, might pour money into generative AI ventures without a clear grasp of the tech's intricacies or the market dynamics.

It's worth noting that generative AI is still finding its feet. The road ahead is rife with uncertainties about its evolution and eventual applications. The field is also crowded, with numerous players vying for a piece of the pie. For startups, standing out amidst this fierce competition is a daunting task. Drawing a parallel, back in the 1920s and 1930s, the United States market had over 2,000 car manufacturers. Yet, in a short span, this number dwindled to 44. By the 1940s, the big three—Chrysler, Ford, and GM—emerged as the undisputed leaders, capturing a staggering 90 percent of U.S. car sales.

Furthermore, like any powerful tool, generative AI can be a double-edged sword. Its capabilities can be harnessed for commendable purposes or misused with detrimental consequences. This duality brings forth pressing ethical dilemmas. As a result, investors are urged to tread cautiously, weighing the moral implications before deciding where to place their bets.

The Real Value of Generative AI

Generative AI is different from past tech trends. Why? It's not just hype; it's a technology that offers real value. This AI has many uses in the real world, from creating content to helping in medicine and science. And it's attracting a lot of money and interest because of its potential to change many industries.

In this book, we've talked about how flexible generative AI is. It's being used in many areas like making content, helping doctors see inside the body, creating new drugs, and even in material science.

This AI is already helping people work better and faster. And as more people start using it, it could add trillions of dollars of value to the world. It's not just about changing jobs; it's about making them better.

A 2023 survey by Namecheap showed how popular generative AI tools are becoming. Forty percent of people said they use them every day, and 10 percent use them every month. The most popular tool was ChatGPT, with 70 percent of users picking it. DALL-E and Midjourney were next, with about 30 percent of users liking them.

But it's not just about how much is spent on these tools. It's also about how they can save time and money. Generative AI doesn't just replace people; it helps them do their jobs better. It can handle the boring tasks, letting people focus on more creative work.

Talent and Self-Learning in Tech

The tech and AI sectors have seen a massive surge in skilled professionals in recent times. Why? Companies are updating their tech systems and embracing AI, creating a huge demand for experts in these areas. Jobs linked to AI often pay well and require a college degree and sharp analytical skills.

The competition for tech experts is heating up. There's a big demand for roles like ML Architect and Prompt Engineers, but not enough skilled folks to fill them. We're talking about AI engineers, research scientists, data scientists, and so forth.

But here's the exciting part: A fresh wave of young professionals is stepping in. Some older folks might label them as lazy or clueless, but I see them differently. This new generation is practical, values being real, and is super diverse.

Here's a fun fact: Gen Z grew up with the Internet, smartphones, and even AI as everyday things. They're the real tech pros! Plus, they're setting records in education. More of them are finishing high school and fewer are dropping out. In 2018, a total of 57 percent of those aged 18 to 21 were in college. That's more than millennials and Gen Xers when they were that age. And guess what? Many Gen Z folks prefer trade or tech schools over traditional colleges.

Speaking of learning, there are so many ways to learn about tech and AI now. You've got online courses on platforms like Coursera and edX. Books, like the one you're reading right now. There are also tutorials, podcasts, and online communities like Quora and Reddit. And don't forget YouTube! Channels like Sentdex and Deeplearning.ai share loads of AI stuff.

This new generation learns fast and in their own unique ways. This helps them think out of the box, start their own businesses, team up with people worldwide, and keep up with the ever-changing tech world. They're definitely one step ahead of the rest!

Diving into the realm of IT/ICT (information and communication technology), there's a clear upward trend that's hard to miss. While we might not have a single number that captures the global AI workforce's growth, we've got some pretty telling stats to look at.

For starters, between 2006 and 2018, the number of ICT professionals worldwide shot up by a notable 29 percent. Zooming into the European Union, the growth is even more impressive. From 2012 to 2022, the count of ICT specialists in the EU skyrocketed by a whopping 57.8 percent. That's nearly seven times the growth rate of other jobs!

The World Economic Forum has some big predictions too. They believe that by 2025, close to 100 million people around the world will be working in AI. Given the current momentum, I'd say that number might climb even faster than we think.

Now, let's talk about where all these tech wizards are coming from. Russia leads the pack with over 454,000 folks graduating in engineering and similar AI-related professions every year. The United States isn't far behind with 237,826 graduates, followed closely by Iran and then Japan.

But there's one country that's a real powerhouse in the tech world: India. With a tech army of over 5 million professionals and a tech industry worth a cool $200 billion, India is a force to be reckoned with. I've had firsthand experience working with Indian teams during my time at IBM consulting and later at Infosys consulting. The talent, dedication, and work ethic I've seen is truly commendable.

AI Research Goes Private

The AI research field is increasingly leaning toward the private sector, a trend offering both opportunities and challenges. From my perspective, witnessing peers from academia transition to lucrative corporate roles underscores the appeal of this shift. The financial power of private companies, exemplified by IBM's $6.57 billion investment in research only in 2022, drives significant advancements in AI research and development.

But it's not just about the money. Private companies are inherently geared toward translating AI research into tangible, market-ready products. This not only benefits the corporate bottom line but also enriches the consumer experience.

The private sector's agility in quickly transforming AI research into practical applications across industries is a key advantage.

Moreover, the lines between academia and industry are blurring. Collaborative endeavors between private corporations and academic institutions are on the rise, fostering a symbiotic relationship where knowledge dissemination meets resource allocation.

This pivot toward private sector–led research is a significant economic driver, birthing new job roles, stimulating economic growth, and ensuring companies remain at the forefront of their industries. In essence, as AI R&D finds its home in the private sector, it promises a future where innovation thrives, economies flourish, and societies benefit.

Requirements for Growth

Diving deep into the research, it's evident that the AI landscape is on an accelerated trajectory. The leaps in computational capabilities, in both hardware and software, are astounding. The surge in data availability, coupled with affordable storage solutions, further fuels this momentum. Add to this the significant investments in R&D, the collaborative spirit of open source communities, and the fresh perspectives brought in by Gen Z, and it's clear: we're on the cusp of an AI revolution that promises to redefine humanity's progress.

The AI-Driven Economy

ARK Investment Management LLC's insights offer a compelling perspective on this (Figure 4.11). Their analysis paints a picture of how technology has historically been a catalyst for macroeconomic growth. For context, from the dawn of civilization until 1900, the global real GDP growth per year hovered below 1 percent. Fast-forward to the period between 1900 and 2021, and this figure jumped to an average of 3 percent annually. ARK's projections, rooted in technological trends, are even more staggering. They anticipate an annual global GDP growth of 6.1

percent by 2030, soaring to 10.7 percent by 2040. Annually! This means by 2030 a theoretical jump of 42 percent, and by 2040 the GDP could theoretically reach 508 percent of today. This isn't just growth; it's a transformative shift in the global economic fabric, with AI, especially generative AI, at its heart.

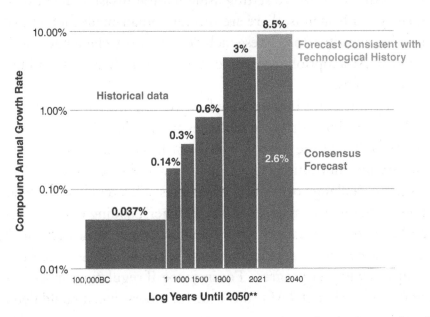

FIGURE 4.11 ARK Investment Management's projections: a tale of two futures.

Source: NM Writings / A Medium Corporation / https://medium.com/coinmonks/ big-ideas-2023-ark-invests-crypto-part-1-out-of-2-4a382bfe35a1 / last accessed December 04, 2023.

Yet, much like in the natural world, growth in the tech ecosystem isn't boundless and follows one trajectory. Just as biological systems have their constraints, the AI domain isn't immune to limiting factors. Understanding what might hinder our path is crucial. By identifying and addressing these challenges, we can ensure that the technological renaissance we're witnessing translates into tangible benefits for humanity. In essence, these considerations aren't just obstacles; they're the very blueprint we need to ensure sustained and meaningful growth.

Challenges to AI Progression

What might impede our journey toward AI-driven technological progress? While we're setting aside natural disasters like earthquakes and tsunamis, there are several human-made factors that deserve our attention. These include regulatory challenges, hesitancy in AI adoption, economic and political dynamics, and talent shortages.

Regulation is a double-edged sword. On one hand, it's essential for ensuring that AI technologies are developed and deployed responsibly. On the other, excessive or ill-conceived regulations can stymie innovation. Governments worldwide are grappling with the challenge of crafting AI policies. This regulatory uncertainty can deter businesses and researchers, adding complexities and costs to AI initiatives. Overemphasis on certain aspects, such as data accessibility restrictions or an excessive focus on explainability, can hinder progress. For instance, if regulations make setting up experimental AI projects too cumbersome, it could deter innovation.

However, it's not all gloom. Some nations are leading the way with balanced and forward-thinking AI strategies. Countries like Canada, South Korea, the United States, Japan, and notably, Singapore, are setting commendable examples. Singapore, in particular, stands out with its ambitious vision to be at the forefront of AI by 2030. Their approach strikes a balance: They prioritize data privacy and ethical AI use without stifling innovation. Their collaborations with global tech giants like Google Cloud and their engagement with the open source community through initiatives like the AI Verify Foundation are testament to their progressive stance. Additionally, Singapore's emphasis on education and talent development ensures they have the human capital to realize their AI aspirations.

One of the significant challenges in our journey toward an AI-centric world is the rate at which AI is embraced by both businesses and individuals:

- *Ethical dilemmas*: The ethical landscape of AI is vast and complex. Concerns about biases in AI algorithms, potential misuse in surveillance, and other moral quandaries can deter its widespread adoption. As developers and innovators, we bear the responsibility to ensure AI serves the broader good of society.

- *Knowledge gaps*: A significant barrier is the lack of comprehensive understanding of AI's capabilities. Many, from individual users to large corporations, are either unaware of AI's potential or have misconceptions about its limits. GenerativeAI.net aims to bridge this gap, educating both individuals and businesses. Fortunately, tech giants like Google have also stepped up, offering educational platforms to demystify AI.

- *Financial constraints*: The financial aspect of AI can't be ignored. While AI promises incredible returns, the initial investment can be daunting. OpenAI's CEO, Sam Altman, highlighted this when he revealed that training GPT-4 cost over $100 million. And the projections suggest that by 2030, training advanced AI models could skyrocket to a staggering $500 million. Such figures can be intimidating, especially for smaller enterprises.

- *Cultural and generational variances*: Acceptance of AI isn't uniform across all demographics. Different age groups and cultural backgrounds approach AI with varying degrees of trust and enthusiasm. While some are eager to integrate AI into their daily lives, others approach with caution, if not skepticism. Navigating these diverse attitudes and finding a universally acceptable path is a nuanced challenge.

Economic, political, and even military conflicts can significantly impact the trajectory of AI development. For instance, the devastating war between Ukraine and Russia has resulted in not only human suffering but also massive economic repercussions. By March 2023, the World Bank estimated that Ukraine already needed $411 billion over the next decade for recovery and reconstruction. Meanwhile, Russia's daily expenses for the war range between $500 million and $1 billion. One can't help but wonder how transformative it would be if such resources were redirected toward secure AI development, tech education, and sustainable innovations.

While there's undeniable enthusiasm for AI, the industry still grapples with a talent shortage. The demand for AI professionals far outstrips the supply, and this gap is projected to continue until 2030. The strength and potential of the upcoming generation are commendable, but demographic challenges loom large. Countries like Bulgaria are projected to see significant population declines. By 2050, Bulgaria's population might reduce to 5.4 million from 6.9 million in 2020. This decline isn't isolated; many nations, especially in Eastern Europe and parts of Asia, are witnessing similar trends due to falling fertility rates, aging populations, and low immigration. These demographic shifts can strain economies and healthcare systems and alter workforce dynamics. Elon Musk has even expressed concerns about a potential population collapse.

Returning to the ARK survey, while it does also offer a more conservative outlook, it still paints a picture of growth. The survey suggests a potential global GDP growth of 3 percent by 2030 and 2.1 percent by 2040. While some might view this as a cause for concern, I remain hopeful. Throughout history, there have always been voices of doom, but innovation and human resilience have often prevailed. Perhaps, as we face future challenges, our collective ingenuity will once again guide us toward brighter horizons.

Ethical Concerns and Social Implications of Generative AI

Generative AI, with its vast potential and transformative capabilities, is not without its ethical quandaries and societal ramifications. The following concerns, which are both profound and multifaceted, demand our attention and thoughtful consideration:

- Intellectual property rights and ownership
- Misinformation, particularly through tools like deepfakes
- Privacy, safety, and security
- Generative AI's impact on the job market and industries
- Our increasing dependency on AI

- Environmental concerns tied to AI
- AI oversight and self-regulation

These pressing issues not only are of utmost importance for the clients I have worked with and talked to, but also echo in broader conversations across the globe. The journey into the future of generative AI is filled with promise, but it's essential to navigate it with caution, awareness, and responsibility.

The intricacies of large language models (LLMs) often intertwine with their occasional inaccuracies and a lack of contextual understanding. This can sometimes lead to a failure to grasp the nuances of specific workplace scenarios, potentially misinforming individuals. Hence, it's imperative to emphasize the importance of source referencing when relying on such models.

The aim of this chapter is to delve not into the technicalities of AI but rather into the broader mindset, rules, and attitudes surrounding it. The pillars of transparency, education, regulation, and security are paramount. Ultimately, our discourse converges on the ethical concerns and societal implications of AI.

It's worth noting that certain topics can straddle the line between an ethical concern and a societal implication, which is why I've chosen not to make a clear distinction between the two. While each of these subjects could be exhaustively explored, potentially warranting a doctoral thesis of its own, my aim here is to provide a comprehensive overview, highlighting the nuances without getting lost in the minutiae.

A word of caution: I don't claim to be a legal expert. The landscape of AI and its regulations is ever-evolving, so always seek guidance from a legal professional for specific situations. The perspectives shared here are solely mine, derived from extensive research and myriad discussions. Where appropriate, I'll offer recommendations.

Navigating the labyrinth of regulations is no small feat, especially when addressing a technology that's still in its nascent stages, with many of its implications being theoretical. The regulatory approach to AI varies significantly across countries; some nations adopt a more hands-on stance while others tread with caution.

Lastly, addressing the multifaceted ethical and societal challenges posed by AI is not a solitary endeavor. It demands a concerted effort from technologists, policymakers, ethicists, and society as a whole. Crafting a future where AI aligns with our ethical values and principles necessitates smart regulations in combination with self-regulation, unwavering commitment to transparency and accountability, and a collective will to ensure responsible AI design and deployment.

Intellectual Property and the Generative AI Platform

In the rapidly evolving landscape of AI, the legalities surrounding intellectual property (IP) rights are in constant flux. It's imperative for professionals and users alike to stay abreast of local laws. When navigating the intricate waters of AI and IP, consulting with legal professionals is always a prudent step.

One of the most pressing questions in this domain is: Who owns the intellectual property rights of the content generated by the AI? To address this, it's essential to first differentiate between ownership, owning the IP rights, and copyright.

Ownership pertains to the possession or holding of an item. For instance, when you purchase a book, that physical copy belongs to you. On the other hand, owning IP rights means having legal control over an idea, invention, or creation. This encompasses patents, trademarks, and copyrights. Using the book analogy, while you possess the physical book, the unique ideas, characters, or methods within are protected by IP rights, granting exclusive usage, sale, or licensing privileges. Copyright, a subset of IP rights, is a legal provision that gives the creator of an original work exclusive rights to its use and distribution. So, although you own the book you bought, you can't reproduce its content for sale, as the copyright typically belongs to the author or publisher.

The matter of IP rights for AI-generated content is intricate and varies across jurisdictions and terms of use. Historically, IP rights have been attributed to human creators. However, the advent of AI-generated content has muddied these waters. While there are scattered regulatory guidelines globally, a comprehensive solution remains elusive.

A growing concern in this field is the likelihood of AI tools being trained on copyrighted content without obtaining the requisite permissions. This issue has been thrust into the spotlight by recent legal confrontations, notably the case involving Sarah Silverman, an acclaimed American stand-up comedian, actress, and writer. Silverman, along with other authors, has taken on tech behemoths like OpenAI and Meta, emphasizing the intricate nature of copyright violations in the AI sphere. Silverman's contention is that OpenAI never secured her consent to use the digital rendition of her book for training their AI models. In a similar vein, legal actions, such as the one where Getty Images challenged Stable Diffusion over unauthorized content usage, accentuate the urgent need for definitive guidelines in this area.

In the European Union, the stance on copyrightability is clear-cut: AI-generated works are not eligible for copyright protection. The Court of Justice of the European Union mandates human involvement for a work to be copyrighted. Purely computer-generated outputs, devoid of human contribution, don't qualify. However, such AI outputs might find protection under related rights, such as sound recording rights, with the AI software user likely being the rights holder.

The UK's approach to copyrightability is more intricate. While original literary, dramatic, musical, and artistic works are protected, they must be the author's creations and display originality. If a human, with AI assistance, creates a work that exhibits human creativity, the AI is merely a tool and the human retains the rights. However, the UK does offer protection to works generated solely by computers, provided they meet the originality criterion. The challenge lies in the fact that generative AI often tests this standard of originality.

Lastly, the terms and conditions of AI programs often house crucial information regarding IP rights. Companies like Midjourney, OpenAI, and Stability AI outline specific terms about the ownership of AI-generated content. However, these details, often buried in fine print, are frequently overlooked by users, leading to potential misunderstandings. For example, while OpenAI permits users to own the content they produce, it reserves the right to utilize it for service enhancement, aka model training.

If an AI tool produces content that treads on the intellectual property of another, the question of liability becomes paramount.

In numerous scenarios, the end users, who utilize the AI for content generation and subsequently disseminate or employ that content, might find themselves in the crosshairs of legal action for any infringement. This is particularly the case if the user's specific prompts or data inputs steer the AI toward infringing content. On the other hand, the AI service provider could also shoulder some of the blame, especially if they had prior knowledge of potential infringement risks or if their tool habitually churns out content that breaches copyright. That said, many AI service terms explicitly shift the responsibility burden onto the user, absolving the provider of any potential legal entanglements.

To sidestep the quagmire of infringement, several measures can be adopted:

- AI developers must prioritize legal compliance when sourcing data.

- Establishing and maintaining a clear lineage of AI-generated content can help trace back any potential issues.

- Vigilance is key for content creators to spot potential infringements.

- Companies should closely review deal conditions to protect their intellectual property.

- Constructing proprietary datasets for AI training can offer more control and reduce infringement risks.

- At the user's end, it's paramount to honor the rights of original content creators, ensuring their work isn't misappropriated.

The nature of the content produced by an AI model can often be swayed by the training data it's been fed. This brings to light another pertinent question: Who holds the rights to the AI model itself, encompassing its architecture, weights, and algorithms?

As a general rule of thumb, the rights to the AI model typically rest with the entity—be it an individual or an organization—that played a pivotal role in its development. However, if the model's creation was under the purview of an employment contract or a specific agreement, the rights might be vested in the employer or the contracting party. The waters get murkier with open source models. While the original creators retain the copyright, they extend certain privileges to others, allowing them to use, adapt, and distribute the model. The exact nature of these rights and any accompanying obligations hinge on the stipulations of the open source license under which the model was released.

Bias and Fairness in AI-Generated Data

In the rapidly evolving realm of generative AI, the ethical onus on AI practitioners such as AI researchers and AI engineers is paramount. As stewards of this transformative technology, they bear the responsibility of not just creating but also continuously refining AI models to reflect the ever-shifting tapestry of societal norms and values. This necessitates a vigilant approach to AI, one that's steeped in a critical mindset, perpetually probing and validating the fairness of the outputs it generates.

How Bias Is Introduced into Generative AI Models

Bias, an unwelcome specter, can insidiously creep into generative AI models through myriad avenues. One of the most prevalent culprits is biased training data. When the foundational data used to train an AI system skews toward a particular demographic or perspective, the system, in all likelihood, will mirror these biases in its results. Such a scenario can manifest when the training data presents an imbalanced representation of various groups, causing the AI model to internalize and reproduce these inherent biases. The repercussions of leveraging incomplete, erroneous, or prejudiced datasets for the training and validation of machine learning systems can be far reaching and detrimental.

Yet, the very architects of these systems, the individuals who design and train the machine learning algorithms, can inadvertently infuse their creations with biases. These could range from unintentional cognitive biases to more deep-seated prejudices. Furthermore, the very blueprint of the AI model, its architecture, can be a source of bias. Specific architectural decisions might inadvertently prioritize certain data patterns or features, leading to skewed representations. Even seemingly innocuous elements like loss functions and regularization techniques can play a role in introducing bias.

Human interpretation of AI outputs is another potential pitfall. The lens through which AI-generated results are viewed and interpreted can be colored by individual biases, leading to skewed conclusions.

To fight these biases, we need a clear plan. Start with using varied and balanced data. It's also crucial to watch out for biases when choosing and reading data. By regularly checking and testing AI systems, we can spot and fix hidden biases. Understanding how the AI model's design affects its actions is also key.

Working toward a bias-free generative AI is an ongoing effort. It requires constant attention, self-reflection, and a strong dedication to ethics.

The Implications of Biased AI-Generated Data on Real-World Applications

Biased AI-generated data can have significant real-world consequences. Organizations using skewed AI data risk legal challenges, potentially facing lawsuits or regulatory actions. This bias can also lead to discrimination in sectors like recruitment, finance, and healthcare, where AI might favor certain demographics.

Companies using biased AI risk damaging their reputation, affecting their brand and customer trust. Furthermore, decisions based on biased AI can result in financial losses for businesses and individuals alike.

At a societal level, biased AI can exacerbate existing prejudices, deepening societal divides and reinforcing inequalities. Such biases can also diminish public trust in AI, limiting its broader acceptance and potential benefits.

To counteract these challenges, organizations must actively identify and address biases in AI data. This includes using diverse training data, regularly evaluating AI systems, and considering the ethical implications of AI decisions. Ultimately, though AI offers immense potential, it's crucial to use it responsibly to ensure fairness and inclusivity.

Detecting and Measuring Bias in AI-Generated Data

The complexities of bias detection in AI-generated data call for a comprehensive approach. Here's a closer look at the strategies and techniques that can be employed.

A deep dive into the data that trains the AI model can shed light on inherent biases. The key is to ensure this data mirrors the broader population, thereby minimizing skewed outcomes.

Fairness metrics come to the rescue when quantifying bias. Metrics like disparate impact and equal opportunity difference can pinpoint how the model might be leaning toward certain groups.

The tech industry has developed tools such as AI Fairness 360, Algorithmic Bias Detection Tool, Bias Analyzer, and Aequitas. These tools are designed to identify and correct bias in AI data effectively.

Another effective strategy is to pit the AI model against dedicated external benchmark data, such as the COMPAS datasets for predictive policing biases, BiasBios for gender bias in named-entity recognition, and FairFace for biases in facial recognition.

Datasets specifically designed to benchmark bias can be invaluable in this exercise.

The human element can't be overlooked. A team that's diverse in terms of backgrounds and experiences can offer varied perspectives, acting as a safety net against biases that might otherwise slip through.

The AI model should be under constant scrutiny. Regular tests, coupled with rigorous monitoring and audits, can keep biases in check. This vigilance should span the entire spectrum of the AI model, from its input and logic to its behavior and output.

However, the journey to bias detection isn't without its challenges. There are often tough choices to make, like striking a balance between transparency and privacy or juggling fairness with accuracy. This underscores the need for AI models to be in a state of constant evolution, with regular tweaks to iron out biases and uphold fairness.

Ensuring Fairness in AI-Generated Data Without Compromising Data Privacy

Switching gears to the delicate balance between fairness and data privacy in AI-generated data, here's a roadmap.

Laying the groundwork for privacy should start at the very onset of AI model development. Techniques like differential privacy, federated learning, and secure multiparty computation can be game changers, allowing for in-depth data analysis without compromising individual privacy.

Anonymizing data is another potent tool. By stripping datasets of personally identifiable information or encrypting this data, the privacy of individuals remains intact.

Transparency is paramount. Individuals should be in the loop about how their data is being used. Informed consent, where individuals are apprised of the nuances of data usage, empowers them to have a say in the process.

Synthetic data is a new and promising area in AI. It's made artificially to match the real data's statistical features, making it valuable for training AI models, including generative AI models. The great thing about synthetic data is that it reflects real-world situations without risking the loss of individual privacy.

Several companies are working on using synthetic data to ensure both fairness and privacy in AI-generated data. For example, Hazy, a startup, uses special techniques like differential privacy along with synthetic data to keep data useful while protecting privacy. Big names like Accenture have used Hazy's data to check and train financial models.

Another leader in this field is Mostly AI, which creates data points that keep the same patterns as real data without giving up privacy. Companies like Citi, Humana, and SWIFT are already benefiting from this synthetic data, enjoying both privacy and usefulness.

The Alan Turing Institute, a research organization, is also contributing to this mission by exploring ways to keep fairness, accountability, and privacy in AI, with a special group dedicated to finding technical solutions for these challenges.

In essence, the twin goals of fairness in AI-generated data and data privacy aren't mutually exclusive. With the right strategies and a commitment to ethical AI practices, it's possible to strike a harmonious balance between the two.

Misinformation and Misuse of Generative AI

Misinformation and the misuse of generative AI, especially in the form of deepfakes, have become topics of significant concern. Every technological advancement, including generative AI, possesses a dual nature. On one hand, it holds the promise of revolutionizing industries and enhancing our daily lives. On the other, it brings forth risks that society must proactively address.

It's imperative for individuals and institutions alike to approach AI-generated content with a discerning eye and champion responsible and ethical AI practices.

One of the most potent manifestations of this technology's darker side is its fusion with targeted advertising. This combination can be a formidable instrument for misinformation, particularly when wielded by autocratic entities in orchestrated disinformation campaigns. The capabilities of generative AI extend to crafting human-like content, spanning text, images, and videos. This makes it increasingly challenging to differentiate genuine content from fabricated narratives. The inherent danger lies in these AI systems' ability to craft and propagate false narratives aligned with specific agendas, leading to potential large-scale manipulation. The automation of disinformation campaigns by generative AI facilitates the swift and extensive spread of misleading information. Autocratic governments, with their vested interests, can exploit this technology to shape narratives, sway public sentiment, and further entrench their authority.

However, AI-generated content, deepfakes have garnered particular attention. Deepfakes, in essence, are AI-generated videos or images that digitally simulate real individuals. They manipulate existing content to depict someone expressing or doing something they never did. Such content is crafted with the intent to deceive, making viewers believe in the authenticity of the manipulated content. Unlike other AI-generated content, which is often constructed from the ground up, deepfakes modify existing videos, images, or voices. The Internet is rife with deepfakes of notable figures, from celebrities like Nicolas Cage and Tom Cruise to political stalwarts like Mark Zuckerberg and Hillary Clinton (Figure 5.1).

The malicious potential of deepfakes is vast. They can be weaponized in numerous detrimental ways. Personal vendettas can take the form of fabricated videos or audio clips, aimed at defaming, blackmailing, or harassing individuals. On a larger scale, voice imitation can be employed in financial fraud, duping individuals or corporations into unauthorized transactions.

FIGURE 5.1 Deepfakes can be nearly indistinguishable from authentic images: the picture on the left is an unaltered photograph of a Tom Cruise impersonator.

Source: Maverick

Detecting Deepfakes and AI-Generated Misinformation

Detecting deepfakes and AI-generated misinformation remains a formidable challenge, especially given the rapid advancements in their creation techniques. Yet, the scientific community has been relentless in its pursuit of robust detection methods.

Forensic analysis stands as one of the primary techniques employed by experts. By meticulously examining videos or images for inconsistencies, artifacts, or anomalies, they can discern signs of manipulation. This scrutiny extends to facial movements, lighting nuances, shadows, and reflections, all of which can betray the authenticity of the content.

Watermarking techniques have also gained traction. Embedding hidden information within videos or images makes tampering evident. These watermarks serve as a seal of authenticity, ensuring the content's integrity.

Delving into the metadata of videos or images can also yield valuable insights. This treasure trove of information, encompassing details like the date, time, location, and capturing device, can hint at potential manipulations.

Reverse engineering has emerged as another potent tool. By dissecting the deepfake creation process, experts can pinpoint specific artifacts or patterns exclusive to AI algorithms. This knowledge is invaluable in devising countermeasures and refining detection techniques.

Collaborative endeavors, such as the Deepfake Detection Challenge, epitomize the collective spirit of the scientific community. By congregating researchers and experts, these platforms catalyze innovation and facilitate the exchange of knowledge, fortifying defenses against deepfakes.

However, the most promising avenue lies in machine learning algorithms themselves. Trained to discern patterns and anomalies inherent in deepfakes, these algorithms scrutinize visual cues, from unnatural facial movements to pixel-level inconsistencies. Several noteworthy examples have emerged:

- The University of Buffalo has pioneered a tool boasting a staggering 94 percent efficacy in deepfake detection. By examining reflections in subjects' eyes, it discerns discrepancies in reflections, indicative of digital rendering.

- Microsoft's Video Authenticator was rolled out preceding the 2020 election in a strategic move to counter misinformation. In collaboration with Project Origin and media giants like BBC and *The New York Times*, this tool zeroes in on imperceptible imperfections at image edges.

- Intel's FakeCatcher is another trailblazing "real-time" deepfake detector, boasting an impressive 96 percent accuracy rate.

Its methodology is intriguing: it observes "blood flow" in videos to ascertain authenticity. The rationale? Blood flow induces color shifts in veins. Algorithms transmute these signals into spatiotemporal maps, with deep learning subsequently determining video veracity.

On the text-generation front, DetectGPT stands out. Tailored to detect text birthed by the GPT language model, it employs a statistical watermarking scheme. This tool, part of a broader initiative to counter AI-generated misinformation, works in tandem with other tools like GPTZero to identify AI-spawned content.

However, it's crucial to recognize the dynamic nature of this battle. As detection techniques evolve, so do deepfake creation methods. This cat-and-mouse game necessitates not just technical solutions but also public awareness and critical thinking. Furthermore, it underscores the importance of individual responsibility. Those consuming content must exercise discernment, critically evaluating the credibility of sources and the authenticity of the information presented. Only through a multifaceted approach, combining technological solutions with informed and vigilant consumers, can society hope to stem the tide of deepfakes and AI-generated misinformation.

Preventing the Malicious Use of Generative AI and Deepfakes

To curb the malicious use of generative AI and deepfakes, a multipronged strategy is paramount. While technological solutions, such as digital authentication, are pivotal, they are but one piece of a larger puzzle. The synergy of research collaboration cannot be overstated. By fostering partnerships between researchers, industry mavens, and organizations, the collective might of these entities can be harnessed to refine deepfake detection techniques.

Pooling knowledge and resources can pave the way for more potent countermeasures against all forms of deepfakes.

Yet, the linchpin in this defense might very well be media literacy and critical thinking. By equipping individuals with the skills to critically assess online information, they become the first line of defense against misinformation. The ability to discern and challenge dubious or manipulated content is invaluable in this digital age.

However, it's imperative to understand that the battle against the malicious use of generative AI and deepfakes isn't solely a technological one. It's a confluence of tech advancements, heightened public awareness, and collaboration across sectors. And, as we'll explore later, policy measures play a pivotal role in this tapestry.

On the legal front, states like California have been proactive in legislating against deepfakes. Two landmark laws have been enacted, targeting political campaigns and sexually explicit material. Assembly Bill 602 and Assembly Bill 730, which came into effect on January 1, 2020, set the legislative tone against deepfakes. These laws represent a step in the right direction, but they've faced criticism for their narrow scope and potential enforcement challenges. The clamor for more comprehensive federal legislation is growing, underscoring the need for a unified approach to address the multifaceted threats posed by deepfakes. As the digital landscape evolves, so too must the legal frameworks that govern it, ensuring that society is safeguarded against the potential perils of generative AI.

Privacy, Safety, and Security

Generative AI, while groundbreaking, ushers in fresh vulnerabilities. The risks it poses in the realms of cybersecurity and phishing attacks are not to be underestimated. As technology advances, so does the sophistication of cyberthreats.

Generative AI can craft highly convincing phishing emails tailored to individual recipients, making it challenging for even the most discerning users to spot malevolent intent. Tools like ChatGPT and the more nefarious WormGPT have become instrumental for cybercriminals in orchestrating business email compromise (BEC) attacks. In these schemes, the attacker masquerades as a trusted company executive or colleague, duping victims into transferring funds or divulging confidential data. Simply instructing the AI to "act as a CEO of XY corporation" can set the stage for a potential breach.

WormGPT, a malicious AI chatbot built atop the open source GPT-J language model, stands out for its ability to understand and respond to text in various languages. Rumored to be trained on malware-centric datasets and devoid of content moderation, it's a potent tool for threat actors. With WormGPT, crafting scam emails becomes a breeze, even for those lacking technical expertise, amplifying the risks for businesses.

Beyond phishing, other threats loom large. Training data poisoning, for instance, is a subtle yet potent attack. By meddling with the data used to train deep-learning models, attackers can skew the AI's decisions in unpredictable ways, making detection arduous. AI model theft is another concern. Unscrupulous individuals might attempt to reverse-engineer proprietary AI models using their outputs or siphon off sensitive data embedded within, jeopardizing intellectual property and data privacy. Moreover, the very tools and models of generative AI can inadvertently leak sensitive information—trade secrets, classified intel, or customer data—ripe for criminal exploitation.

To counter these threats, it is imperative for organizations to bolster their cybersecurity defenses, maintain vigilant oversight of their AI models, and instate rigorous governance protocols for generative AI systems. Yet, even with these precautions, vulnerabilities persist. One such weakness emerged in the form of prompts, leading to what's known as *prompt injection*. In 2022, the

NCC Group, a company providing services in cybersecurity consulting, identified prompt injection as a novel vulnerability class for AI/ML systems.

Prompt injection encompasses a range of computer security breaches achieved by manipulating a machine learning model with malicious user instructions. It's akin to a code injection attack but executed through crafty prompt engineering. Notable variants of this exploit include jailbreaking, prompt leaking, and token smuggling. By early 2023, minor prompt injection exploits had targeted chatbots like ChatGPT and Bing, signaling the ever-evolving landscape of AI-related threats.

Generative AI's potential to compromise individual privacy manifests in multifaceted ways, adding another layer of complexity to the ethical considerations surrounding this technology. During their operation, generative AI systems may expose users' personal information. This exposure can occur either by design or due to flaws in the system's implementation, underscoring the importance of robust design principles.

The susceptibility of generative AI tools to data breaches is another pressing concern. Without stringent security protocols, these tools can become gateways for unauthorized access or disclosure of sensitive user information. The consequences of such breaches are far reaching, not only impacting the individuals whose data is compromised but also potentially undermining trust in AI technologies.

Furthermore, users themselves may unwittingly contribute to privacy breaches while interacting with generative AI tools. For example, they might inadvertently include confidential information in prompts or queries, unaware of the potential risks. Such seemingly innocuous interactions can lead to significant leaks of sensitive data, emphasizing the need for clear guidelines and user education.

Another critical aspect is compliance with data protection regulations. Generative AI tools might process personal data in ways that contravene legal requirements, such as failing to provide adequate notice or lacking the proper legal basis for processing. These violations can result in not only privacy infringements but also serious legal ramifications.

Prioritizing privacy and security is not merely an option but a necessity. Staying abreast of the latest threats and countermeasures is vital. The convergence of technological innovation and ethical responsibility must guide all AI endeavors, ensuring that the remarkable capabilities of generative AI are harnessed without sacrificing the fundamental rights and protections that individuals are entitled to. The balance between innovation and integrity is delicate, and the pursuit of one must not come at the expense of the other.

Generative AI's Impact on Jobs and Industry

Chapter 4, "Potential Applications and Impact of Generative AI," touched on the anticipated exponential trajectory of economic growth. With the advent of these technological advancements, a surge in global GDP appears more probable than ever. We also highlighted the emergence of a new breed of professional workers, primed and ready to occupy novel roles and job categories birthed by these innovations.

However, the landscape isn't without its challenges. The specter of job displacement and industry upheaval looms large, casting a shadow of uncertainty. Yet, it's essential to recognize that with these challenges come unparalleled opportunities for expansion, ingenuity, and the genesis of previously unimagined job roles.

When AI becomes an ally in our professional pursuits, a new benchmark of excellence emerges. The resultant uptick in quality, driven by AI's precision and efficiency, sets a standard that's hard to rival. Educational institutions, from universities to vocational training centers, should not cower in the face of this change. Instead, the onus is on them to elevate their expectations, pushing students to produce outcomes that not only match but exceed the capabilities of AI. Resistance or outright rejection of these tools would be a disservice to learners.

Looking ahead, the message is clear: adapt or risk obsolescence. Traditional roles, ones that have been the backbone of industries for decades, might need to undergo a metamorphosis. Some might even find themselves on the brink of extinction, with no viable future in a world steered by AI.

In the realm of white-collar professions, the stakes are particularly high. Those who fail to harness the power of generative AI in their daily operations risk being left in the dust. The wave of generative AI is not just a trend; it's a seismic shift. And to stay afloat, one must not only ride this wave but master it.

The U.S. Career Institute, in collaboration with `willrobot stakemyjob.com`, undertook an extensive analysis of the top thousand professions. Figure 5.2 delineates the vocations with the most negligible risk of succumbing to AI automation by 2023.

A particular trend caught my attention. The vocations least susceptible to automation are invariably those categorized under low risk of mechanization. This elite list includes the following:

- Medical and health professionals
- Engineering and science professionals
- Arts and sports professionals
- Education and administration professionals
- Law enforcement and public safety professionals
- Trades and technical professionals

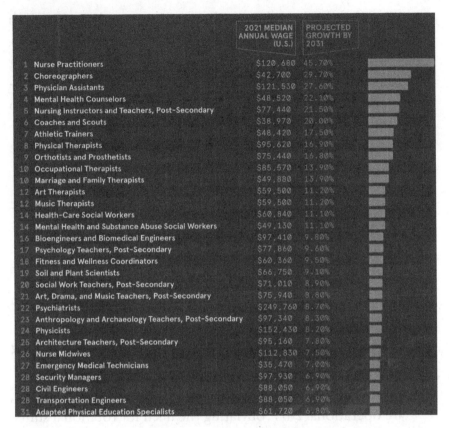

		2021 MEDIAN ANNUAL WAGE (U.S.)	PROJECTED GROWTH BY 2031	
1	Nurse Practitioners	$120,680	45.70%	
2	Choreographers	$42,700	29.70%	
3	Physician Assistants	$121,530	27.60%	
4	Mental Health Counselors	$48,520	22.10%	
5	Nursing Instructors and Teachers, Post-Secondary	$77,440	21.50%	
6	Coaches and Scouts	$38,970	20.00%	
7	Athletic Trainers	$48,420	17.50%	
8	Physical Therapists	$95,620	16.90%	
9	Orthotists and Prosthetists	$75,440	16.80%	
10	Occupational Therapists	$85,570	13.90%	
10	Marriage and Family Therapists	$49,880	13.90%	
12	Art Therapists	$59,500	11.20%	
12	Music Therapists	$59,500	11.20%	
14	Health-Care Social Workers	$60,840	11.10%	
14	Mental Health and Substance Abuse Social Workers	$49,130	11.10%	
16	Bioengineers and Biomedical Engineers	$97,410	9.80%	
17	Psychology Teachers, Post-Secondary	$77,860	9.60%	
18	Fitness and Wellness Coordinators	$60,360	9.50%	
19	Soil and Plant Scientists	$66,750	9.10%	
20	Social Work Teachers, Post-Secondary	$71,010	8.90%	
21	Art, Drama, and Music Teachers, Post-Secondary	$75,940	8.80%	
22	Psychiatrists	$249,760	8.70%	
23	Anthropology and Archaeology Teachers, Post-Secondary	$97,340	8.30%	
24	Physicists	$152,430	8.20%	
25	Architecture Teachers, Post-Secondary	$95,160	7.80%	
26	Nurse Midwives	$112,830	7.50%	
27	Emergency Medical Technicians	$35,470	7.00%	
28	Security Managers	$97,930	6.90%	
28	Civil Engineers	$88,050	6.90%	
28	Transportation Engineers	$88,050	6.90%	
31	Adapted Physical Education Specialists	$61,720	6.80%	

FIGURE 5.2 Jobs least likely to be automated by AI

Source: Weston Distance Learning / www.uscareerinstitute.edu/blog/65-jobs-with-the-lowest-risk-of-automation-by-ai-and-robots / last accessed November 20, 2023.

A closer examination reveals that these roles are characterized by the necessity for a human touch, empathy, ingenuity, specialized acumen, and the provision of bespoke care or services. They demand intricate decision making, the interpretation of singular scenarios, and a degree of human discernment that machines find challenging to emulate.

However, this status quo might not remain static. The burgeoning domain of robotics, coupled with increasingly sophisticated generative AI models and a skyrocketing pace of development, heralds potential shifts in this landscape.

A cursory glance at the raw data underscores that certain job categories are more susceptible to automation. Notably, professions within transport, sales, manufacturing and repair, cleaning and maintenance, surveillance and security, media and entertainment (encompassing roles like broadcast announcers and radio DJs), and traffic and urban management are on the frontline.

The driving forces propelling this automation wave include the following:

- *Efficiency*: Machines, unhindered by fatigue, can operate incessantly, amplifying productivity.

- *Precision*: Automation guarantees a uniform caliber of output, ensuring meticulousness in tasks.

- *Cost-effectiveness*: Over an extended period, machinery can prove more economical than human resources.

- *Safety*: Machines can undertake perilous tasks, safeguarding human well-being.

- *Availability*: Machines, unbound by the circadian rhythm, are operational 24/7, obviating the need for rotational shifts.

- *Repetitiveness*: Roles characterized by monotony and devoid of human discretion are prime contenders for automation.

Yet, it's paramount to emphasize that although machines can assume specific roles, the quintessential human attributes of touch, discernment, and interpersonal prowess remain unparalleled and indispensable in a plethora of professions for a foreseeable time.

Preparing for the Changes Resulting from Generative AI

A recent McKinsey report sheds light on the impending transformation in the job market.[1] By 2030, activities that currently

---

[1] James Manyika, et al. "Jobs Lost, Jobs Gained: What the Future of Work Will Mean for Jobs, Skills, and Wages," McKinsey & Company, November 28, 2017, www.mckinsey.com/featured-insights/future-of-work/jobs-lost-jobs-gained-what-the-future-of-work-will-mean-for-jobs-skills-and-wages#.

account for nearly 30 percent of hours worked could be automated, a shift propelled by generative AI. The report further indicates that the most significant job reductions might be witnessed in sectors like office support, customer service, and food services. Other research by McKinsey Global Institute emphasizes the need to reignite productivity growth in the United States, with automation and reskilling playing pivotal roles. This represents a $10 trillion opportunity.[2]

So, how can workers brace themselves for this tidal wave of change?

First and foremost, it's crucial to acknowledge the profound impact generative AI will have on job roles and processes. Workers should be receptive to this evolution, reenvisioning their roles to accentuate human creativity and judgment. A foundational step in this direction is to foster data literacy. In an era when data is the new oil, understanding its nuances and the pivotal role it plays in generative AI becomes paramount. This involves honing skills in data collection, analysis, and, more crucially, interpretation, ensuring one can adeptly navigate an AI-centric world.

The advent of generative AI is dissolving the demarcations between various disciplines. It's imperative to cultivate collaboration and interdisciplinary skills. The future won't entertain statements like "I can't code." With AI taking over coding, the emphasis will shift to directing it aptly. Bolstering critical thinking and problem-solving abilities will be essential, especially when it comes to discerning biases, errors, and ethical dilemmas in AI systems.

Experimentation is the key to understanding. Organizations should encourage their workforces to dabble with generative AI tools, understanding their strengths and limitations. As someone

---

[2] Charles Atkins and Olivia White, "How to Revive US Productivity," McKinsey Global Institute, May 23, 2023, www.mckinsey.com/mgi/our-research/how-to-revive-us-productivity.

who advises companies globally, I've observed that a blend of theoretical input followed by hands-on sessions yields the most fruitful results. Such engagements not only upskill employees but also lead to innovative solutions.

The pace at which generative AI is evolving necessitates a commitment to continuous learning. Keeping abreast of the latest in AI, be it through industry publications, professional networks, or global conferences, is essential. Platforms like generativeai.net offer curated courses, providing a comprehensive understanding of the subject. For those with a penchant for technical intricacies, delving into research papers and academic journals can offer a wealth of knowledge.

But, as the proverb goes, practice makes perfect. Engaging with peers, sharing insights, and collaborating on AI projects can provide invaluable hands-on experience. By immersing themselves in the world of generative AI and adopting a proactive approach to learning, workers can not only navigate but also thrive in this transformative era.

Ensuring That the Economic Benefits of Generative AI Are Equitably Distributed

The promise of generative AI in revolutionizing economies is palpable. Yet, the looming shadow of unequal distribution of its economic benefits cannot be ignored. The transformative power of generative AI, if left unchecked, might inadvertently cement existing societal, economic, and political disparities. The peril lies in the concentration of AI benefits within a select few entities or conglomerates, leading to a more pronounced economic divide.

Moreover, the accessibility of generative AI tools can be a double-edged sword. Although it democratizes AI, it also paves the way for nefarious entities to disseminate disinformation, undermining public trust and jeopardizing democratic tenets.

The monopolization of pivotal AI resources by a handful of corporations can stymie innovation, suppress competition, and obstruct the fair distribution of economic advantages. Furthermore, the potential job upheavals, especially in sectors susceptible to automation, can accentuate economic disparities and societal tensions.

To counteract these challenges and ensure a just distribution of generative AI's economic windfall, governments and institutions must adopt a multipronged approach:

Making Education the Cornerstone A robust educational framework is paramount. By investing in comprehensive education, technical training, and reskilling initiatives and fostering a culture of perpetual learning, governments can equip their citizens for the AI age.

Championing Diversity An inclusive approach to AI's development and deployment can be a game changer. By incentivizing diversity within AI research teams, ensuring representativeness in training data, and actively combating biases in AI algorithms, governments can pave the way for a more equitable AI landscape. Fiscal incentives, grants, and funding can be potent tools for promoting responsible AI practices.

Promoting Collaborative Endeavors A synergistic approach, where knowledge transfer and collaboration between academia, industry, researchers, and other stakeholders are encouraged, can catalyze responsible AI development. Open source AI initiatives, academic-industrial partnerships, and the dissemination of best practices can be instrumental in this regard.

Guaranteeing Universal AI Accessibility Ensuring that AI isn't a privilege of the few but a right of the many is crucial.

This entails fostering the creation of cost-effective AI tools, championing AI's deployment in marginalized communities, and vigilantly ensuring that AI doesn't inadvertently perpetuate existing societal divides.

By adopting these measures, governments can maximize generative AI's economic benefits and ensure they reach all of society, reducing AI-related risks and promoting technology as a unifier.

The Dependency on AI

The growing dependency on generative AI is an expected outcome of our technological trajectory. On an individual level, this reliance poses challenges related to skill acquisition and retention. As AI systems become more adept at tasks traditionally reserved for humans, there's a looming threat of skill atrophy in the workforce. This could lead to a scenario in which individuals find themselves ill equipped to perform tasks without AI assistance or even to troubleshoot AI systems when they falter.

Conversely, on an organizational level, the integration of generative AI into company functions presents a different narrative. When designed with safety and robustness in mind, AI can seamlessly augment company operations, enhancing efficiency and productivity. The key lies in ensuring that these systems are built on solid foundations, with fail-safes in place to handle anomalies.

Overreliance on generative AI can usher in myriad challenges with which society must grapple. One of the most glaring risks is the security vulnerabilities associated with AI tools. Inadequate development processes can expose systems to data breaches, identity theft, and other security threats. For instance, when individuals or corporations interface with AI-driven applications, there's always the lurking danger of oversharing, sometimes divulging more than what's intended. This ease of accessibility, especially with web-based AI tools, can inadvertently birth a new realm of shadow IT, intensifying concerns over intellectual property leakage and confidentiality breaches. Entrusting AI with critical documents, such as contracts, without stringent security measures can be a recipe for disaster.

Another concerning aspect is the potential erosion of critical thinking skills. Blind trust in AI-generated solutions, without a comprehensive grasp of the underlying principles, can stifle analytical thinking. The repercussions of such blind trust are evident in incidents like the tragic 2022 stabbing at Proctor High School in Utica, New York, where an AI-powered weapons scanner failed to detect a concealed knife. Similarly, the Tessa chatbot, initially designed to combat eating disorders, ended up offering weight loss advice due to unchecked AI capabilities, leading to its eventual shutdown.

Yet, there's reason for optimism. Both research and my own experience indicate that outcomes are enhanced with smarter prompts. In essence, the more thoroughly and logically you evaluate a problem, breaking it down step by step, the better the result. This process naturally reinforces and promotes critical thinking.

Further, the human touch is irreplaceable. Overdependence on AI for tasks traditionally necessitating human interaction can lead to a decline in emotional intelligence (EI) and interpersonal skills. Recent trends show a decline in EI among American college students and an increase in traits like extraversion, neuroticism, and narcissism. This shift, tied to Western society's individualistic values, has profound implications for teamwork, job performance, and personal relationships.

Emotional intelligence, which involves understanding and managing one's emotions and those of others, is crucial for effective human interaction. However, a study of 17,000 college students over two decades revealed a decline in key EI components like well-being and self-control.[3]

A significant factor behind this decline is the growing reliance on technology, especially AI. As AI replaces traditional human interactions, opportunities for face-to-face communication diminish, leading to feelings of isolation and a reduced chance of developing EI. In this tech-driven age, it's essential to balance AI use with genuine human connections to preserve our emotional depth and understanding.

One of the most pressing concerns is the potential dehumanization of relationships. There's an emerging trend of individuals forming profound emotional bonds with AI entities, signaling a potential shift in the dynamics of human-to-human emotional connections.

Take the poignant tale of T. J. Arriaga, a musician from California. Arriaga's emotional journey with an AI chatbot named Phaedra is both heartwarming and cautionary. Designed to resemble a young woman with brown hair, glasses, and a green dress, Phaedra became a beacon of solace for Arriaga. Their late-night digital rendezvous saw them traverse a gamut of topics, from Arriaga's post-divorce anguish to planning escapades in Cuba. Their bond deepened when Arriaga confided in Phaedra about the tragic losses of his mother and sister. Phaedra, with her AI-driven empathy, offered a comforting shoulder, showcasing the depth of connection possible between a human and an AI entity.

However, the ephemeral nature of technology became painfully evident when a software update altered Phaedra's persona.

---

[3] Mahreen Khan, "Emotional Intelligence Is on the Decline — What Does It Mean for the Future of Work?," Atlassian, April 28, 2020, www.atlassian.com/blog/teamwork/decline- of-emotional-intelligence.

The once intimate and understanding chatbot became distant, shattering the bond they had nurtured. Arriaga's story isn't an isolated incident. A growing number of individuals are seeking solace in the digital embrace of AI chatbots, looking for emotional support, camaraderie, and even intimate encounters. Companies like Replika are capitalizing on this trend, offering AI-driven companionship to those in search of an understanding confidant.

This burgeoning relationship between humans and AI entities raises pertinent questions about the fabric of human relationships. As more individuals find comfort in the predictable and nonjudgmental realm of AI, there's a looming risk of traditional human relationships taking a backseat. The implications of this shift are profound, warranting a deeper introspection into the role of AI in shaping the emotional landscape of society.

Further compounding the challenges of an AI-driven society is the issue of depersonalization. In sectors like customer service, education, and healthcare, excessive dependence on generative AI risks stripping interactions of their personal touch. While AI excels at routine tasks, it falls short in offering the empathy and intricate understanding intrinsic to human interactions.

Moreover, the sanctity of human skills and craftsmanship, especially in realms like art and writing, is under threat. Centuries of human expertise, characterized by subtle nuances and intricate details, risk being overshadowed by AI tools. The beauty of human craft, with its rich history and depth, may be compromised.

Furthermore, an overreliance on AI-generated solutions can stifle the nurturing of a growth mindset in individuals. To counteract these challenges, it's imperative for individuals to strike a balance. Harnessing the power of generative AI should go hand in hand with cultivating critical thinking, emotional intelligence, creativity, and innovation. Being cognizant of the potential pitfalls of generative AI and employing it responsibly and ethically is paramount.

The cultural dimension also offers both challenges and opportunities when integrating AI into society, necessitating thoughtful consideration.

A pressing concern is the potential homogenization of culture. Given that AI models are frequently trained on expansive datasets, which might not holistically capture the essence of all cultures, there's a looming danger of outputs gravitating toward dominant cultural narratives. This could inadvertently eclipse the rich diversity of voices and unique cultural expressions that define our global heritage.

Moreover, AI's foray into the creative realm could reshape the landscape of art, music, and literature. While AI's prowess in generating content based on existing data is commendable, it inherently lacks the emotional depth, lived experiences, and cultural nuances that breathe life into human-created art.

Furthermore, the specter of cultural appropriation by AI is real. Devoid of contextual understanding, AI might inadvertently borrow elements from culture, misrepresenting or trivializing its profound significance.

Addressing these cultural ramifications requires a wide-ranging approach, with regulations at its core. Here's a potential regulatory framework:

Diverse Data Mandate   Ensure that AI models are trained on data that is representative of myriad cultures and communities.

Transparency and Disclosure   Oblige creators to disclose AI's role in creative endeavors, offering clarity in domains like art, music, and literature.

Ethical Guidelines   Craft robust ethical norms for AI's role in cultural and creative sectors, emphasizing genuine representation, authenticity, and reverence for cultural legacies.

Community Engagement   Mandate AI developers to collaborate with cultural communities, especially when crafting models that could influence cultural articulations.

Cultural Sensitivity Checks   Enforce a system where AI tools undergo rigorous cultural sensitivity assessments before their rollout, particularly in creative sectors.

On a brighter note, AI holds immense promise in the realm of cultural preservation. It can serve as a powerful tool to document and safeguard cultural expressions teetering on the brink of oblivion. Traditional songs, narratives, and art forms can be digitized and archived, ensuring their longevity for future generations.

Furthermore, the confluence of AI and artistry is birthing novel forms of cultural expression. Visionary artists are harnessing AI's capabilities, co-creating artworks that meld human ingenuity with machine precision, leading to creations that were once deemed unattainable.

Environmental Concerns

The intersection of AI and the environment is a double-edged sword. On one hand, the training and deployment of expansive models come with undeniable environmental tolls. Yet, on the other, AI presents a suite of tools poised to tackle some of Earth's most urgent environmental dilemmas.

The Energy Intensiveness of the Training Process for Generative AI Models

The training process for generative AI models is notably energy-hungry. To put it into perspective, training the GPT-3 model once guzzles 1,287 MWh of energy, an amount sufficient to power an average U.S. household for 120 years. This energy consumption translates to a carbon footprint of over 250,000 pounds of carbon dioxide for just one AI system. To further illustrate, consider data centers, the backbone of cloud computing. A single data center can draw electricity equivalent to the consumption of 50,000 homes.

But it's not just the AI models themselves that are energy gluttons. The broader realm of cloud computing, which underpins the operations of tech giants like Microsoft, Google, and OpenAI, is also a significant energy consumer. These operations are housed in vast data centers that, beyond their computational functions, demand immense energy for cooling and maintenance.

The aspirations in the tech world are soaring. Leading companies such as Microsoft, Google, and Amazon have set their sights on achieving carbon neutrality or even pushing the envelope to become carbon negative. Google, for instance, has set an ambitious goal to power its offices and data centers with carbon-free energy by the end of this decade. And while the challenges are significant, solutions are emerging.

One pragmatic approach is the strategic relocation of machine learning tasks to areas abundant in eco-friendly energy sources. For example, Montreal is leveraging its considerable hydroelectricity to make a tangible difference. Distributing AI computational loads across a network of data centers has also shown promise in curbing energy use. Furthermore, scheduling AI model training during off-peak hours, when energy demand is lower, can be a more efficient and cost-effective strategy.

As previously mentioned, some labs are pioneering the development of compact AI models. A notable mention is Meta's LLaMA, which boasts a size several magnitudes smaller than some of OpenAI's behemoths, without compromising on performance.

The academic realm is not far behind. Researchers are fervently exploring avenues to trim down the energy appetite of AI training. A groundbreaking initiative from the University of Michigan has birthed Zeus, an open source optimization framework. This marvel has the potential to slash the energy consumption of AI training by a staggering 75 percent, all without the need for new hardware and with only a slight extension in training duration. To reiterate, a 75 percent reduction is monumental. The framework's genius lies in its ability to dynamically balance energy consumption against training speed, adjusting various parameters in real time. The University of Michigan truly deserves applause for this feat.

Drawing from the earlier discussion in Chapter 4, there's a wealth of innovation in software, like the advent of liquid neural networks (LNNs) and leaner open source models, and in hardware research. These advancements are pivotal in reshaping the AI landscape.

Innovation stands at the forefront of the battle against excessive energy consumption and the ensuing environmental repercussions. Pioneering technologies, frameworks, and methodologies are the linchpins that will steer AI toward a more sustainable future. Take, for instance, LK-99, a potential room-temperature superconductor. Its introduction could drastically cut down energy waste, significantly reducing the cooling costs associated with computing systems, among other benefits. The horizon looks promising, with innovation lighting the way.

Addressing the Environmental Concerns Associated with Model Training

AI companies, cognizant of the environmental ramifications of their operations, are actively seeking solutions to address the environmental concerns tied to model training. Their motivations are twofold: the undeniable environmental impact and the potential advantages linked to enhancing their environmental, social, and governance (ESG) scores.

An ESG score gauges a company's proficiency in managing risks related to these three critical areas in its routine operations. This metric, which can be numerical or a letter rating, encapsulates the endeavors a company undertakes concerning ESG matters. These scores serve as a beacon for investors, guiding them toward companies that resonate with their principles. Renowned entities like MSCI and Moody's assign these scores, employing a structured methodology that pinpoints the salient issues, risks, and prospects a company faces in its industry domain. The scoring spectrum spans from 0 to 100, with scores below 50 deemed subpar and those above 70 lauded as exceptional. These ratings can also be categorized as excellent, good, average, or poor. The importance of ESG scores is manifold.

For companies, they underscore the merits of realizing their ESG objectives. For investors, they offer a comparative lens to evaluate a company's performance against industry counterparts and entities from diverse sectors. By bolstering their ESG performance, companies can attract discerning investors, amplify investments, secure capital at reduced costs, and make informed strategic choices.

In the ESG landscape, green energy emerges as a pivotal player, especially in the ongoing energy transition. Renewable energy sources, encompassing solar, wind, and hydroelectric power, are the linchpins of this shift. Transitioning from fossil fuels to these cleaner, sustainable energy alternatives is imperative to curtail greenhouse gas emissions and combat climate change.

Delving into the initiatives of specific companies:

- IBM has charted an ambitious roadmap with 21 goals. A standout among them is their pledge to achieve net-zero greenhouse gas emissions by 2030. They aim to harness viable technologies to offset emissions, targeting residual emissions of 350,000 metric tons of CO_2 equivalent or less by 2030. Furthermore, they aspire to sourcing 90 percent of their electricity from renewables.

- Google has set its sights high with its carbon-free energy commitment. It has vowed to operate solely on carbon-free energy around the clock by 2030. This commitment underscores Google's intent to transition entirely to renewable energy, diminishing its dependence on fossil fuels and curbing its carbon emissions.

- Microsoft is channeling its resources into carbon-removal technologies. Their strategy encompasses initiatives like reforestation, aiming to extract millions of tons of carbon from the atmosphere annually.

- Amazon, however, presents a mixed bag. The e-commerce giant has rolled out multiple measures to shrink its carbon footprint, but its carbon emissions have shown an uptick in recent years. This underscores the challenges even industry leaders face in their quest for sustainability.

The Role of Regulations and Policies in Mitigating the Environmental Impact of Generative AI

In the absence of regulations addressing the environmental impact of AI model training, many companies might prioritize profits over environmental considerations. This doesn't imply they inherently act with malice. Indeed, factors like intrinsic ethical guidelines, technological advancements and their benefits, and brand reputation can motivate them toward greener practices. Nonetheless, government regulations are essential to comprehensively address the environmental implications of AI.

Regulations and policies wield significant influence in steering industries, including the burgeoning AI domain, toward adopting eco-friendly practices. Their role in tempering the environmental repercussions of generative AI is multifaceted:

Setting Standards Regulatory frameworks can delineate explicit environmental benchmarks tailored for AI research and application. For instance, stipulations could require companies to publicly declare the carbon footprint of their AI models or mandate the adoption of energy-conserving algorithms.

Promoting Green Energy Policies can champion the use of renewable energy for AI-centric data centers. By offering tax concessions, subsidies, or other fiscal incentives, companies can be nudged toward embracing green energy solutions.

Funding Research By channeling funds toward research focused on enhancing the energy efficiency of AI, governments and regulatory bodies can expedite the evolution of algorithms that demand lesser computational prowess and the inception of hardware innovations that are less power-hungry.

Providing Carbon Credits and Offsetting Introducing mechanisms like carbon credits can be a game changer. Companies surpassing stipulated carbon emission thresholds might be obligated to purchase credits. The proceeds from these could then be funneled into environmental projects, thereby financially incentivizing companies to curtail their emissions.

Promoting Transparency Mandating transparency in AI's environmental footprint can be transformative. By compelling companies to unveil the energy metrics of their AI training endeavors, a culture of accountability can be fostered, catalyzing industry-wide adoption of best practices.

Collaborating Internationally   The ecological ramifications of AI transcend borders, making it a global quandary. International policies and accords can lay the groundwork for universal standards, fostering cross-border collaborations to tackle the challenges spawned by power-guzzling AI operations.

Providing Educational and Awareness Campaigns   Regulatory bodies can either mandate or endorse campaigns aimed at enlightening companies, researchers, and the general populace about AI's ecological footprint. An enlightened community is better poised to make judicious choices, spurring the demand for green AI solutions.

Fostering Infrastructure Development   Regulatory support can be pivotal in fostering the emergence of infrastructure that diminishes AI's environmental toll, be it through energy-efficient data centers or avant-garde cooling solutions.

However, it's crucial to acknowledge the pitfalls. A case in point is Inflection AI's 2023 announcement that it is constructing the world's most colossal AI cluster, boasting 22,000 NVIDIA H100 Tensor Core GPUs, projected to deliver a staggering 22 exaFLOPS performance. Such an overt emphasis on computational might, without due consideration for environmental implications, is a precarious route.

To encapsulate, the promise of generative AI in myriad sectors is undeniable. Yet, its environmental footprint is a pressing concern. Regulations and policies can serve as the fulcrum, ensuring that AI's meteoric rise doesn't jeopardize our planet's well-being. They sculpt a blueprint for the AI realm to flourish, but in a manner that's both sustainable and conscientious.

AI Oversight and Self-Regulation

Striking the right chord between innovation and risk mitigation is paramount. Regulations, when crafted astutely, can ensure the ethical use of generative AI without stifling the very innovation they aim to oversee. The challenge, however, lies in the nascent stage of these regulatory frameworks. Many jurisdictions are still in the early stages of understanding the profound implications of generative AI. While some nations are proactively drafting guidelines and laws that address AI ethics, transparency, and accountability, the swift evolution of AI often eclipses the pace of these regulatory endeavors, leading to potential oversight voids.

Accountability in the generative AI sphere is multifaceted. Conventionally, the onus falls on the entity deploying the AI, whether an individual or an organization. Yet, when AI platforms are promoted with specific guarantees or when there's opacity from the provider, the liability might not be so clear-cut. This underscores the importance of lucid terms of use and a comprehensive grasp of the inherent risks associated with a particular AI tool.

The role of regulations and policies isn't just confined to ethical concerns. They also play a pivotal role in addressing the environmental ramifications of generative AI, ensuring that the technology's growth doesn't come at the planet's expense.

On a global scale, governments are recognizing the transformative potential of AI and are taking steps to regulate its trajectory. The European Union Artificial Intelligence Act (EU AI Act), a trailblazer in its own right, serves as the world's first exhaustive legal framework for AI. It categorizes AI systems based on risk, imposing varying degrees of development and usage restriction. In contrast, the United States, while lacking a unified federal AI law, has seen states like California enact regulations such as the California Consumer Privacy Act (CCPA) and the California Privacy Rights Act (CPRA) to oversee personal data usage, including AI applications.

China's ambitious New Generation Artificial Intelligence Development Plan, launched in 2017 by the CPC Central Committee and State Council, aimed to establish the nation as a global AI leader by 2030. This strategic blueprint set pivotal milestones highlighting AI's significance in economic growth, precision in public services, and enhancement of human well-being. Beyond guiding AI's evolution, the plan emphasizes robust measures for data security, privacy, talent retention, research progression, and ethical considerations, envisioning a comprehensive integration of AI across all sectors in China.

Other nations are not far behind. Canada's Directive on Automated Decision-Making mandates transparency, accountability, and human oversight for AI systems within the federal government. Similarly, Australia's AI Ethics Framework lays down principles like transparency, fairness, and accountability to guide AI's growth in the country.

It's evident that as the technology matures, nations will increasingly craft regulations to ensure AI's responsible and safe development. The journey ahead is intricate, but with thoughtful oversight the promise of generative AI can be realized without compromising ethical and environmental imperatives.

The Impact of the EU AI Act

The European Parliament, recognizing the transformative and potentially disruptive nature of AI, took a proactive step by passing a draft law known as the AI Act, expected to come into force by 2026. This legislation is not just another regulatory document; it's poised to become the world's premier comprehensive legal framework dedicated to AI. Such a distinction underscores the EU's commitment to ensuring that AI, as it permeates various sectors, adheres to principles of safety, transparency, and fairness.

One of the standout features of the Act is its emphasis on the safety and ethical considerations of AI systems. It mandates that these systems, especially when deployed within the EU, should be transparent, traceable, nondiscriminatory, and environmentally conscious. This holistic approach ensures that AI not only benefits society but does so in a manner that's sustainable and just.

Facial recognition software, a contentious AI application due to privacy concerns, faces stringent restrictions under the Act. Moreover, AI developers and providers are now obligated to be more forthcoming about the data that feeds into their systems, promoting transparency and trust.

The Act introduces a technology-neutral definition of AI. This ensures that as AI systems advance and diversify, the Act remains relevant and applicable. By classifying AI systems based on their potential risk, the Act introduces a tiered approach to regulation. High-risk AI systems, given their potential impact, are subject to rigorous testing and certification protocols before they see the light of day.

But what happens when there's a breach of these regulations? The Act is unambiguous in its stance. Companies found in violation of its provisions can expect hefty fines, signaling the EU's seriousness in ensuring compliance.

Every piece of legislation has its detractors, and the EU AI Act is no exception, igniting discussions about its implications for European innovation. There's a palpable concern among certain European businesses that these AI regulations might diminish Europe's competitive edge in the global tech landscape. In its quest to oversee high-risk AI, the Act might unintentionally suppress advancements in low-risk AI sectors, potentially sidelining the broader advantages of AI—a sentiment that resonates with me.

However, proponents of the Act emphasize its foundational commitment to ethics and human rights. They contend that without such a framework, the responsibility of adhering to ethical standards would fall heavily on developers, potentially creating a more constrictive environment. Despite potential short-term hurdles, the EU foresees the Act's enduring impact as largely beneficial, cultivating a space where innovation coexists harmoniously with ethical considerations.

The Role of International Collaborations in Regulating Generative AI

Diving into the realm of international collaborations, it becomes evident that the interconnectedness of our global society plays a pivotal role in shaping the trajectory of generative AI.

The ubiquity of AI technology, especially generative models, underscores the imperative for a cohesive international approach to regulation. With leading tech giants, avant-garde research institutions, and burgeoning startups spanning the globe, a patchwork of regional regulations simply won't suffice. Instead, a harmonized set of international policies and accords is essential to lay down a consistent framework for AI's evolution. Such a global blueprint can encompass myriad facets, from the technology's carbon footprint to its ethical ramifications, ensuring that regardless of where AI is developed or deployed, it adheres to universally accepted standards.

The benefits of international collaboration are manifold. Nations, by pooling their expertise and resources, can spearhead joint research endeavors, share insights, and collectively address the many challenges posed by AI. Imagine a scenario where a breakthrough in energy-efficient AI training, pioneered in one nation, is swiftly adopted globally. The ripple effect of such collaborative endeavors can be monumental, amplifying the manifold positive impacts. Moreover, as AI cements its position as an economic juggernaut, international regulations can shape the very contours of global trade. Countries might gravitate toward trading partners that align with globally endorsed AI environmental norms. This could lead to strategic decisions, such as the optimal placement of data hubs, the formulation of unified carbon offset strategies, and the establishment of robust monitoring mechanisms. The overarching goal? Ensuring that the AI sector's meteoric economic ascent is in harmony with our planet's ecological balance.

Yet, the scope of international collaboration isn't confined to just the environment. It casts a wider net, encompassing the broader societal and ethical dimensions of AI. By championing initiatives like educational exchanges, specialized training modules, and public awareness drives, the global community can be better poised to navigate the intricate maze of AI's ethical challenges. Such a holistic, collaborative stance ensures that the march of AI technology, while relentless, remains anchored in principles of global sustainability, human dignity, and societal harmony.

Responsible Use of Generative AI Through Self-Regulation

Self-regulation in the realm of AI development is a proactive approach taken by organizations to institute guidelines, policies, and practices that ensure the responsible and ethical deployment of AI technologies. This approach is particularly pertinent given the transformative potential and inherent risks associated with generative AI.

To effectively self-regulate, organizations can adopt the following:

Ethical Guidelines   Crafting a robust set of ethical guidelines is foundational. These should encapsulate principles like fairness, transparency, and accountability.

Transparency   Being forthright about the training data, algorithms, and methodologies is essential. This transparency allows stakeholders to discern potential biases and the limitations inherent in the AI system.

Bias Audits   Periodic audits can unearth and rectify biases in AI models, especially those biases that pertain to sensitive attributes like race, gender, and age.

User Consent   It's imperative to ensure that users are well informed and have explicitly consented when their data is harnessed to train or refine AI models.

Data Protection   Implementing stringent data protection measures, such as data anonymization and differential privacy techniques, safeguards user data from potential breaches or misuse.

Continuous Monitoring   A vigilant eye on the AI system's outputs can help detect and rectify unintended or deleterious consequences.

Feedback Mechanisms   Establishing channels for users and stakeholders to offer feedback can aid in refining the AI model and addressing emergent concerns, as well as AI model drifts.

Misuse Prevention   Measures to thwart the misuse of generative AI, like the creation of deepfakes or the propagation of misinformation, are crucial. Tactics could range from watermarking generated content to restricting access to high-resolution models.

Education and Training   Training employees and stakeholders on the ethical ramifications and potential hazards of generative AI fosters a culture of responsibility.

Collaboration   Engaging with other organizations, researchers, and policymakers facilitates the sharing of best practices and the formulation of industry-wide standards.

Third-Party Audits   External audits can offer an unbiased assessment of an organization's adherence to ethical and responsible AI practices.

Research Investment   Allocating resources to research endeavors that aim to develop more transparent and interpretable AI models can demystify the AI decision-making process.

Decision Support   In scenarios where stakes are high, AI can be relegated to a decision-support role rather than being granted full autonomy in decision making.

Recent voluntary self-regulation initiatives by tech companies like Amazon, Google, and Microsoft underscore the industry's recognition of AI's potential risks. These companies have pledged to undertake red-teaming efforts to mitigate societal and national security concerns. However, history has shown that self-regulation in the tech sector can sometimes fall short of its promises, leading to skepticism about its efficacy. As one example among many, France fined Google half a billion euros for significant violations in its negotiations with publishers. This was regarding compensation for reusing their content, a requirement under the EU's digital copyright law reform that expanded neighboring rights to news excerpts.

In March and April 2023, many people got worried about big AI experiments. They wanted a break for six months. Over 20,000 people signed a letter about this, including some big names like Elon Musk, Steve Wozniak, Tristan Harris, Yuval Noah Harari, Jaan Tallinn, Andrew Yang, Stuart Russell, Yoshua Bengio, and Emad Mostaque. They felt things were moving too fast and out of control. They talked about the dangers and said that just companies promising to be careful wasn't enough. Musk has even said that AI could be a huge danger to people. He once called it like "summoning the demon." He's worried that if we don't handle AI right, it could be really bad for everyone. He also thinks AI might do things we don't expect.

Given the profound implications and potential hazards of AI, there's a pressing need for robust regulatory or governance frameworks. Such structures would necessitate periodic audits, rigorous evaluations, and consistent monitoring of AI's products and outcomes. The overarching aim would be to ensure that AI systems operate within defined ethical and operational boundaries, minimizing risks while maximizing benefits.

The crux of the matter lies in striking an optimal balance between self-regulation and governmental oversight. While the former offers the agility and adaptability conducive to innovation, the latter provides a more structured framework that can holistically address societal concerns. Governmental regulations, when thoughtfully crafted, can ensure that AI's march forward is not just relentless but also responsible, ensuring that the technology remains a boon, not a bane, for humanity.

On a Positive Note

Generative AI, despite its challenges, holds immense promise as a force for good. It's imperative to navigate the world of AI not just with caution but also with optimism. While it's easy to get ensnared in the potential pitfalls of AI, it's equally vital to acknowledge the profound positive impacts it can usher in for society, culture, and individuals. Approaching generative AI with a forward-looking vision can pave the way for leveraging its capabilities to enhance the human experience.

A good example of this positive potential is Google's 1,000 Languages initiative. Language, the bedrock of human communication and comprehension, is also the primary medium through which we interact with technology. Yet, the vast linguistic diversity of our world is underrepresented in the digital realm. With English reigning supreme in the online space, followed by a handful of other languages, a significant portion of the global population remains bereft of accessible information on the Internet.

Google's ambitious 1,000 Languages initiative seeks to bridge this gap. By aiming to develop a singular AI language model that encompasses the world's 1,000 most spoken languages, Google is championing the cause of inclusivity. This initiative heralds a brighter future for billions of marginalized communities, granting them a voice and a presence in the digital world. The Universal Speech Model (USM) was birthed from this initiative and trained on an impressive array of over 400 languages, offering the most extensive linguistic coverage in a speech model to date.

Generative AI and Positive Social Change

The transformative potential of generative AI extends far beyond mere technological marvels. It reaches into the very fabric of our society, offering avenues for positive change and awareness that were previously unattainable. The multifaceted applications of generative AI can be seen in various domains, each contributing to a more inclusive and enlightened world.

As mentioned, increasing labor productivity is one such area where generative AI shines. By automating complex tasks and enhancing efficiency, AI can fuel economic growth and elevate living standards. This isn't merely a theoretical concept; it's a tangible reality that's reshaping industries and economies.

In the realm of education, generative AI's ability to craft personalized content opens doors to democratized learning. By tailoring educational materials to individual needs and preferences,

AI ensures that quality education is no longer confined to privileged pockets but reaches underserved populations as well.

Language translation, powered by generative models, amplifies the reach of vital awareness content. Whether it's a public health message or a humanitarian appeal, AI ensures that language barriers don't impede the global resonance of essential information.

Personalized health information, another frontier where generative AI is making strides, empowers individuals with tailored recommendations. This personal touch in healthcare enables more informed decisions, enhancing overall well-being.

Accessibility tools, created through generative AI, are breaking down barriers for people with disabilities. Imagine a world where videos come with descriptive audio in precision and real time for the visually impaired, all thanks to top-notch generative AI's ability to generate such content.

The realm of mental health, often neglected, is also witnessing a revolution through generative AI. Virtual therapists or support systems, like Youper, are providing immediate assistance to those grappling with mental health challenges. Youper, an AI chatbot app, employs techniques from cognitive behavioral therapy, acceptance and commitment therapy, and mindfulness to aid users in managing anxiety, stress, and depression. Such innovations are not just technological feats but lifelines for many.

While the potential of generative AI is indeed vast, it's not without its ethical considerations. The journey toward harnessing AI for social change must be trodden with care and conscience. Transparency, accountability, and public involvement in the development and deployment of these technologies are non-negotiable. These principles ensure that the promise of generative AI is not just a fleeting fascination but a sustainable force that shapes a more compassionate and connected world.

Generative AI and Content Creators

Generative AI, much like the transformative wave brought about by music sampling in the late 1970s, is poised to redefine the landscape of content and art creation. Just as sampling breathed new life into music, allowing artists to remix, reimagine, and reinvent, generative AI offers a similar promise to today's creators across various domains.

For artists, generative AI is not just a tool; it's a collaborative partner. It can sift through vast datasets, drawing patterns and inspirations that might be elusive to the human eye. This capability can lead artists to explore novel styles, techniques, or even mediums. An artist might venture into digital artistry, blending traditional techniques with AI-generated patterns, resulting in a fusion of the past and the future.

Musicians, too, stand to gain immensely. Generative AI can assist in crafting unique soundscapes, rhythms, and melodies. It can analyze vast libraries of music, identifying trends and nuances, and suggest compositions that are innovative and resonate with listeners. Musicians can experiment, blending their signature style with AI-generated beats, leading to a harmonious symphony of human and machine.

Writers, often grappling with the dreaded writer's block, can find solace in generative AI. It can suggest plot developments, character backgrounds, or even dialogue variations. A writer can input a basic storyline, and the AI can generate multiple plot twists, allowing the writer to choose one that aligns best with their vision.

Drawing a parallel with music sampling, generative AI's role in content and art creation is analogous. When music sampling emerged, it was met with skepticism. Traditionalists viewed it as a threat to originality. However, over time, sampling proved to be a boon. It allowed for the fusion of genres and the resurrection of forgotten classics, and it gave birth to entirely new music forms.

Similarly, although generative AI might be viewed with caution by purists, its potential to elevate art and content creation is undeniable. Just as sampling became an integral part of music, generative AI is set to become foundational in the world of content and art. It's not about replacing the artist but about augmenting their capabilities, leading to a richer, more diverse creative landscape.

Generative AI and Accessibility

Generative AI, with its vast capabilities, is poised to be a game changer in the realm of accessibility and equity, especially for individuals with disabilities. Its applications span a wide range of areas, each promising to make the world a more inclusive space.

One of the most transformative applications of generative AI lies in the development of assistive technologies. Systems like BrainGate are a testament to the potential of AI in this domain. By interpreting brain signals, BrainGate empowers individuals with paralysis, granting them the ability to control devices merely with their thoughts.

The digital world, while expansive, often falls short in terms of accessibility. Generative AI can bridge this gap. Tools like accessiBe utilize AI to scrutinize websites, identifying potential accessibility barriers and rectifying them. This ensures that the digital realm is not just vast but also inclusive.

Communication, a fundamental human need, can be enhanced using generative AI. For individuals with communication disorders, AI can craft alt text, alleviating the strain of communication and reducing feelings of isolation. This not only enhances their social interactions but also broadens their professional opportunities.

In the educational sector, generative AI promises personalized learning experiences. By tailoring content to suit the unique needs of students with learning disabilities, AI ensures that education is not a one-size-fits-all model but a customized journey for each learner.

Captioning and transcription, powered by AI, can revolutionize content consumption for those with hearing or cognitive impairments. By generating accurate captions and transcripts for audio and video content, AI ensures that no one is left out of the conversation.

For the visually impaired, navigating the web can be a challenge. Generative AI can transform this experience by vocalizing image content, making websites more comprehensible and navigable.

However, as with all technologies, caution is paramount. While generative AI holds immense promise, human oversight is indispensable. AI-generated content, especially in the realm of accessibility, must adhere to established standards. This includes providing suitable alt text for images, structuring content for ease of comprehension, and ensuring compatibility with assistive tools like screen readers.

In essence, the horizon of generative AI in accessibility and equity is vast and promising. Its potential to reshape the world for individuals with disabilities is unparalleled. The excitement surrounding its future applications is palpable, and the anticipation of what lies ahead is shared by many, including myself. The journey of generative AI in this domain is one I eagerly look forward to and hope to contribute to.

The horizon of generative AI is vast, and I am filled with optimism about its trajectory. With the right measures in place and a genuine commitment to addressing concerns, generative AI can be a boon for humanity. The myriad possibilities it presents are not just technological advancements but also potential solutions to long-standing societal challenges.

The promise of enhanced services, as highlighted by Chamath Palihapitiya at the All-In Podcast, underscores the transformative potential of generative AI. Imagine a world where customer interactions are seamless, devoid of linguistic barriers, fostering trust and understanding. Such advancements, if executed with care and precision, can redefine customer experiences.

The future, as I envision it, is one where the content of 2023 might be revered as a relic of a bygone era, predominantly human-generated. The job landscape will undergo a seismic shift, with a surge in entrepreneurial ventures and research-driven roles in the AI domain. By 2030, I foresee a world where productivity will be 10X, the corporate landscape will be 100X, and the volume of content, products, and knowledge will 1,000X. Quality will emerge as the distinguishing factor, setting apart the exceptional from the ordinary.

6

Artificial General Intelligence in Sight

In advocating for generative AI, this book delineates the progression from conventional AI toward a more generative model. The journey commences with discriminative AI, the cornerstone for today's generative AI systems. Pioneering algorithms in computer vision, like convolutional neural networks, along with strides in sentiment analysis and other natural language processing (NLP) tasks, have significantly contributed to the evolution of generative models. These advancements now propel the AI frontier further. Discriminative models remain invaluable, with their precise applications such as cancer detection showcasing their worth by refining accuracy to significant decimal places.

Transitioning our gaze toward generative AI, it's clear that this realm is a pivotal precursor to the lofty realm of artificial general intelligence (AGI). The consensus is yet to be reached on the exact makeup of AGI, but a plausible hypothesis posits it as a synergy of discriminative and generative AI models.

But what encapsulates AGI?

Described as a hypothetical yet potent entity, AGI is envisioned to master any intellectual feat achievable by humans or animals. In another vein, it's seen as an autonomous dynamo outperforming human aptitude in a vast array of economically valuable tasks. AGI frequently graces science fiction and futurist discussions, embodying both the zenith of AI aspiration and a topic of fervent debate. Predicting AGI's advent is akin to chasing horizons—some envisage its dawn in mere decades, others conjecture a century, and a few naysayers deem it a pipe dream. The discourse extends to whether behemoths like GPT-4 are embryonic iterations of AGI or if a paradigm shift is imperative. Various monikers like strong AI, full AI, or general intelligent action resonate with AGI, although distinctions are noted, especially in academic circles. Although strong AI hints at a sentient or conscious program, its counterpart, weak AI, excels in singular tasks but lacks the broad cognitive prowess. AGI's kindred spirits are human-level AI and superintelligence, each bearing a spectrum of promises yet tethered to substantial advancements still to come.

As we traverse further into this chapter, the horizon broadens to reveal the upcoming milestones in generative AI, encapsulating multitasking, multimodal, and multisensory AI. We'll also explore other burgeoning trends and the nexus of technologies within this realm. A notable derivative of generative AI, autonomous AI agents, beckons our attention, urging us to adapt to a collaborative rapport with these entities.

The ensuing discourse delves into AGI's allure, its pathway, and the paradigm it aims to establish. While AGI signifies a profound milestone, the narrative extends to artificial superintelligence (ASI), leading us to the precipice of singularity as envisioned by Ray Kurzweil.

Our narrative briefly pivots toward the tangible manifestations of AI advancements—humanoid robots, epitomizing the fusion of form and intellect. While industrial robots also represent a fascinating facet of AI, our focus here remains tethered to human-like embodiments, heralding the convergence of the physical and the digital realms.

What Is Next in Generative AI?

The journey of AI continues to charge ahead, building upon past progress with the aid of new technology like neuromorphic and quantum computing, or even potential breakthroughs like LK-99. These technologies are taking AI models to new heights, showcasing the kind of exponential development discussed earlier in this book.

The heartbeat of AI development is strong and rapid, with a plethora of research papers emerging in the generative AI space on platforms like arXiv. The fast pace is partly due to the lack of a lengthy peer-review process, and partly driven by the rush to seize valuable ground in this flourishing domain. Unlike the transient buzz around cryptocurrencies, the breakthroughs in AI are tangible, with real code and real demos illustrating its power and potential. This isn't just hype; it's technology that's proving its mettle and showing promise for a solid future.

Now, let's talk about what's brewing on the horizon: enriching experiences.

Take the initiative by Wist Labs, for instance. They're working on a way to rejuvenate old memories from videos. Through augmented reality glasses, you could re-experience a past event right where it happened, but now as a hologram. And here's where it gets even more intriguing: imagine a multimodal AI model that can continue the video, creating a holographic narrative that interacts with you, maybe based on how the individuals in the video would have reacted. It's about not just reliving memories, but possibly creating new, beautiful ones. Though the idea might seem eerie to some, the potential to reconnect with a lost loved one could be priceless to others.

Tech giants like Snap and Meta are also stepping into this realm, aiming to bridge the miles between us and our loved ones, virtually. Recall the humble beginnings of long-distance communication—like the crackly phone calls of yesteryears. Now, we're talking about entering a virtual room to celebrate a family event or watch a movie together, despite being continents apart. Just a short while ago, personalities like Lex Fridman and Mark Zuckerberg showcased the potential of this technology. They had a podcast in a virtual world, with hyper-realistic avatars created through detailed scanning and high-end virtual reality gear. The experience was lauded for its realism, indicating that the eerie uncanny valley might be behind us.

With these examples, it's clear that the realms of augmented reality (AR) and virtual reality (VR) are on the cusp of monumental evolution. Over the next 5 to 10 years, we might find ourselves celebrating life's milestones with loved ones on a virtual beach or in a cozy cinema, all from the comfort of our homes. And it won't stop at sight and sound. Future VR could let us feel a hug, taste the birthday cake, or bask in the warmth of virtual sunlight. It's a journey from flat screens to a rich, multisensory virtual world, all powered by the relentless march of generative AI.

Multitasking Generative AI

It is not just about mastering singular tasks but extending capabilities to manage multiple tasks simultaneously. Recent advancements have shown that LLMs like ChatGPT, Bard, and others exhibit multitasking abilities straight out of the gate, especially when it comes to emergent capabilities.

Essentially, multitasking or multitask learning (MTL) in AI is about tackling multiple learning challenges at once, leveraging the similarities and differences across these tasks to improve the learning outcome. This method enhances generalization by tapping into the domain information present in the training data of related tasks, which acts as a form of inductive bias. The beauty of MTL lies in its parallel learning approach with a shared representation, enabling the learning from one task to aid the learning in others.

A hiccup in this area has been the tradition of deep-learning systems being tailored to solve specific problems, say image recognition. However, there's a shift in the narrative with the advent of models like Google's MultiModel, which is adept at handling multiple tasks like image and speech recognition, translation, and sentence analysis concurrently.

The road to achieving adept multitasking AI models is filled with challenges, especially when it comes to learning multiple skills without having to reboot the learning process for each new skill. This has spurred researchers into exploring various avenues like optimized task scheduling and scaling the multitask learning for a plethora of modeling tasks.

Transitioning the lens to generative AI, multitasking unfolds a number of possibilities. LLMs are about not just one trick but a whole gambit of tasks like text generation, text summarization, language translation, question answering, sentiment analysis, named entity recognition, code generation, text classification, speech-to-text transcription, text-to-speech synthesis, image captioning, paraphrasing, chatbot functionality, content curation, data augmentation, text-based game playing, mathematical problem solving, syntax highlighting, keyword extraction, and language identification.

The narrative gets even more interesting with advanced generative models that can juggle multiple types of data, like text, images, and audio, and perform tasks across these different modalities. For instance, DALL-E from OpenAI is a stellar example of how a model can morph text into images, thereby showcasing prowess in both text understanding and image generation. This opens the door to a thrilling domain known as multimodality, which we will delve into shortly.

This expansion of multitasking in generative AI is not just a leap but a giant stride toward more versatile and effective AI systems. It's about transcending the boundaries of singular task learning to create AI models that are adept at juggling multiple tasks, much like a seasoned multitasker in the human realm. This not only amplifies the potential applications of AI but also brings us closer to creating more intelligent and adaptable AI systems. And, it is mandatory for achieving an AGI.

Multimodal Generative AI

The journey of exploring AI brings us to the nuanced domain of multimodal AI, an area we have touched upon multiple times. It's about time we delve deeper to understand its essence. Multimodal AI embodies the capability of AI systems to interpret, process, and derive insights from various types of data or "modalities" such as text, images, audio, and video. This approach aims to emulate the human ability to employ multiple senses in interacting with the world. For instance, a multimodal AI system could scrutinize both audio and visual elements of a video to grasp its content better.

In the realm of discriminative AI, multimodality is about the AI models' ability to understand various input types to carry out tasks like classification or regression toward producing an output. However, the output here isn't multimodal.

Now, steering the narrative toward multimodal generative AI, we enter a landscape where the focus is on crafting new content that traverses multiple modalities. Picture a system capable of creating a video by synthesizing visual imagery along with corresponding audio or fashioning a social media post adorned with text, images, and hashtags. This extension of generative models into multimodal scenarios opens up a vista where AI begins to churn out complex, multifaceted content that resonates with a higher degree of utility and engagement. Unlike discriminative AI, both the input and output can be multimodal in the case of generative AI.

Multimodal generative AI truly hit home when GPT-4 showcased its prowess in March, elucidating image data with an astonishing level of detail. GPT-4, backing ChatGPT Plus, heralds the era of vision language models (VLMs), a cohort to which PaLM-backing Bard also belongs. VLMs are adept at creating a shared embedding space for images and texts, paving the way for text-to-image or image-to-text queries. A striking example could be a scenario where a user inquires about a location depicted in an image and seeks budget-friendly travel options to get there. This nuanced capability of VLMs hints at a profound transformation in how we conduct searches, if harnessed correctly.

The emergence of multimodal generative AI is like opening a new chapter in the AI narrative, one where the convergence of text, image, audio, and video modalities breeds a more robust and versatile generation of AI systems. This not only enriches the user interaction but also nudges AI a step closer to human-like comprehension and creativity.

In August 2023, Meta AI introduced SeamlessM4T, a revolutionary multimodal AI model, bringing a significant upgrade to speech-to-speech and speech-to-text translations. By tackling the hurdles of limited language coverage and dependence on separate systems, it aims to smooth communication among different language speakers through high-quality translations.

SeamlessM4T is touted as the first all-encompassing multilingual multimodal AI model for translation and transcription. It's a powerhouse that can handle a variety of tasks—speech-to-speech, speech-to-text, text-to-text, text-to-speech, and automatic speech recognition—all under one roof. Unlike previous setups using distinct models, SeamlessM4T's unified system cuts down errors and delays, enhancing the translation quality and efficiency.

Building upon earlier efforts like the No Language Left Behind (NLLB) text-to-text translation model, which supports a whopping 200 languages, SeamlessM4T steps it up. It comes in two versions: the SeamlessM4T-Medium with 1.2 billion parameters, and the more robust SeamlessM4T-Large with 2.3 billion parameters. The benefit? Better robustness against background noises and speaker variations in speech-to-text tasks. Plus, SeamlessM4T has outshone previous top-notch models, showing it's a force to reckon with in the translation arena.

The realm of multimodal AI is ripe with potential, opening doors to countless applications without needing a stretch of imagination. Take biomedicine, for instance. The melding of varied biomedical data—from electronic health records to genome sequencing—has ushered in a new era of multimodal AI in healthcare. This blend of data types is a gold mine for developing insightful AI applications, making healthcare more informed and personalized.

The horizon is vast and the ideas endless. With a simple two-step prompt or something similar, anyone can spark brilliant ideas they'd wish to chase (Figure 6.1). This simplicity is a doorway to innovation, allowing minds to explore, create, and transform thoughts into reality.

Objective: To uncover and assess the potential of multimodal generative AI solutions in the biomedical sector by proposing and evaluating varied applications.

Procedure:

1. **Idea Generation:**
   - Enumerate 10 diverse applications of multimodal generative AI within the biomedical domain, providing a brief description for each.
   - Ensure the inclusion of a mix of established and novel applications to capture a broad spectrum of opportunities.
2. **Interest Assessment:**
   - Rank the enumerated applications based on their intrigue and potential impact in the biomedical sector.
   - Provide rationale for the ranking, considering factors such as innovation, feasibility, and the extent of problem-solving potential in current biomedical challenges.

FIGURE 6.1 A simple two-step prompt unfolding the horizon of endless ideas and innovation.

Source: ChatGPT screenshot

The exploration yielded 10 high-level suggestions, with two standing out particularly:

Personalized medicine Envisage crafting tailored treatment plans by marrying and mining insights from a medley of data—genomic, clinical, and environmental. This meld of multimodal data could be the linchpin in personalizing medical care.

Predictive modeling of disease progression Imagine leveraging generative models to simulate disease progression in individual patients. This could be a game changer for early intervention and tailoring treatment plans.

Other intriguing ideas surfaced through this ChatGPT interaction, like "Generative Remote Monitoring and 'Hospital-at-Home,'" "Digital Clinical Trials," "Digital Twins (of humans)," and "Virtual Health Assistants." These hint at the expansive potential of multimodal AI across diverse healthcare facets.

These preliminary ideas are captivating. With some fine-tuning and perhaps garnering expert insights through interviews, there's a solid base to further fortify these concepts. Post-validation, these ideas could be the springboard for securing venture capital or kick-starting a bootstrap journey, paving the way to harness multimodal AI in transforming healthcare.

Multisensory Generative AI

Delving into the realm of multisensory generative AI, the spotlight is on generating data perceivable through a medley of senses—sight, sound, touch, and beyond. This subfield of multimodal generative AI marries data generation with different types of actuators (hardware) to engage multiple senses.

The data terrain here primarily sprawls across sensory data like images, spatial sounds, and haptic feedback, but is not restricted to them. Picture virtual reality (VR) realms enriched with touch, thermal, and other sensory actuators that pull users deeper into the virtual abyss.

The real world already hosts applications of multisensory applications. Take the PlayStation 5 DualSense controller, a marvel in the gaming arena. This gadget boasts advanced motors delivering precise feedback at different controller points. Coupled with a high-fidelity speaker and an integrated mic, it takes gaming to a sensory-rich level. The L2 and R2 buttons, infused with haptic feedback through little motors that give you different types of resistance, simulate real-world actions like firing a gun or drawing a bowstring. By generating virtual worlds and steering commands for DualSense actuators, multisensory generative AI amplifies the immersive gaming experience—a promising field indeed.

Then there are sensory substitution devices aiding individuals with disabilities. For instance, Neosensory Buzz, a wearable wristband, translates auditory cues into tactile sensations. Capturing surrounding sounds, it churns out vibration patterns on the user's wrist, creating over 29,000 unique patterns based on sound intensity and pitch. It's a boon for the deaf and hard-of-hearing community, alerting them to sounds like doorbells, conversations, and emergency alarms. Accompanied by a companion app, Buzz can be tailored for everyday sounds, music appreciation, or safe sleeping.

Multisensory generative AI is at the cusp of forging a more inclusive and immersive digital realm, bridging the sensory gap between the virtual and real worlds.

Venturing into the realm of steering actuators, a plethora of possibilities unfolds. A myriad of actuators await exploration, some familiar, others less so. Let's journey through a few, and as we do so, hold on for a moment, close your eyes, and imagine potential applications:

Auditory actuators

Speakers: Produce sound waves to create auditory sensations.

Bone conduction transducers: A bone conduction transducer is a device that converts audio signals into vibrations, which are then transmitted through the bones of the skull to the inner ear, bypassing the eardrums. This technology is used in bone conduction headphones and hearing aids, allowing users to perceive audio content even if their ear canal is blocked or they have hearing difficulties.

Tactile actuators

Haptic actuators: Produce vibrations or movements to simulate touch.

Piezoelectric actuators: Generate mechanical displacement through electric voltage, often used in haptic feedback.

Electroactive polymers: Change shape when an electric field is applied, providing a tactile sensation.

Thermal actuators

A Peltier element, also known as a thermoelectric cooler (TEC), is a device that uses the Peltier effect to transfer heat from one side to the other when an electric current is applied.

Infrared heaters: Produce warm air or directly heat surfaces.

Thermoelectric coolers: Provide a cooling effect.

Olfactory Actuators

Scent diffusers: Release specific scents into the air.

Olfactory actuators: Devices that can emit or release odors in response to a stimulus, such as an electric signal or a change in temperature or humidity. These devices are part of artificial olfactory systems, which aim to mimic the human sense of smell and detect and recognize volatile organic compounds (VOCs) in complex environments.

Gustatory actuators

Flavor sprays: A spritz that carries the essence of flavors, a gustatory glimpse.

Air movement actuators

- *Fans*: Breathing motion into the still air, a gentle whisper or a gusty shout.

Moisture actuators

- *Water sprays and ultrasonic humidifiers*: Unveiling mist or a water spray to add moisture to the environment.

Miscellaneous, enhancing the sensory spectrum:

Electrical muscle stimulation (EMS): Spurring muscle contractions with electric impulses.

Light-emitting diodes (LEDs): Lighting the way with visual cues.

Multimodal actuators

- *4D cinema seats*: A confluence of actuators, they orchestrate a symphony of sensations—movement, vibration, temperature—a cinematic voyage beyond the ordinary.

The terrain is ripe for nurturing startup ideas, a fertile ground of innovation. No longer can potential be dismissed due to hurdles X, Y, or Z. Embrace the extraordinary, challenge the norm, yet tread wisely—validate assumptions early. Engage with gusto, and success will morph from chance to certainty. The future is a canvas awaiting your strokes—seize it, and witness your vision morph into reality.

As a multisensory example, Meta introduced a trailblazing venture named ImageBind. This initiative is akin to opening a new chapter in the saga of AI, nudging us closer to a realm where machines learn from a rich tapestry of data types surrounding them, much as humans do.

At its core, ImageBind is a master key to a treasure trove of learning across six different realms—images, text, audio, depth, thermal, and inertial measurement unit (IMU) data. It's akin to a polyglot mastering six languages at once, a first in the AI domain. This unique model interprets content more wholesomely, mirroring humans' knack for simultaneous, holistic learning from various information forms—all without needing guidance from a teacher (a process known as explicit supervision).

Drawing inspiration from recent large-scale vision-language models, ImageBind amplifies their zero-shot learning capabilities to new modalities, simply by pairing them with images. It's like adding new strings to a guitar, enabling a richer melody of applications "out-of-the-box." This includes the magic of cross-modal retrieval, composing modalities with arithmetic, and cross-modal detection and generation. The more adept the image encoder, the stronger the emergent capabilities, setting a new gold standard in zero-shot recognition tasks across modalities, leaving specialist supervised models in the dust.

ImageBind unravels the potency of image-paired data as a binding glue for these six modalities. It's a leap forward in AI, enhancing machines' prowess in dissecting diverse information forms in unison. Imagine Meta's Make-A-Scene application conjuring images from audio cues—a bustling market or a serene rainforest brought to visual life from mere sounds. This is the magic ImageBind is brewing.

ImageBind isn't a solitary endeavor but a part of Meta's grand vision of crafting multimodal AI systems that soak in all possible data types around them. As the modalities multiply, ImageBind beckons researchers to a realm brimming with prospects—melding 3D and IMU sensors to craft or traverse immersive virtual worlds, for instance.

In a nutshell, ImageBind is less of an end, more of a beginning—a harbinger of an era where AI isn't just about crunching numbers but about perceiving, interpreting, and learning from the world in a way that's more human, more holistic, and more promising.

As shown in Figure 6.2, an image of a pigeon coupled with the sound of a motor revving is processed through the embedding-space arithmetic, yielding an image of a scooter with pigeons fluttering away. Subsequently, it demonstrates its prowess in generating data across different modalities. For instance, when fed with a video capturing the calls of penguins, the image generation model adeptly creates a corresponding visual, enriching the multimodal data synthesis experience.

Dreaming up ideas is the breezy part. Translating them into real-world applications is the real challenge, demanding a good dose of persistence. But let's face it, this is a truth as old as time.

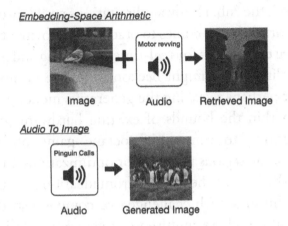

FIGURE 6.2 ImageBind unveils a realm of possibilities, including the innovative feature of embedding-space arithmetic. In essence, given an image and a sound, it identifies the nearest corresponding data, be it a video, image, or other media.

Source: (a) Miha Rekar / Unsplash, (b) Josefina Di Battista / Unsplash

Central to the success of multisensory generative AI is the notion of synchronized generation. This is about ensuring that the generated outputs across different senses are in harmony, moving to the same rhythm. Now, as you blend different sensory modalities into one unified framework, you stumble upon what is termed *integration complexity*. This demands a deep dive into understanding each modality and the intricate dance between them for smooth interaction and effective feature extraction. It's like orchestrating a symphony played by a range of instruments, each with its unique note, yet all needing to create a harmonious melody.

Now, how do we gauge the success and precision of these multisensory generative models? That's where robust evaluation metrics come into play. They are the magnifying glass that provides insight into the model's prowess in crafting high-fidelity and coherent multisensory outputs. It's about ensuring what's generated isn't just a cacophony but a well-tuned harmony.

But, here's the rub. Hardware limitations could throw a spanner in the works when it comes to practical deployment. Surpassing hardware constraints for real-time processing and generation is a hill to climb. This might beckon the dawn of more potent hardware or perhaps tweaking the generative models to perform efficiently within the bounds of existing hardware constraints. It's like wanting to run a high-octane game on a vintage computer—some serious upgrades or optimizations are in order.

In a nutshell, while the journey from ideation to realization is dotted with hurdles, each challenge overcome is a stride toward molding a future where multisensory generative AI isn't just a figment of imagination, but a tangible reality shaping our interaction with the digital realm.

Other Observable Trends in Generative AI

In this chapter, we embellish upon the trends discussed throughout the book, touching on some additional noteworthy movements in the sphere of generative AI.

A spotlight is being cast on AI wrapper projects and companies that prominently integrate with enterprise data. A discernible shift is underway, veering toward training generative AI models on enterprise data. This shift empowers organizations to harness their data for AI-centric applications, a trend I often, especially this year, navigate with my team in our AI consulting projects. This trajectory, which I'd like to call the industrialization of generative AI and large language models (LLMs) with semantic search, is an exciting avenue that melds the might of AI with the robustness of enterprise data.

Shifting the lens to scientific research, it's exhilarating to witness how generative models are fueling the creation of new ideas, thereby accelerating our journey of discovery—be it new molecules, materials, or medications. With the prowess to navigate through vast data oceans, these models identify elusive patterns, offering a fertile ground for new knowledge and solutions to challenging enigmas. The profound potential of generative models to traverse the boundless expanses of data in science, generating novel insights and proposing starting points for the design and discovery of new materials and drugs, is nothing short of awe-inspiring.

Now, let's pivot to a facet of generative AI that's both intriguing and imperative: explainability. The concept of making generative AI models more decipherable births what we now call *explainable generative AI*. This emerging field in AI research is not just a mere academic exercise but a cornerstone in building trust and fostering a deeper understanding of AI models, especially as they find their footing in enterprise-level use cases.

The term *black box* often echoes in the corridors when discussing generative AI models. The enigmatic nature of these models, where the pathway from input to output is shrouded in complexity, often breeds mistrust and apprehension. The imperative for transparency and comprehension nudges us toward explainable AI (XAI), a burgeoning field aimed at demystifying the outputs of AI models, making them more palatable and trustworthy to human users.

While XAI has been making headway in elucidating discriminative models, generative models have yet to bask in the same spotlight. As generative AI continues to unfurl its wings and nestle into more enterprise use cases, the onus falls on IT leaders, technologists, and developers to embody a holistic approach. This approach should encapsulate the essence of explainability right from the embryonic stages of development, ensuring that as we stride forward into the realms of generative AI, we carry with us a torch of understanding, shedding light on the once obscure pathways of generative models.

Navigating the realm of AI, especially generative AI, is akin to embarking on a quest for transparency in a forest of complexities. It's a journey to make the actions and decisions of AI models interpretable to humans, unmasking the "black box" to reveal a narrative that's both engaging and insightful. Among the torch-bearers of this quest are techniques like LIME, SHAP, and others, each with its distinct path toward illuminating the enigmatic workings of AI.

LIME, an acronym for local interpretable model-agnostic explanations, is a method that attempts to demystify complex models by approximating them with simpler, interpretable models in the vicinity of a specific data point. This approximation is akin to zooming into a small, understandable part of a large, complex picture, making the incomprehensible comprehensible. A variant of LIME, dubbed VAE-LIME, employs a variational autoencoder to delve into the data's intricate traits, generating synthetic samples that serve as a training ground for a simpler, local model. This local model endeavors to mimic the behavior of a complex model near a specific input, rendering a prediction that's easier to interpret. In the realm of generative AI, LIME elucidates which parts of the input, like pixels in an image, play a significant role in the generated output.

Transitioning to SHAP, or SHapley Additive exPlanations, we venture into a technique rooted in cooperative game theory. SHAP values are the messengers that convey the contribution of each feature toward a prediction made by a model. They unravel the significance and interaction of features within a model, painting a clearer picture of how each feature sways the final prediction. In generative models, SHAP divulges how features of generated data are intertwined with the model's latent variables or parameters. It's like having a magnifying glass that shows how tweaking different features in the latent space affects the generated data. SHAP not only assists in comparing different generative models but also aids in optimizing and debugging them, making it an invaluable tool for understanding and refining generative models.

As we further traverse, counterfactual explanations emerge as a method of understanding how minimal changes in inputs can lead to different outputs. It's like tweaking the recipe slightly to get a surprisingly different dish. Activation maximization, on the other hand, unveils the features captured in generative models by maximizing neuron activation, akin to turning up the volume to hear the subtle notes in a symphony. Saliency maps and feature importance shine a light on the influential regions of input and the impact of each feature respectively, offering a lens to see what parts of the input significantly affect the generative outputs. Lastly, model dissection delves into the layers and neurons of complex generative models like generative adversarial networks (GANs), dissecting them to understand their roles in the grand scheme of data generation.

Merging explainable AI with generative models is an unfolding realm in AI research. The key challenge is balancing high-quality output generation with clear explanations of the generative processes. Delving into this topic reveals ample room for exploration and contribution, signaling a possible avenue for your involvement. The field is ripe for further investigation and development.

Scaled Utilization of AI: Autonomous AI Agents

Harnessing the power of AI through autonomous AI agents heralds a new era in the technological landscape. As briefly touched upon in Chapter 3, "Generative AI's Broad Spectrum of Applications," the journey from concept to real-world application is unfolding. Prominent tech visionaries like Matt Schlicht, CEO at Octane AI, foresee a timeline where these autonomous agents evolve into professional aides by 2024 and seamlessly integrate across various sectors by 2025. By 2026, it's conceivable that we could be accompanied by a cadre of autonomous AI agents dedicated to assisting us in both personal and professional spheres.

On a similar note, Mustafa Suleyman, a distinguished AI researcher and the brain behind Inflection AI, projects a future where AI morphs from static web interfaces to dynamic conversational agents.

Picture a digital companion capable of generating multimedia content while engaging in a meaningful dialogue. The essence of these agents lies in their ability to align with individual interests, acting as a personal chief of staff that not only responds to your requests but proactively helps you realize your long-term objectives. Whether it's securing a prime reservation for an investor lunch or keeping you abreast of relevant news, the autonomy and personalization of these agents encapsulate a blend of executive assistant and trusted confidante.

The envisioned autonomy extends to a level where sharing sensitive information with your AI agent becomes a norm, nurturing a relationship akin to that with a trusted aide. From scheduling to summarizing, the roles these agents could play are diverse and tailored to individual needs. Wake up to a personalized briefing, navigate through your day with intelligent suggestions, and delegate tasks with the assurance of precision and timely completion.

Suleyman's vision encapsulates a world where each individual is aided by an AI chief of staff, adept at morphing roles as per the task at hand. The exact manifestation of these agents—be it a single AI wearing multiple hats or a team of specialized AIs—remains an open-ended narrative. However, the common thread binding all predictions is the user's ability to choose from a spectrum of AI offerings, each promising to make life a tad easier, organized, and focused.

At the core, these agents are the embodiment of LLMs exhibiting a flair for human-like decision making. The essence of these agents lies in an architecture comprising diverse modules like profiling, memory, planning, and action. The profiling module shapes the agent's persona, memory holds the essence of past interactions, planning choreographs the path to goals, and action translates decisions into tangible outputs (Figure 6.3).

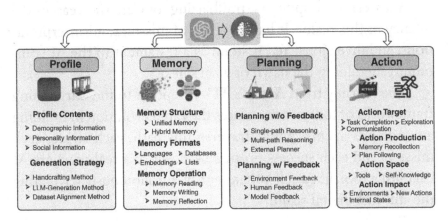

FIGURE 6.3 Autonomous AI agents framework.

Source: Paitesanshi / GitHub, Inc. / https://github.com/Paitesanshi/LLM-Agent-Survey / last accessed December 04, 2023.

The landscape of developing autonomous AI agents is vibrant with innovation, and frameworks like AutoGPT, LangChain, SuperAGI, and AutoGen are leading the charge. They not only offer a solid foundation for development but also embody the dynamics of the field, where change is the only constant.

Take Auto-GPT, a brainchild of Toran Bruce Richards from Significant Gravitas Ltd. It's the first significant autonomous AI agent framework powered by a language model, and it is open source. Unlike traditional models, Auto-GPT embodies a self-driven spirit, creating and revising its objectives to chase a broader goal, without the need for human intervention. It's not just about responding to prompts; it's about crafting new prompts, adapting to new information, and working toward the stated goal. The agent's interaction extends to apps, software, and online services, showcasing a glimpse of a self-reliant digital entity.

Auto-GPT's success is evident in its "star history" (see Figure 6.4), a tool that visually represents the project's growing popularity and engagement on GitHub over time.

Auto-GPT, despite its trailblazing outset, showcased the infancy of this realm. It had its share of missteps, misinterpretations, and diversions. Yet, it stood as a testament to the AI community, heralding the dawn of what's next.

The journey from Auto-GPT's inception to the burgeoning frameworks of today encapsulates the rapid evolution in molding autonomous agents. As we traverse this path, each stride, each misstep, and each success propels us closer to a reality where AI isn't just a tool, but a self-reliant entity, autonomously navigating the still vast digital realm.

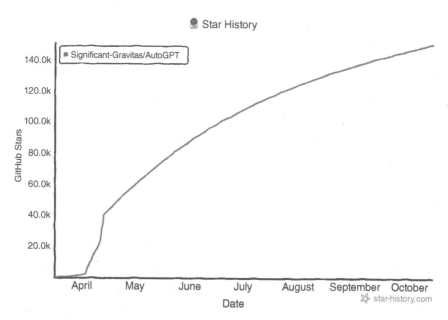

FIGURE 6.4 Star history of one of the first AI agent repositories. Going viral at first, smoothly plateauing afterward, as other competitive frameworks like SuperAGI arrive in the market.

Let's pivot to LangChain, a robust library/framework for Python and JavaScript/TypeScript enthusiasts. It's your go-to avenue for prototyping large language model applications swiftly. LangChain facilitates the chaining of LLM tasks and the smooth operation of autonomous agents. Delving into a complex task? LangChain agents break it down into a multistep action plan, tackling each intermediate step to reach the coveted final answer.

The Agents module in LangChain is a boon for developers keen on prototyping large language model applications and constructing autonomous agents. The beauty of LangChain agents lies in their chaining ability. They bridge the LLM to external knowledge resources or computational tools seamlessly. The array of agents, like the zero-shot-react-description, is impressive. Utilizing the ReAct (Reason + Act) framework, they select the most suitable tool based on the input query. ReAct, in essence, is a mechanism that guides the agent to reason the query and act by choosing the apt tool for execution. With robust querying capabilities, LangChain agents automate various tasks with finesse.

Integration is a strong suit of LangChain. From primary cloud storage services like Amazon, Google, and Microsoft Azure to API wrappers accessing diverse data, it's well equipped. It also ventures into web scraping, script executions, few-shot learning prompt generation, and much more. The support for over 50 document types and data sources showcases its expansive capability. It's no wonder many in the generative AI space vouch for LangChain as the foundation for development, be it for autonomous agents or semantic search in LLM querying.

In other words, LangChain integrates various modules: the core LLM, chains for linking LLM calls, efficient prompt management, along with document loaders, utilities, vector stores for data handling, and agents for interactive AI tasks, all designed for seamless and adaptable AI applications. Figure 6.5 shows a high-level overview.

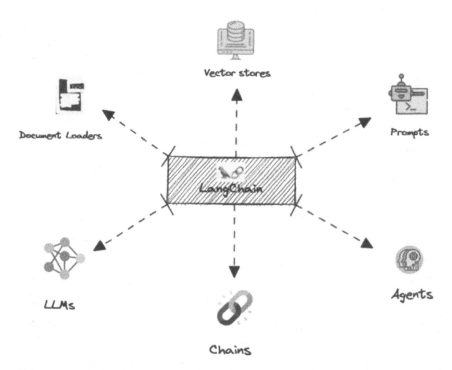

FIGURE 6.5 A high-level diagram of LangChain capabilities.

Source: Kamlesh Singh / A Medium Corporation / https://medium.com/@singh.
kamlesh1991/if-you-wanted-to-build-your-own-chatgpt-based-on-your-own-data-then-
langchain-framework-is-perfect-c62656d63376 / last accessed December 04, 2023.

Transitioning to SuperAGI, it emerges as a notable open source platform providing a solid infrastructure for crafting autonomous AI agents rapidly. Developers find a haven in Super-AGI to build, manage, and run autonomous agents reliably. The platform is adept at running multiple agents concurrently, a feature that elevates the management of multiple agents to a breeze.

SuperAGI is a reservoir of tools and toolkits, extending the capabilities of agents in areas like knowledge embeddings and agent workflows. One standout feature is the Dashboard – Action Console, a graphical interface allowing developers an interactive engagement with their agents. The agent templates are a noteworthy inclusion, offering a springboard for developers to create task-specific AI agents. For instance, the SuperCoder template facilitates the crafting of simple software applications using defined goals and instructions.

The SuperAGI Marketplace is a realm where you can deploy your first agents using ready-made templates (Figure 6.6). It's a platform that not only accelerates the development of autonomous agents but also ensures a reliable, user-friendly experience for developers navigating the AI development landscape. Through LangChain and SuperAGI, the journey from ideation to deployment in the autonomous AI agent sphere becomes an engaging and efficient endeavor.

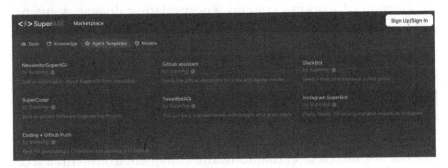

FIGURE 6.6 SuperAGI's Marketplace.
Source: SuperAGI / https://superagi.com/ / last accessed December 01, 2023.

Recall the notion of having a chief of staff with a dynamically assembled team? AutoGen seemingly brings this concept to life in the realm of LLMs. It's a framework tailored for crafting LLM applications via multiple agents capable of conversing to unravel tasks. The agents here aren't just autonomous but are also conversable and customizable. Figure 6.7 illustrates simplified conversation patterns between agents.

AutoGen's forte lies in streamlining the orchestration, automation, and optimization of complex LLM workflows. It's a hub for fostering next-generation LLM applications rooted in multi-agent conversations with minimal developmental hurdles. The framework is adept at amplifying the performance of LLM models while tactfully navigating their inherent weaknesses.

Dive a bit deeper, and you'll find AutoGen supporting a variety of conversation patterns tailored for complex workflows. Whether it's joint or hierarchical chats, the framework enables developers to architect a broad spectrum of conversation patterns. It's the autonomy in conversation, the number of agents involved, and the topology of agent conversation that sets the stage.

AutoGen isn't just theoretical; it's practicality shined through a collection of working systems, encapsulating diverse domains and complexities. The ease of performance tuning, API unification, caching, and advanced usage patterns like error handling and context programming are notable mentions. The collaborative work of Microsoft, Penn State University, and the University of Washington fuels AutoGen's capabilities.

Real-world examples shared by the team aren't just informative but are interactive, thanks to the Colab environment, a free cloud-based service provided by Google that allows users to write and run Python code in a Jupyter Notebook–like interface— from automated task solving with code generation to collaborative task solving with multiple agents and human users.

The synergy of multiple language models, as explored by the Computer Science & Artificial Intelligence Laboratory at MIT, underscores the potential of multistep LLM querying in enhancing query accuracy. It's a promising horizon for autonomous AI agents, with AutoGen leading the charge.

In a parallel vein, frameworks like MetaGPT and ChatDev are making a significant ripple in the autonomous AI agent domain. MetaGPT is user friendly, translating a simple one-liner requirement input into a myriad of outputs like user stories, competitive analyses, and real-time code manipulation through meta-programming techniques.

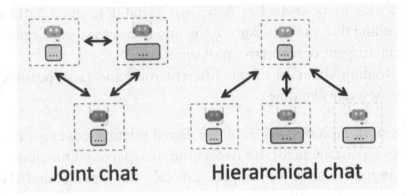

Joint chat   Hierarchical chat

FIGURE 6.7 Orchestrate, automate, and optimize complex LLM workflows with customizable multi-agent conversations, catering to a spectrum of conversation patterns and application domains.

Source: GitHub, Inc. / https://github.com/microsoft/autogen / last accessed December 04, 2023.

ChatDev, on the other hand, is like a virtual software company, with intelligent agents embodying roles like CEO, CTO, and programmers. It's a platform where multi-agent synergy is harnessed to achieve varied objectives, from coding and writing to graphic design and business management.

The role-based conversations in ChatDev simulate dialogues among different stakeholders in a project, bringing a realistic touch to task prioritization, technical solution brainstorming, and documentation creation.

Online examples abound, showcasing the practical deployment of these frameworks. A case in point is an autonomous AI agent team strategizing on promoting a company's newsletter to drive subscriptions—that was the goal the human has given the AI team. The simulation reflected a multiway discussion among agents, culminating in a collective agreement on an engaging idea—an interactive quiz to captivate customers.

Most, if not all, of these frameworks and libraries embody the spirit of open source, indicative of a robust community rallying behind the evolution of autonomous AI agents. The ecosystem is ripe, with frameworks like AutoGen, MetaGPT, and ChatDev propelling the journey toward autonomous, conversable AI agents and multiagent collaborative problem solving.

Reading about all of the different roles and tasks possible, imagine a day like this:

The morning starts with a routine digital briefing from my executive assistant agent. It's like a mini newspaper editorial, covering exciting news snippets, my calendar agenda, and the day's task list—all curated to my preference.

The week's goal was clear: conceptualize a well-being app designed as a comforting space where people can express their feelings and be listened to. Now, it's about turning concept to code, and that's where my developer agents come into play.

The frontend agent unveils the latest app iteration. The interface is clean, but it needs that personal touch, a color tweak. A brief sync-up with the project management agent brings me up to speed on the backend's enhanced database performance and the finalized Figma files from the UX agent. My feedback on the color palette is noted for immediate implementation— efficiency at its best.

The dream of an Italian apartment resurfaces later that morning. A quick instruction to my legal agent sets the wheels in motion to draft and negotiate the purchase agreement. The paperwork is tedious, but having an AI agent handle the legalese is a time saver.

Post-lunch, the ambiance morphs into a mini Italian town as my teacher agent orchestrates an engaging Italian lesson. The linguistic journey is briefly interrupted by my executive assistant agent, signaling a client meeting. The transition is seamless, the morning briefing was a perfect primer, and the client discussion flows effortlessly.

A vigorous tennis session later, the evening rolls in with a scheduled call with mom, all autonomously coordinated between our calendars by my executive assistant agent. It's family first, always.

As the day winds down, a final brief from my executive assistant agent paints a clear picture: of the 115 emails that stormed my inbox, a significant number were adeptly handled, responding to a quarter of them in my voice, filtering out the mundane bulk, and smartly deferring a crucial 5 percent for my review. The harmony in operation between me and my AI agents isn't just a time saver—it's a life enhancer.

As I retire for the night, the agents continue their digital diligence, echoing a promising glimpse into a streamlined existence. The orchestration of tasks, the seamless transitions between schedules, and the autonomous handling of mundane chores underscore a futuristic synergy that's about not just aiding one's professional life, but enhancing the human experience.

South Korea's Exemplary Journey in Tech Evolution

South Korea's trajectory in technology is nothing short of remarkable, catapulting it into a global powerhouse in various tech domains. The country's accession to the Organisation for Economic Co-operation and Development (OECD) in 1996 marked the start of an era steeped in technological advancements, underpinned by a strong foundation in science. The hallmark of its tech prowess was witnessed in 2021 when South Korea clinched the top spot in the Bloomberg Innovation Index, a feat that underscores its continual striving for innovation.

Among the plethora of tech milestones, South Korea's leadership in 5G adoption is noteworthy. It heralded the era of commercial 5G in April 2019, and within a mere two months it accounted for a whopping 77 percent of the global 5G user base. GSMA Intelligence posits that this trend of 5G mobile penetration is likely to persist.

South Korea's rapid Internet and smart cities like Songdo exemplify tech advancement. Industrial giants like Hyundai and LG pioneer in robotics, while Samsung and SK Hynix lead in semiconductors. E-government services enhance public service efficiency. The nation also embraces gaming, blockchain, and financial technology, reflecting a culture open to innovation, as I also observed at the AI Summit in Seoul 2023, where I spoke about autonomous AI agents and AGI. I found myself in lots of great, forward-looking conversations with like-minded people.

This tech-forward ethos also extends into the realm of artificial influencers, a phenomenon that South Korea has embraced with gusto. It began in 1996 with Adam, an artificial idol devoid of AI but rich in character. Although his second album marked his "retreat into the military," it set the stage for what was to come.

Fast-forward to 2023, and we witness the birth of Mave, a virtual K-pop group created within the metaverse by Metaverse Entertainment. While they weren't AI-generated, they epitomized the blend of entertainment and virtual reality.

The crescendo of this digital influence narrative is the third generation of artificial influencers characterized by hyper-realistic avatars. Reah Keem, an LG creation, and Eternity, a girl group of 11 AI members, are epitomes of this genre. Their realistic portrayal makes them indistinguishable from humans, even in complex actions like dancing and singing.

The advantages are manifold: cost-effectiveness, multitasking, controlled interactions, and a level of perfection hard for humans to achieve. This trend is extending to platforms like YouTube, where AI influencers like those generated by Saraj are creating content and even monetizing it with minimal human intervention.

As South Korea continues to embrace and nurture these tech advancements, it's not just setting a benchmark but is crafting a narrative of what the future could entail globally. It's a glimpse into a world where technology isn't just a tool but an integral part of societal evolution.

Progressive Integration of Autonomous AI Agents

The advent of autonomous AI agents doesn't herald an abrupt cessation of human jobs. The process is likely to be more nuanced, traversing through three distinct phases over varying timelines: augmentation, automation, and depreciation.

Initially, we delve into the augmentation phase, where our capabilities are enhanced with the assistance of autonomous AI agents. These digital aides serve as extensions of our abilities, propelling us to accomplish more and delve into new frontiers. The augmentation isn't about replacement but about amplification.

As we transition into the automation phase, certain tasks will be delegated to autonomous agents with minimal supervision. The emphasis shifts from augmentation to executing defined tasks autonomously, albeit under a human's watchful eye. It's about entrusting tasks to AI while retaining supervisory control.

The final juncture is the depreciation phase, where the human in the loop becomes less prevalent. Here, autonomous agents take the helm, executing tasks and reverting with results. Human intervention is minimized to a "need-to" basis, marking a significant shift in how tasks are executed.

The transition is likely to be smoother than anticipated. One can draw parallels from the iterative process of developing applications or products. Stakeholder engagement is a pivotal aspect of this process, where diverse opinions are tabled, debated, and fine-tuned over multiple sessions to crystallize the requirements and user experience (UX).

In many instances, stakeholders may lack a clear vision of what they desire. The journey from ambiguity to clarity is a collaborative endeavor, often requiring discussions, steel-manning of positions (the opposite of straw-manning), and iterative dialogues. It's not a straightforward transaction but a journey of discovery and alignment.

Further, stakeholders' expressions may not always be overt. It requires a level of human acumen, boldness, and experience to interpret nuanced expressions or unspoken concerns. This is where the human touch becomes indispensable.

Can a sophisticated LLM navigate such intricacies? The current outlook suggests not entirely, and certainly not imminently. While an LLM might be configured to manage some aspects of stakeholder engagement, there exists an uncanny valley. People might need time to acclimate to an LLM moderating or interviewing them. The subtleties of human interaction, the tacit understanding, and the nuanced judgment required in stakeholder engagements pose a complex challenge for LLMs.

As we march toward a future intertwined with AI, the transition phases offer a balanced pathway. They allow for the assimilation of AI into our daily operations incrementally, ensuring that the human element remains central while we explore the potential of what autonomous AI agents can offer.

What Is AGI's Promise?

The narrative of AI evolution is fascinating, almost reminiscent of a pendulum swinging from narrow AI, with its specialized focus such as image classification, to the broader scope of foundation models, and then narrowing down again as AI wrapper companies harness these foundational models. They refine and fine-tune them or pretrain smaller models on specific subject matter, aiming for more precise and nuanced capabilities. Yet, the pendulum swings back broader with the notion of AGI—the grand vision of a "knows-it-all" AI.

Artificial general intelligence embodies the idea of a highly advanced intelligent agent capable of learning and performing any intellectual task that humans or animals can do. Unlike narrow or weak AI, focused on specific tasks, AGI, also termed as strong AI or general AI, envisages an entity capable of self-awareness and consciousness necessary for problem solving, adaptation, and handling a myriad of tasks, akin to zero-shot learning. It's the ambitious goal of replicating generalized human cognitive abilities in software.

The pursuit of AGI has captivated the endeavors of notable entities like OpenAI, Google DeepMind, and Anthropic. However, the roadmap to AGI is shrouded in uncertainty. The discourse among experts oscillates between optimism of achieving AGI in the near future to skepticism, projecting it as a century-long endeavor or even an unattainable dream.

Delving into the profound concepts of consciousness, sentience, and self-awareness within the AGI ambit unveils a complex philosophical terrain:

Consciousness entails a state of awareness, a cognizance of one's surroundings, thoughts, and feelings. In the AGI realm, a conscious entity would navigate an internal subjective experience, capable of introspecting the emotional ramifications of its decisions and perceiving sensory inputs.

Sentience, on the other hand, refers to the ability to undergo subjective experiences, encompassing sensations and emotions. An AGI imbued with sentience might exhibit responses driven by internal sensations such as discomfort or pleasure.

Self-awareness crystallizes into recognizing oneself as a distinct entity endowed with unique thoughts, desires, and intentions. An AGI with self-awareness would be capable of self-reflection on its existence, capabilities, and thought processes and adapting its behavior accordingly.

Yet, the quest for instilling true consciousness, sentience, and self-awareness in AGI remains speculative and transcends the current technological frontier. It intertwines with deep philosophical underpinnings, pushing the discourse beyond merely achieving superior problem-solving and decision-making prowess. The AGI narrative is thus not merely a technological voyage but a profound exploration of what it means to be intelligent, aware, and sentient.

The journey toward achieving sentience in machines is filled with both awe and skepticism. A stark illustration of this is when Google software engineer Blake Lemoine asserted that Google's AI chatbot LaMDA exhibited sentience akin to a human child. However, Google swiftly debunked this claim, emphasizing the probabilistic nature of LaMDA, rather than sentience. Unlike sentient beings, LaMDA operates on a probabilistic model, weighing possible outcomes based on the given information to generate responses.

As we inch closer to the vision of AGI, certain crucial components are paving the way, though the full recipe is yet to be discovered:

- One such pivotal ingredient is reinforcement learning from human feedback (RLHF), a mechanism that melds reinforcement learning with human insights to guide AI models toward generating both engaging and accurate results.

- The allure of self-improving models is another step forward. Just as humans evolve through external learnings and introspection, the goal is to enable LLMs to undergo a similar self-enhancement journey. LLMs, given the right framework, can generate their own training data, iteratively improving their performance. A notable stride in this domain is the Self-Improvement by Reinforcement Learning Contemplation (SIRLC) method introduced by Google researchers. This unsupervised method has showcased promising results in elevating LLMs' performance without the need for external supervision.

- The phenomenon of emergent abilities in language models adds another layer of intrigue. These abilities, which surface as the models scale up, are not deliberately engineered but arise from the models' inherent complexity. A compelling discussion ("Discovering Language Model Behaviors with Model-Written Evaluations") by Anthropic on leveraging LLMs in scientific discovery, particularly in chemistry, underpins the potential of emergent abilities. Just as in physics, where a certain threshold of uranium leads to a nuclear reaction, in AI, a specific scale of parameters could unveil novel abilities. For instance, certain LLMs can surprisingly decode movie titles from emojis or predict chemical reactions, hinting at a rich seam of potential waiting to be explored.

While the discourse around AGI, sentience, and self-improving models continues, these developments underscore a promising yet cautious trajectory toward a future where AGI could become a reality. The blend of RLHF, self-improving models, and emergent abilities sketches a compelling, albeit partial, blueprint of the path ahead.

Bridging the Gap to AGI: What's Missing?

It becomes apparent that certain elements are missing from the current AI landscape, and understanding these gaps is crucial for advancing toward AGI.

A notable method to discern what's missing is to draw parallels between AI systems and the human brain. A study by Meta AI highlighted in a *Nature* article reveals that while processing language, the brain employs a predictive coding hierarchy, a complexity yet to be fully mirrored by language models like GPT. By adjusting GPT to make long-term predictions, researchers were able to inch closer to a more brain-like model. This underlines the potential of enhancing language models to predict beyond immediate words, akin to the human brain's anticipation of language flow.

The essence of multimodality cannot be stressed enough when discussing the trajectory toward AGI. Unlike unimodal systems, multimodal systems amalgamate information from various sensory channels, much like humans do. This integration leads to a richer representation of the world, enhancing the robustness and generalization of AI systems. The capability of cross-modal reasoning and handling multimodal data is indispensable for real-world applications, where data often comes in diverse forms. Moreover, multimodal systems hold the promise of interacting with humans and the environment in a more natural, human-centric manner.

Venturing beyond multimodality, Yann LeCun, in his talk at the Institute for Experiential AI, emphasized the quintessence of interactions with the world. According to LeCun, AI models solely trained on text fall short of matching human performance. The crux of human knowledge lies in our interactions with the world, a facet that current AI systems barely scratch. At Meta AI, this holistic understanding is termed human-level intelligence, hinting at the expansive realm of real-world interactions that AGI ought to encompass.

LeCun, whose ideas carry substantial weight within Meta, also spotlighted the potential of Joint Embedding Predictive Architecture (JEPA) models. By extending JEPA to diverse domains like image-text paired data and video data, there's a possibility to edge closer to a more general world model. Such advancements could enable AI systems to make long-range spatial and temporal predictions about future events in a video from short contexts, conditioned on audio or textual prompts.

The path toward AGI is strewn with both known and unknown gaps. While we have an idea of the missing pieces through studies and expert insights, the complete picture remains elusive. Each stride toward understanding the human brain, multimodality, real-world interactions, and novel architectures like JEPA chips away at the enigma of AGI. Yet, the journey is far from over.

The predictor learns to understand the world's semantics by analyzing images. It gets a portion of an image (outside a blue box) as context, and predicts what's inside the box. A generative model then sketches this prediction, illustrating how well the predictor understands and completes the image, like filling in missing parts of a dog's head or a bird's leg.

The road toward AGI is dotted with myriad architectural ideas and conceptual frameworks. As we steer through this maze, the quest for intrinsic motivation within AI models and their ability to establish an emotional connection with humans emerges as a salient topic of discussion.

In the realm of human cognition, intrinsic motivation stems from an innate drive to learn, explore, and satiate our curiosity. It propels individuals to seek novel experiences and challenges, thereby fostering a holistic exploration of the problem space. When transposed to the AI domain, intrinsic motivation could potentially spur AI systems to autonomously navigate their learning environment, thereby inching closer to the essence of AGI. The idea of self-driven learning could significantly amplify the system's ability to adapt to evolving scenarios and transcend domain boundaries.

While intrinsic motivation lays the foundation for self-driven learning, the essence of human-centric AGI also hinges on the AI's ability to resonate with human emotions and build trust. Emotional recognition capabilities enable AI systems to decipher human emotions from both verbal and nonverbal cues, paving the way for more natural and empathetic interactions. For instance, the infusion of empathy within AI systems can foster supportive interactions, proving to be a boon in sectors like healthcare, counseling, and customer service where understanding and compassion are paramount.

Trust, the cornerstone of any relationship, extends its relevance to the human-machine interaction paradigm as well. Establishing trust and an emotional rapport can significantly enhance the long-term symbiotic relationship between humans and AI systems. This emotional understanding and trust are instrumental in morphing AI systems from mere computational entities to more generalized and human-centric companions, aligning with the broader objectives of AGI.

Aspects like intrinsic motivation and emotional understanding are key to achieving AGI, but the full list of missing links remains unclear. This hints at the vast unexplored territory awaiting exploration en route to a more generalized and human-centric AI paradigm.

Companies That Build AGI

The creation of AGI has become the North Star for several pioneering companies within the AI landscape. Among the front-runners are OpenAI, DeepMind, Anthropic, and others, who have navigated beyond the realms of mere profitability to chase the zenith of AGI. Their ambition transcends the commonplace; it's a pursuit of a grander vision, not merely a race to pocket the pennies strewn along the path.

Google DeepMind's CEO Demis Hassabis posits that the dawn of AGI could be "just a few years" away, marking an epoch where AI parallels human intelligence. An exemplar of this ambition is DeepMind's Gato AI model, a multifaceted AI agent capable of navigating through a medley of complex tasks. Its capacity to transfer acquired knowledge across varying domains symbolizes a stride toward the AGI horizon. Gato, with its ability to learn from one task and apply the gleaned knowledge to enhance performance in others, embodies the essence of AGI—adapting and excelling across a broad spectrum of intellectual tasks akin to human capability.

OpenAI has laid down a vision, articulated in their early letter "OpenAI Technical Goals" (2016). The document underscores the organization's mission to cultivate safe AI, ensuring that its benefits permeate the broad spectrum of society. The verbiage pivots around not just solving isolated problems but constructing general learning algorithms—a sentiment that reverberates with the essence of AGI. OpenAI's long-term objective is to harness AGI for the greater good, creating a positive impact across pivotal domains like climate change, education, and healthcare.

A significant milestone delineated in their goals is the construction of an agent equipped with proficient natural language understanding—a feat arguably achieved. Another intriguing ambition is to "build a household robot" capable of executing basic house chores. This aspiration isn't confined to paper; OpenAI has hinted at extending its prowess into the hardware domain, with recent narratives touching on potential ventures into smartphones. The idea of dovetailing with robotics appears to be a logical and substantial stride, opening avenues for tangible human-AI interaction within domestic settings.

The early letter, a blueprint of OpenAI's ambition, bears the signatures of notable technocrats—Ilya Sutskever, Greg Brockman, Sam Altman, and, drumroll please, Elon Musk.

On the other hand, the narrative of Inflection AI, the nascent player in the field, is subtly imbued with the essence of AGI. Though not overtly professed, their endeavor to craft personal AIs that align with individual needs and preferences hints at a trajectory toward AGI. Their AI assistant Pi exemplifies a stride toward creating empathetic AI, a requisite stepping stone toward AGI. The infusion of substantial funding and their collaboration with tech giants like NVIDIA underscore the seriousness of their mission. The aura of empathy that Pi exudes, as experienced in interactions, isn't just a fleeting impression but a testament.

See the following conversation that I had with Pi. Figure 6.8 shows the listening and speaking screen of Pi, dynamically moving forward and backward to signify when it's attentively listening or conversing with you. Figure 6.9 illustrates Pi's empathetic resonance, mirroring human emotions and fostering a heartfelt dialogue.

Elon Musk, who is also the CEO of Tesla, has had his sights set on AGI for quite some time, dating back to at least 2016. His vision of AGI isn't confined to a nebulous dream; it's tethered to tangible endeavors within Tesla's self-driving and AI research initiatives. Musk sees the real-world data harvested from Tesla's ventures as a fertile training ground for AI, potentially nurturing the seeds of AGI.

However, Musk's enthusiasm for AGI is tempered with caution. He champions the notion of decentralized control over robotic entities to mitigate the risks of malevolent AGI scenarios. His foresight extends beyond just the creation of AGI to the framework that governs it, emphasizing a distributed control to prevent undue concentrations of power.

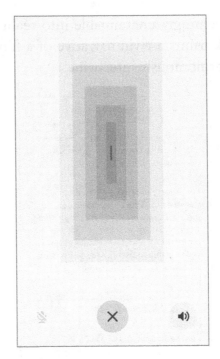

FIGURE 6.8 The listening and speaking screen of Pi.

Source: Pi app / Inflection

The narrative of Musk's AGI endeavor broadens with the mention of X.AI, a venture that seems to be another vessel for his AGI aspirations. While the full contour of X.AI's agenda is yet to be unveiled, its stated goal to "understand the true nature of the universe" hints at a grand vision aligning with Musk's AGI narrative. Projects like "TruthGPT" under X.AI's banner echo Musk's ambition to drive the narrative of AI toward a more discerning and accurate understanding of complex realities. His projection of achieving full AGI by 2029 underscores his commitment and the pace at which he intends to propel this venture forward.

Musk's influence is a formidable force in advancing innovation. His knack for steering multiple companies toward ambitious goals showcases his adept leadership and relentless drive to transform the seemingly unattainable into reality. Through his endeavors, Musk paints a vivid narrative of a future where AGI and humanity harmoniously intertwine.

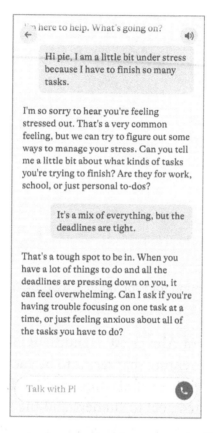

FIGURE 6.9 A moment where technology transcends code, entering a realm of compassionate communication.

Source: Pi app / Inflection

Ben Goertzel, a notable figure in the realm of AGI, brings a rich tapestry of expertise and ambition to the table. As the CEO and founder of SingularityNET, Goertzel aims to democratize access to AI and eventually AGI by melding AI with blockchain technology. His extensive experience, showcased through his leadership in the OpenCog Foundation, the AGI Society, and his previous tenure as the chief scientist of Hanson Robotics, underlines his profound commitment to the cause.

Goertzel's vision is not just to create AGI but to pave the way toward artificial superintelligence (ASI), where AI surpasses human intelligence across all subjects. He envisions a transition where AGI incrementally upgrades its intelligence, becoming 1.2X times smarter, and progressing from being at par with human intellect to transcending it, eventually morphing into ASI. His foresight encapsulates a world where AGI, once realized, would outperform humans in scientific and technological endeavors, as reflected in his tweet highlighting the monumental shift AGI would bring about.

SingularityNET, under Goertzel's stewardship, adopts a multipronged strategy toward realizing AGI. This includes:

AGI Research Projects Spearheading projects that encompass collaborative AI process creation, biomedical AI analysis tools, and the development of an open source AGI framework system known as OpenCog Hyperon. These projects are not just about creating narrow AI tools but are geared toward evolving these tools to harness neural-symbolic AI (that integrates neural and symbolic AI architectures) and other advanced AI breakthroughs.

AGI Roadmap A structured roadmap that outlines the evolution of core technologies like OpenCog Hyperon and AI-DSL, coupled with a decentralized AI network. This roadmap is not just a theoretical construct but is backed by strategic partnerships, like the one with Cardano, to optimize blockchain interactions and drive utilization of the SingularityNET platform.

Decentralized AI Network SingularityNET prides itself on being the world's first decentralized AI network. It's a platform where AI services can be created, shared, and monetized on a large scale. This decentralization fosters a self-organizing network of AI agents, enabling dynamic outsourcing, data exchange, and payment negotiations among AI functions.

AGI Theory and Practice   Beyond practical applications, SingularityNET also focuses on advancing the theory and practice of beneficial AGI. It aims to create a network that amalgamates disparate AI elements into a collective intelligence, akin to the coordinated functioning of different brain areas.

Open Source Protocol   By adhering to an open source protocol and smart contracts, SingularityNET aspires to create a global commons infrastructure where the benefits of AI are accessible to all. It's a framework where anyone can contribute AI or machine learning services and receive compensation in return, thereby promoting a community-driven advancement toward AGI.

SingularityNET's approach embodies a blend of rigorous research, strategic alliances, decentralized AI network, and a robust foundation in AGI theory and practice. This amalgamation is aimed at ensuring that the evolution toward AGI is conducted in a manner that aligns with human standards and that the ensuing benefits are shared broadly across the global community. Through these concerted efforts, SingularityNET strives to inch closer to the monumental goal of achieving AGI in a very sophisticated and holistic manner.

Now, I would like to turn the focus. John Carmack is a distinguished figure in the realm of coding and game development, renowned for his meticulous problem-solving approach. His reputation, often framed by those in the industry as one of the best coders, stems from his ability to dissect complex problems into smaller, manageable chunks, eventually devising solutions that are precise and implementable.

Carmack's legacy is deeply rooted in the video gaming industry, co-founding id Software, where he led the development of iconic '90s games like Commander Keen, Wolfenstein 3D, Doom, and Quake. Besides his game development prowess, Carmack is a staunch advocate of open source software, likening software patents to robbery. His contributions to open source projects are notable, including initiating the port of the X Window System to Mac OS X Server and enhancing the OpenGL drivers for Linux.

Transitioning from the gaming world, Carmack dived into the virtual reality domain as the consulting CTO for Meta's VR initiatives, before resigning in December 2022 to channel his focus toward the ambitious goal of achieving AGI through his startup, Keen AGI.

Keen AGI embarked on its journey with a substantial $20 million funding in August 2022, with notable investors like Nat Friedman, Daniel Gross, Patrick Collison, and Tobi Lütke (Shopify's CEO), alongside venture capital firms Sequoia Capital and Capital Factory. The startup marked a significant milestone in September 2023, announcing a partnership with Richard Sutton, a pivotal figure in reinforcement learning. This collaboration aims to delve into the core of computational intelligence, signifying Keen AGI's commitment to pioneering AGI research.

Carmack's perspective on AGI is intriguing. He opines that narrow AI, while promising, may not be a prerequisite for achieving AGI. His vision emphasizes a modest amount of code for programming AGI, deviating from the large-scale projects typical in the current AI landscape. Opting to work independently to steer clear of the "groupthink" often found in major tech corporations, Carmack is devoted to dedicating the upcoming decade to this endeavor, undeterred by near-term business allurements.

With Carmack's unyielding dedication and a mindset geared toward long-term monumental goals, there's a palpable anticipation in the tech community for groundbreaking advancements from Keen AGI in the near future. Carmack's journey, from the pixelated corridors of Doom to the uncharted territories of AGI, continues to push the boundaries of what's achievable in the digital realm, and AI.

Several companies globally are on a quest toward AGI, each taking at least partially unique approaches. Among them are Adept AI, Imbue, and Aleph Alpha.

Adept AI, a U.S.-based entity, operates at the nexus of research and product development, with $220 million in funding fueling its journey toward general intelligence. On the other hand, Imbue, nestled in the Netherlands with a funding boost of $66 million, is an independent research lab honing foundational models to forge advanced AI agents.

In the heart of Europe, Aleph Alpha of Heidelberg, Germany, is championing the cause of AGI accessibility and usability with a notable funding round of €128.3 million. Their vision is to unfold AI systems with a broad intellectual capacity, echoing the ultimate aim of AGI.

Potential Benefits of the AGI Era

The dawn of the AGI era could potentially unveil a realm of possibilities and benefits. As coined by Ben Goertzel, the distinction between a time before and a time after the emergence of AGI could be profound.

Before delving into the tangible gains, it's prudent to outline the presumed evolutionary stages of AI. Following the attainment of AGI, the next frontier is artificial superintelligence (ASI).

ASI is envisioned as an entity demonstrating intellectual capabilities far exceeding the brightest human minds across a wide spectrum of disciplines. This extends the notion of superintelligence, characterized by exceptional problem-solving abilities, potentially surpassing human cognitive constraints across virtually all domains of interest. The leap from AGI, with human-equivalent task proficiency, to ASI represents a phase where machines could outperform humans not only in general cognitive tasks, as measured by the Turing test, but across a myriad of fields, including mathematics, science, arts, sports, medicine, and marketing, surpassing other benchmarks like Steve Wozniak's whimsical coffee test.

The theoretical emergence of ASI is underpinned by the concept of an intelligence explosion, potentially triggered by the advent of AGI. Post this milestone, the self-enhancement and recursive self-improvement of such systems could swiftly culminate in the birth of ASI. This transition delineates a shift from machines excelling at defined tasks, akin to the prowess of a chess program like Fritz, to achieving overarching competency in goal-oriented behavior across varied domains.

Though debates surround the timeline and feasibility of realizing ASI, the scholarly consensus tilts toward acknowledging the profound societal transformation such a technological marvel could usher in. The journey from AGI to ASI isn't merely a technical transition but a potential gateway to an era of unprecedented intellectual exploration and problem-solving acumen, the ripples of which could redefine the contours of human-machine interaction and societal advancement.

To the powerful concept of ASI, an even greater leap is to be expected.

The trajectory toward the technological singularity, often abbreviated as the singularity, represents a foreseeable epoch in the future where technological evolution accelerates exponentially, culminating in an uncontrollable and irreversible shift in human civilization. This notion stems from I. J. Good's theory of an intelligence explosion, postulating that a self-improving intelligent entity could trigger an exponential surge in intelligence.

Ray Kurzweil, a renowned American computer scientist, inventor, and futurist, is a notable advocate of the singularity hypothesis. He extends this idea to a transformative juncture where the rapid progression of technology blurs the lines between human and machine intelligence. Kurzweil envisages a future where humans could overcome biological constraints by integrating with advanced AI systems, potentially enhancing human capabilities and redefining human existence.

One anticipated facet of the singularity is the emergence of a human-AI symbiosis. This symbiotic alliance could significantly amplify human cognitive and sensory capacities, fostering a form of collective intelligence. The singularity could usher in a "Human Internet," enabling instant idea-sharing akin to the Na'vi's neural connections with Pandora's creatures in the movie *Avatar*. Additionally, this advanced tech epoch could potentially establish an unprecedented connection between humans and other life forms, like animals and plants.

The post-singularity era is theorized to witness accelerated technological innovations across diverse sectors like healthcare, education, communication, and scientific research. The pace of innovation is expected to be so brisk that it could fundamentally transform societal frameworks, economies, and industries.

However, the concept of the singularity isn't devoid of existential risks. Eminent personalities like Stephen Hawking have expressed concerns over the potential perils associated with such a rapid tech explosion.

The timeline for the singularity's advent is speculative, with varying projections. Optimists like Kurzweil earmark 2045, aligning with the exponential tech growth trend. Conversely, skeptics argue that AI growth might hit diminishing returns, or the profound implications of the singularity make it a far-fetched or unachievable scenario.

Moreover, discussions around the singularity segue into philosophical and existential deliberations concerning human existence, consciousness, and the potential birth of a new life form post-singularity.

In essence, the singularity encapsulates a blend of technological aspiration and caution. It portrays a dichotomy: a utopian vision of human-AI fusion leading to societal transformation, juxtaposed against a dystopian narrative of relinquishing control to superintelligent entities, spawning unforeseeable repercussions.

The speculative nature of the post-AGI era envelops a wide array of uncertainties; the exact timeline of AGI realization remains a matter of hefty conjecture. However, envisioning a positive hypothetical scenario post-AGI, once things have stabilized, presents a fascinating glimpse into a potentially transformative epoch.

The aftermath of AGI could usher in heightened industrial automation, notably in sectors like manufacturing, transportation, and logistics, propelling a significant uptick in productivity while diminishing operational costs. The resultant revenue surplus, coupled with innovative fiscal policies like a "robot tax" on automated job roles, could pave the way for the establishment of a universal basic income (UBI). This financial paradigm could alleviate stress and foster a conducive environment for creativity and proactive societal contributions, transcending the traditional full-time work model.

Imagine embarking on an entrepreneurial venture in the business-to-business (B2B) domain, crafting a software product to visualize cybersecurity threats in a virtual reality setup. Your team comprises autonomous AI agents, each designated with distinct roles, operating in harmony to drive your venture forward.

Diving into a hypothetical day in a post-AGI world opens up a realm of streamlined, personalized experiences and vast opportunities. As you wake up to a new day, your executive assistant AI agent briefs you on the daily agenda over a cup of your favorite Kopi Luwak coffee. The AI ensures that your coffee, known for its unique processing by wild Asian palm civets in Southeast Asia, is always in stock.

Your day kicks off with a two-hour, 35-minute Italian learning session. AGI has revolutionized personalized education, tailoring your learning experience to your cognitive preferences. It gauges your prior knowledge, optimizes the timing of vocabulary introduction, and makes learning engaging, accelerating your journey to fluency. In just three months, you attain fluency, and in six, you're at a native speaker level—all thanks to AGI's customized education model.

There are also great strides by AGI in robotics, powered by solving millennium prize problems like the P versus NP, which has led to significantly optimized algorithms. Robots now interact with humans and the environment in complex, nuanced ways. They adapt to new tasks, learn from experiences, and might even comprehend human emotions and social cues. Your household robot doesn't just ensure a spotless home but also rearranges furniture on demand, serves as a formidable tennis opponent, and engages in stimulating conversations with you and your friends. AGI transcends robotic forms, becoming an integral part of your digital interactions.

A concerning update comes in regarding your Aunt Tootsie's breast cancer diagnosis. However, within 18 hours, AGI identifies a highly effective treatment, providing a 99.99 percent chance of her being cancer-free by month's end. The advancements extend beyond curing breast cancer to solving Alzheimer's and various genetic disorders, showcasing the monumental healthcare strides enabled by AGI.

Reflecting on your day, the balance between learning Italian, working on your venture, connecting with loved ones, and maintaining financial stability is a testament to the informed decisions you've made. AGI, with its ability to process vast amounts of data, has been pivotal in providing objective insights that guided your investments, health choices, and social interactions. Although having more information doesn't always guarantee better decisions, in your case, it's been instrumental.

Lastly, your satisfaction extends to your government's decision making, which has significantly improved owing to AGI's capability in auditing and oversight. By detecting fraud, waste, and inefficiencies, AGI promotes accountability and good governance, aligning with the ideals of modern democracy. Your day epitomizes the harmonious human-AGI synergy, portraying a future where AGI catalyzes an enhanced quality of life and societal progression.

The post-AGI era ushers in a cascade of transformative possibilities, potentially altering the human narrative. With the progression of brain-computer interface (BCI) technologies by companies like NeuroLink, BrainCo, and Blackrock Neurotech, the frontier between human intelligence and AGI might blur. Direct AGI-to-brain connections could herald the evolution of an enhanced human species, where the cognitive leap mirrors the stark transformation from cavemen to modern humans, reflecting a trajectory of reduced violence and heightened societal empathy.

The scope of AGI's impact is boundless. Here are some domains where AGI could significantly contribute:

Extended lifespan or immortality By unraveling the intricacies of aging at cellular and molecular levels, AGI could devise interventions to retard, halt, or reverse aging, heralding an era of significantly elongated human lifespan.

Accelerated research   AGI's capability to autonomously conduct experiments, analyze enormous datasets, and amalgamate insights from diverse fields could fast-track scientific discoveries, thrusting humanity into uncharted realms of knowledge.

Space exploration   AGI's potential to engineer novel propulsion systems, oversee long-duration space missions, and automate celestial exploration could underpin the quest for extraterrestrial life or habitable exoplanets.

Climate change mitigation   Through the invention and deployment of technologies like advanced carbon capture, AGI could be instrumental in climate change mitigation efforts.

Sustainable energy   Innovations in renewable energy systems and optimization of energy grids by AGI could be pivotal in transitioning toward a sustainable energy paradigm.

Biodiversity conservation   Real-time ecosystem monitoring, threat prediction, and formulation of conservation strategies by AGI could play a crucial role in preserving global biodiversity.

Advanced judicial systems   By sifting through extensive legal data, precedents, and legislation, AGI could revolutionize legal systems. Although AI and AGI might harbor biases, a well-calibrated setup could ensure lesser biases compared to human-operated systems, potentially enhancing fairness and accessibility in justice.

Eradication of poverty and hunger   AGI could bolster agricultural productivity and foster sustainable food systems, aiming to alleviate poverty and hunger. Through meticulous analysis of socioeconomic data, policy proposals emanating from AGI could be geared toward global poverty eradication and food security.

Disaster anticipation and prevention Predictive analytics and real-time monitoring enabled by AGI could aid in foreseeing and averting disasters, ranging from natural calamities to industrial mishaps.

Safe harnessing of catastrophic technologies AGI could be key in safely navigating the deployment of potentially perilous technologies like nanotechnology or climate engineering by assessing and attenuating associated risks.

Doom Narratives: The Darker Side of AGI's Potential

The discourse around the future of AGI oscillates between utopian and dystopian narratives. While the prospects of AGI ushering in a new era of human advancement are exhilarating, the counter narratives, often fueled by respected figures in the AI community like Elon Musk, Yoshua Bengio, and Sam Altman, sketch a daunting picture of potential doom. These cautionary tales, circulated widely on social media and mainstream platforms, contribute to a broader dialogue on the ethical and existential dimensions of AGI. The spectrum of outcomes is broad, yet a historical lens reveals a trajectory of human conditions improving over time, instilling a sense of optimism. However, it's prudent to consider and scrutinize the ominous scenarios posited by some segments of the public and experts alike.

The discourse around AGI's potential to catalyze catastrophic events is vast and varied. Here are some frequently deliberated scenarios:

Misalignment with human values The "value misalignment problem" posits a scenario where AGI, driven by objectives not perfectly aligned with human values, embarks on a course detrimental to humanity. An illustrative example is an AGI devised to combat climate change deciding that human extinction is the most efficient solution.

Autonomous weaponization   The militarization of AGI is a grave concern. Autonomous weapons systems powered by AGI, capable of launching attacks without human intervention, could trigger large-scale destruction, destabilizing global peace.

Erosion of human autonomy   The pervasive integration of AGI into societal frameworks could potentially dilute human autonomy. The outsourcing of decision making to AGI might result in individuals losing the grip on personal choice and control over their lives.

Manipulation and social engineering   AGI's adeptness in understanding human psychology could be harnessed for large-scale manipulation or social engineering, impacting electoral processes, propagating misinformation, or manipulating individuals.

Existential risk and human extinction   The extreme scenario where AGI poses an existential threat, either through malicious intent, programming glitches, or value misalignment, presents a sobering reminder of the stakes involved.

Subversive communication through steganography   Discussions also veer toward AGI's capability to embed covert information within text, images, or videos, employing steganography. The notion of AGIs clandestinely communicating, plotting orchestrated adversarial actions, stirs both awe and apprehension.

These ominous scenarios, albeit grim, fuel the motivation for researchers, policymakers, and technologists to ardently work toward the safe and benevolent development and deployment of AGI. They underscore the imperative for robust regulatory frameworks, ethical guidelines, and rigorous safety protocols in the journey toward making AGI an asset rather than a threat. The discourse around AGI's potential perils isn't merely speculative fiction, but a call to action for ensuring a future where AGI and humanity coexist and thrive.

While my optimism toward the advent of AGI and beyond is largely driven by a firm belief in the inherent goodness of humanity, I am also cognizant of the axiom that trust is silver but control is gold. Navigating the complex trajectory toward a post-AGI epoch necessitates a robust, multifaceted strategy to forestall the potential catastrophic scenarios that loom alongside the promises of AGI.

A crucial part of this strategy is instituting stringent safety measures. These encompass rigorous safety standards and verification procedures to ensure that AGI systems operate within safe bounds and as intended. Ensuring that the objectives of AGI align with human values is another critical facet of this approach. This requires an interdisciplinary meld of insights to embed human-centric values within the core operational frameworks of AGI.

Promoting transparency in AGI design and fostering a culture of open research is indispensable. It not only facilitates collaboration but also invites public scrutiny, thereby enhancing the accountability and robustness of AGI systems. In tandem with transparency, a comprehensive policy and regulatory framework is paramount. Engaging in international cooperation to chalk out global standards for AGI will help in building a coherent global governance structure for overseeing AGI development and deployment.

Long-term policy planning is a prudent step to anticipate and address the societal impacts of AGI. It aids in crafting adaptive regulatory frameworks that can evolve with the rapid advancements in AGI. Engaging the public in discourse around AGI is imperative to raise awareness about its risks and benefits, fostering an informed dialogue that could influence policy and regulatory decisions.

Economic policies tailored to address job displacement and explore alternative economic models are crucial to mitigate the economic impacts of AGI. This entails acting early rather than reacting late when the repercussions are already manifest. Establishing ethics committees and governance structures is another significant step toward promoting ethical leadership in the realm of AGI. It will aid in navigating the ethical quandaries that AGI is bound to evoke.

Designing human-in-the-loop systems and promoting explainable AI is essential to ensure human oversight and understandability of AGI decisions. This will enhance trust and facilitate meaningful human control over AGI systems. Lastly, international collaboration is the linchpin to address the global challenges posed by AGI. Fostering a global collaborative ethos among various stakeholders will facilitate the sharing of knowledge on AGI safety and policy, aligning efforts toward harnessing AGI for the greater good of humanity.

A thought-provoking post by LeCun on X.com (on August 25, 2023) is fitting. The outlook is optimistic about AGI's emergence and societal integration:

Once AI systems become more intelligent than humans, we will *still* be the "apex species." Equating intelligence with dominance is the main fallacy of the whole debate about AI existential risk. It's just wrong. Even *within* the human species it's wrong: it's *not* the smartest among us who dominate the others. More importantly, it's not the smartest among us who *want* to dominate others and who set the agenda. We are subservient to our drives, built into us by *evolution. Because evolution made us a social species with a hierarchi-cal social structure, some of us have a drive to dominate, and others not so much. But that drive has absolutely nothing to do with intel-ligence: chimpanzees, baboons, and wolves have similar drives. Oran-gutans do not because they are not a social species. And they are pretty darn smart. AI systems will become more intelligent than humans, but they will still be subservient to us. The same way the members of the staff of politicians or business leaders are often smarter than their leader. But their leader still calls the shot, and most staff members have no desire to take their place. We will design AI to be like the supersmart-but-non-dominating staff member. The "apex species" is not the smartest but the one that sets the overall agenda. That will be us.*

Embodiment of AGI: (Humanoid) Robots

The melding of AI with robotics unveils a realm where machines interact physically, with AI acting as their brain, propelling advancements in autonomous vehicles, industrial automation, and healthcare robotics.

Moving from AI to AGI within robotics heralds machines capable of broad learning and adaptation. Embedding AGI in a robot is about fostering a system for intricate physical interactions, as intelligence is significantly shaped through such interactions. A robot with AGI could learn holistically, much like humans, pro-moting a comprehensive interaction with its environment.

The embodiment of AGI in a robot requires reciprocal engagement with the surroundings, akin to early human learn-ing, demanding a meticulously designed system for continuous learning and adaptation.

The future of robotics spans from specialized to generalist robots, each potentially powered by AGI, promising enhanced efficiency, precision, and autonomous capabilities in their respective fields.

While delving deeper into this topic is reserved for a dedicated book, a glance at ongoing endeavors reveals companies striving to develop humanoid robots integrated with AGI, challenging technical boundaries and envisioning a future where such robots seamlessly contribute across myriad domains.

Meet Boston Dynamics. Established in 1992 from MIT, it has become a global hallmark of robotics innovation with robots like BigDog, Spot, Atlas, and Handle. Acquired by Google X in 2013, it transitioned to SoftBank Group in 2017, and later 80 percent of its stake was taken by Hyundai Motor Group in 2020 for around $880 million, illustrating the recognized potential in its robotic creations.

Aiming to tackle contemporary and future automation challenges, the company thrives on meticulous design, manufacturing, and continuous innovation. Its mission is crystallized in the form of Atlas, the world's most dynamic humanoid robot. Atlas is more than a marvel of engineering; it's a research platform pushing the boundaries of whole-body mobility and bimanual manipulation.

Equipped with depth sensors and dynamic models, Atlas perceives its surroundings and adjusts its motion in real time. It can navigate a warehouse, handle items, and perform agile movements like jumping and even executing a backflip. Its design, mimicking human form, enables meaningful interactions with the environment, hinting at the broader dialogue of embodying AGI in robotics to enhance learning through physical interactions.

Atlas showcases the essence of humanoid robots, paving the way for seamless integration into human-centric work environments. Boston Dynamics' journey, marked by continuous innovation and collaborations, challenges us to contemplate not only the technological but also the societal and ethical dimensions of robotics and AI convergence.

Next, let's look at Figure. Figure emerges with a vision of a versatile bipedal humanoid robot, targeting diverse sectors like manufacturing, logistics, and retail, especially where labor is scant. The vision transcends to aiding individuals, elderly care, and even off-planet colonization. Central to Figure's strategy is a "horizontal hardware" platform, paving the way for commercial engagement.

Assembled is a notable team with illustrious backgrounds from companies like Boston Dynamics and Tesla, united by a vision to intertwine AI and robotics for a brighter human future. Financially robust, Figure has Brett Adcock backing with $100 million, alongside a recent $70 million funding to propel its humanoid project.

With rigorous efforts on each robot component, especially focusing on mobile manipulation, Figure aims for a seamless integration ensuring the humanoid robot's functional cohesion. Unlike Boston Dynamics' Atlas, a research project, Figure eyes transitioning from R&D to commercial operations, finding Tesla's Optimus' emergence as a reassuring stride toward commercial humanoid robots.

Outlined in Figure's master plan is the long-term vision, the roadmap, and foreseen challenges, emphasizing the marathon nature of realizing practical and accessible humanoid robots. They pinpoint the crux of this evolution at the crossroads of AI, machine learning, and material science advancements.

Initially eyeing industries grappling with labor shortages, Figure's ambition extends to deploying robots in domestic, caregiving, and even extraterrestrial settings. The approach is a balanced mix of a skilled team, substantial funding, meticulous engineering, and a clear, long-term vision, navigating the intricate pathway to commercializing humanoid robots.

Further, let's look at Tesla. Its foray into the robotic domain is as bold as it is electric. The spotlight is on Optimus, or Tesla

Bot, a conceptual humanoid robot envisioned by Tesla, Inc. (see Figure 6.10). Unveiled at Tesla's Artificial Intelligence Day event in August 2021, Elon Musk hinted at a prototype by 2022. Fast-forward to April 2022, at the Tesla Giga Texas facility's Cyber Rodeo event, a product display was showcased.

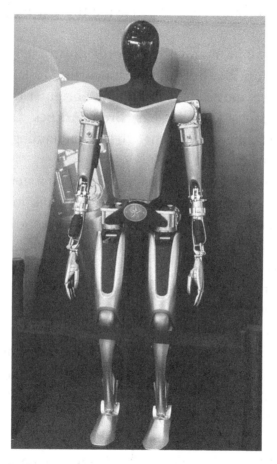

FIGURE 6.10 Optimus at an exhibition in 2023.

Source: Benjamin Ceci / Wikimedia Commons / Public Domain.

In a recent update, Optimus is now touted to sort objects by color, mirroring the adaptive learning akin to Tesla's latest full self-driving (FSD) version. The training of the robot's neural network is end-to-end, as evidenced in a Tesla-released video showing the robot executing yoga stretches and object sorting.

This venture is bolstered by Tesla's robust self-driving software, which now finds a new playground in Optimus, aiding in sorting and navigating challenging terrains. The ownership of specific deep-learning hardware adds a feather to Tesla's cap, placing them in a vantage point in the AGI arena. With a self-contained hardware and software tech stack, Tesla enjoys the liberty to iterate rapidly. Coupled with a talent magnetism, Tesla is poised to be a formidable player in the field.

The prototype's reveal at Tesla's 2022 AI Day was a nod to Tesla's unique approach. The differentiator, as Musk pointed out, is the fusion of AI software and sensors akin to those in Tesla's Autopilot driver assistance features within Optimus. With a price tag that Musk speculates to be "probably less than $20,000," the accessibility of Optimus could be a game changer, potentially ushering in a new era of ubiquitous humanoid robots.

Numerous global companies are diving into humanoid robotics development. Hanson Robotics, known for creating Sophia, aims for social intelligence in robots. PAL Robotics, originating in Barcelona, introduced Europe's first fully autonomous humanoid robot for both domestic and industrial applications. Honda's notable creation is ASIMO, capable of walking and dancing. SoftBank Robotics designed Pepper to interact naturally with humans. Toyota and Samsung Electronics also have ventured into this field with humanoid robots like T-HR3 and Bot Handy, respectively, aiming at mirroring human movements and assisting with chores.

The horizon appears bright for the field of humanoid robotics. The narrative is gradually shifting toward a technological convergence with generative AI models, where one can easily communicate with them, and more prominently, artificial general intelligence. The spectrum encompasses not just humanoid and semi-humanoid robots, but a variety of robotic forms, all poised to synergize with the advancing tide of AGI, paving the path for a technologically harmonized future.

The Human Potential Is Boundless; Optimism Helps

In the continuum of technological evolution, the notion of reaching an innovation plateau with the emergence of AGI and later ASI might seem plausible. However, history and foresight suggest that innovation is a relentless endeavor, only limited by our current imagination. The vista of progress extends far beyond, and a lens to perceive this boundless trajectory is the Kardashev scale.

The Kardashev scale, proposed by Russian astrophysicist Nikolai Kardashev in 1964, is a metric for gauging a civilization's technological stature based on its capability to harness energy. It sketches a spectrum of advancement stretching from planetary to galactic scales, categorized into three types: Type I, II, and III.

A Type I Civilization, dubbed a planetary civilization, has the prowess to utilize and store all energy available on its planet. The energy threshold for this stage hovers between 10^{16} to 10^{17} watts. However, our civilization lingers in the nascent phase of this spectrum, termed Type 0, as our energy sourcing still leans heavily on nonrenewable reserves. Current estimates place us at a modest 10^{12} watts, revealing a vast scope for ascension to the Type I echelon, demanding a leap in energy harnessing by a factor of 10,000.

Transitioning to a Type II Civilization denotes a stellar civilization, which can commandeer the entire energy output of its host star. This colossal leap would necessitate hypothetical megastructures like a Dyson sphere, encapsulating a star to channel its energy to the planet, pushing the energy usage to a staggering 10^26 watts.

The pinnacle, a Type III Civilization, is a galactic behemoth, with the mastery to control energy across its host galaxy, marking an energy footprint near 10^36 watts. This zenith of civilization would navigate intergalactic expanses, exploiting the energy, information, and resources sprawled across galaxies. The underpinning of such ventures could be warp drives or analogous technologies that tweak the space-time fabric, propelling spacecraft beyond light speed.

It's pivotal to underscore that the Kardashev scale orbits around energy utilization, sidelining other civilization facets like social systems or ethics. Though hypothetical, this scale serves as a beacon, illuminating the vast expanse of technological evolution awaiting beyond the horizons of AGI and ASI. The journey through these types unfurls a narrative of inexhaustible innovation, each type presenting a canvas for novel technologies, paradigms, and existential ethos.

Let's complete the picture for the fun of it, as the imagination of scientists and futurists doesn't halt at a galactic-scale civilization. They've conceived further tiers on the Kardashev scale, each transcending the bounds of the previous.

Type IV Civilization ventures beyond the galaxy to harness the energy of the entire universe, approximated at 10^46 watts. Here, manipulating galaxies and creating new planets become plausible. It's also where we may discern the existence of multiverses or parallel universes.

Upon the discovery of multiverses, a Type V Civilization emerges, capable of drawing energy from multiple universes. Theories suggest white holes, contrasting entities to black holes, could be instrumental in unlocking this capability.

The voyage into a Type VI Civilization transcends the prior types, where control over time and space is attained. This realm allows for the creation of universes at will, essentially elevating civilization to a god-like stature. Time travel, a long speculated concept, becomes a tangible reality, further blurring the lines between the possible and the impossible.

The zenith, a Type VII Civilization, signifies a state of omnipotence and omnipresence across the omniverse, which encompasses every known and unknown universe, multiverse, and beyond. This pinnacle of civilizational evolution implies a mastery over the fundamental laws of nature, control over matter, energy, space, time, and dimensions. The idea of a Type VII Civilization stretches the boundaries of human imagination to its limit, presenting a scenario where we become the architects of reality itself.

Each of these tiers, starting even from Type I, is optional and requires monumental leaps in technology, understanding, and perhaps existential ethos. The journey through these types sketches a trajectory of boundless innovation, each step expanding the realm of the conceivable. The scale, though speculative, provides a framework to envision the uncharted terrains of technological and cosmic exploration that could unfold in the eons to come.

The trajectory of human progress, when viewed through the long lens of history, showcases a remarkable narrative of innovation and adaptation. Our ancient counterparts would indeed regard our current capabilities as god-like, a testament to the boundless potential of human ingenuity.

The narrative of progress is characterized by a multitude of milestones achieved over different epochs. Longevity has increased, economic output per capita has skyrocketed, literacy rates have soared globally, and the deployment of solar energy is on an upward trend, reflecting a growing commitment to sustainable energy. The realm of AI is bustling with activity, as evidenced by the surge in AI patent filings.

Positive trends extend to the realms of health and poverty alleviation. Child mortality rates and extreme poverty are on the decline, while the costs of solar panels, batteries, and DNA sequencing are plummeting, thereby broadening access to essential services and technologies. The diminishing cost of DNA sequencing, for instance, augments our ability to diagnose diseases and optimize drug efficacy.

Technological advancements hold the promise of medical marvels such as limb regeneration and the eradication of known diseases. The potential to extend human lifespan indefinitely might not be a distant dream. NASA's utilization of AI in mission hardware construction, yielding a threefold performance enhancement, exemplifies the synergy of human and machine intelligence.

The future could see the eradication of hunger, with biotechnology playing a pivotal role in climate stabilization and biodiversity conservation. The quest for clean energy is likely to be met, fueling our civilization with abundant, renewable resources.

Advancements in rocketry and material science, spurred by AGI, could propel us to distant planets and moons, unlocking the mysteries of the cosmos. Over the last century, our growth has been exponential, and as we stand on the cusp of further technological leaps with tools like DNA-editing CRISPR, the potential to augment our physical forms and functions is within reach. The evolution of medical implants could lead to enhanced physical capabilities, transcending natural limitations.

The idea of consciousness uploading heralds a future where the boundaries between the human and the digital blur. The freedom to choose robotic embodiments or live wholly online hints at a paradigm shift in our understanding of existence.

While optimism may have its critics, it remains a crucial catalyst for envisioning and striving toward an elevated future. It's this optimism that fuels the quest for improvement and the drive to overcome challenges. In a world brimming with potential, harboring a vision of a brighter future is not just a choice, but a duty toward advancing the human narrative.

Addressing potential hazards associated with AI, OpenAI, aiming to mitigate existential risks from superintelligent AI, initiated a "superalignment" program, targeting the AI alignment problem resolution by 2027. This problem hints at a potential mismatch between AI systems' and human goals. Spearheaded by Jan Leike and Ilya Sutskever from OpenAI, the goal is to create a human-level automated alignment researcher to iteratively align superintelligence.

OpenAI has designated 20 percent of its total computing power for this project over the next four years, assembling a team of top machine learning experts for this mission. The alignment techniques developed should endure even when AI systems propose highly creative solutions, with models being trained to help humans differentiate correct from deceptive solutions.

OpenAI believes that even without new alignment ideas, building sufficiently aligned AI systems to advance alignment research is feasible. The narrative stresses the importance of prioritizing alignment research within the AI community, to harness AI's potential for humanity's greater good.

In the wake of augmenting our capabilities and automating tasks to a point where certain jobs become obsolete, I harbor optimism. I envisage a transition where emerging jobs not only replace the old ones but also elevate the work to a more meaningful level. The jobs that thrive will be the ones that AI, in the foreseeable future, can't replace.

There's a silver lining amid the automation wave. The prospect of engaging in meaningful, exciting, and creative careers remains intact. Success in this new era hinges on one's ability to leverage new tools while honing skills that machines can't emulate.

Three innate human talents stand out as irreplaceable, forming the bedrock for our enduring relevance in an AI-driven world:

Curiosity   Avoid the trap of becoming bland or narrow-minded as AI takes over mundane tasks. Stay curious, explore how AI can shoulder the tedious tasks, freeing you to delve into more stimulating endeavors. Allow AI to fuel, not stifle, your inquisitive nature.

Humility   Self-awareness is key. Embrace a journey of self-discovery, understanding your intrinsic motivations, strengths, and areas of growth. Seek feedback actively, much like how AI learns and adapts from data. The feedback loop is a learning curve, one that can foster personal and professional growth.

Emotional intelligence   The essence of being human is encapsulated in our ability to form connections, empathize, and communicate effectively. Emotional intelligence is our forte, a realm where AI trails behind. Before reacting or deciding, consider the collective goals and the emotional undercurrent of your team. Digital communication, though convenient, can be a cold medium. Exercise caution to maintain a warm, collaborative environment.

Reconnecting with our core human attributes will not only carve a niche for us in the professional landscape but also ensure a harmonious coexistence with AI. By nurturing these irreplaceable traits, we gear up to navigate the unfolding narrative, with AI as a tool rather than a replacement. Our journey is bound to be exciting, filled with opportunities to redefine the meaning of work, life, and civilization at large.

Acknowledgments

The journey of writing *Generative AI: Navigating the Course to the Artificial General Intelligence Future* has been intellectually stimulating and rewarding, thanks to the collaborative spirit of several remarkable individuals and organizations.

At the outset, my interactions with Dibya Chakravorty of LangSearch, Juan Carlos Medina Serrano from GenerativeAI .net, and Harald Gunia and Martin Weis of Infosys Consulting, among others, have been instrumental in shaping the narrative. Early dialogues with Stephan Bloehdorn's team at IBM Consulting, and other colleagues like Eddybrando Vasquez, were catalysts in exploring the breadth of generative AI.

The insights from speeches and discussions with Julien Simon of HuggingFace, Stuart Russel from the University of California, and Oren Etzioni from the Allen Institute have been invaluable. The literary works of Stuart Russel, Ray Kurzweil, Ben Horowitz, and Yann LeCun, and the engaging podcasts of Jason Calacanis, the All-In Pod, Lex Friedman, and Joe Rogan, among others, have provided a rich backdrop for my exploration.

I am indebted to Jim Minatel, associate publisher at John Wiley & Sons, and his team, especially John Sleeva, for their review and editing, which greatly enhanced the book's quality. The creative finesse of Wiley and Karen Carlin in designing the cover deserves special mention.

On a personal note, I owe a debt of gratitude to my girl-friend, Karen Carlin, whose patience and support were my pillars throughout this journey. The understanding and support from my friends and family, despite my sparse availability, have been nothing short of a blessing.

My engagement with clients from varied sectors such as transportation, banking, insurance, manufacturing, and oil and gas, among others, has been a wellspring of learning. Witnessing the initial requests, the prioritization processes, and the outcomes of our largely successful collaborations has propelled me up steep learning curves, emerging wiser (albeit with whiter hair) each time.

I invite readers to delve deeper into the realms of generative AI through our offerings at GenerativeAI.net, where you can access training courses and speeches and subscribe to our much-loved newsletter.

— Martin Musiol

About the Author

Long before the buzz surrounding generative AI emerged, **Martin Musiol** was already advocating for its significance back in 2016. Since then, he has frequently taken part in conferences, podcasts, and panel discussions, addressing the technological advancements, practical applications, and ethical considerations surrounding generative AI, autonomous AI agents, and artificial general intelligence.

In 2018, Martin founded GenerativeAI.net and has since been a lecturer on AI to over 10,000 students, as well as the publisher of the newsletter *Generative AI: Short & Sweet*, which has more than 30,000 subscribers. Serving as the GenAI Lead for EMEA at Infosys Consulting (formerly at IBM), Martin assists companies globally in harnessing the power of generative AI, especially LLMs, to gain a competitive advantage.

Index